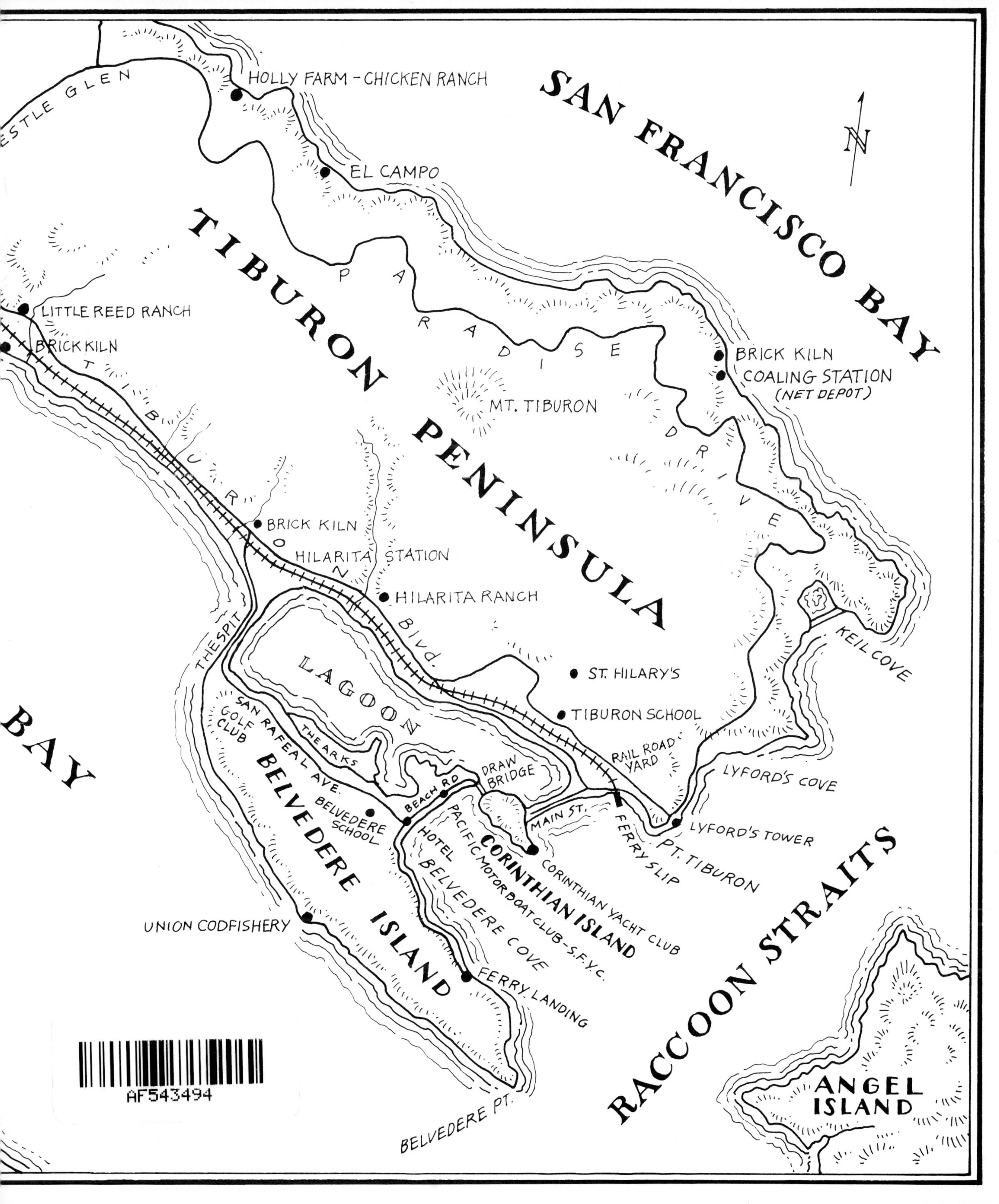
SAN FRANCISCO BAY
TIBURON PENINSULA
HOLLY FARM - CHICKEN RANCH
EL CAMPO
PARADISE DRIVE
LITTLE REED RANCH
BRICK KILN
TIBURON BLVD.
BRICK KILN
COALING STATION
(NET DEPOT)
MT. TIBURON
BRICK KILN
HILARITA STATION
HILARITA RANCH
LAGOON
THE SPIT
ST. HILARY'S
TIBURON SCHOOL
KEIL COVE
BAY
SAN RAFEAL AVE.
GOLF CLUB
THE ARKS
RAIL ROAD YARD
LYFORD'S COVE
DRAW BRIDGE
BEACH RD
MAIN ST.
BELVEDERE SCHOOL
BELVEDERE ISLAND
HOTEL
PACIFIC MOTOR BOAT CLUB - S.F.Y.C.
CORINTHIAN ISLAND
CORINTHIAN YACHT CLUB
FERRY SLIP
LYFORD'S TOWER
PT. TIBURON
BELVEDERE COVE
UNION CODFISHERY
FERRY LANDING
RACCOON STRAITS
ANGEL ISLAND
BELVEDERE PT.
N

SPONSORED BY
THE LANDMARKS SOCIETY OF BELVEDERE AND TIBURON

Both Sides of the Track

A Collection of Oral Histories from Belvedere and Tiburon

Edited by
James Heig and Shirley Mitchell

Historians
Shirley Mitchell and Cathy Debs Epstein

Scottwall Associates – San Francisco, California
1985

Front Cover: Waldo and Jack Ericson, 1914. Courtesy Carol Ericson.

Book Design: James Heig and Shirley Mitchell
Frontispiece Map: Masami Daijogo
Typography: Alphabetics, San Francisco

First Edition

Scottwall Associates
95 Scott Street
San Francisco, California 94117

Printed by Braun–Brumfield Company, Ann Arbor, Michigan.

ISBN 0-9612790-6-0 (hardcover)
ISBN 0-9612790-7-9 (paperback)

A Note To The Reader

Oral history is man's earliest method of passing down a record of events from one generation to the next. An oral history is a telling of personal remembrances, augmented by family legends and hearsay. It strives for truth and accuracy, but is primarily interested in conveying the quality of life, the texture of the times, the unique perceptions of people of an earlier generation.

The idea of collecting oral histories of Tiburon and Belvedere came to Cathy Debs Epstein and me in 1975. We were afraid that the local people's recollections of earlier times would soon be lost by death or failing memories, so we decided to interview some of these people and record their stories.

Our first step was to take a course in oral history technique at College of Marin. We further educated ourselves at the Regional Oral History Office at the Bancroft Library, U.C. Berkeley, the California Historical Society and the National Maritime Museum in San Francisco, the Marin County library and its branches, the Marin County Historical Society, and the Landmarks Society of Belvedere and Tiburon, which made available its large collection of photographs and memorabilia.

We collected these histories with a tape recorder, most of them in 1975 and 1976, a few later. We tried to ask simple, direct questions which would not be intrusive: Where were you born? Why did your family settle here? What was your work? And gradually information began to emerge of its own accord.

The people we interviewed enjoyed sharing their memories with us. They were understandably proud of the fact that their families had helped to shape the community, and were pleased that someone wanted to record and preserve their stories.

As the recordings accumulated, we began to see how much our narrators had in common: memories of the San Francisco earthquake and fire, the 1924 railroad strike, the Depression, Prohibition, the filling and dredging of the lagoon, the trains and ferryboats, Main Street and Beach Road, the yacht clubs, the arks, the dairies. We came to understand that underlying the very different stories was one story, of two towns growing side by side, the inhabitants of both living in a complex social network.

Oral history fills a need in the 20th Century. It serves as a link between the present and the not too distant past, described in a very human and understandable way. Such a glimpse into the past can give young people, or the newcomer to the community, a true sense of belonging. It can also help in the future task of preserving landmarks, legends, and history.

We want the reader to know and enjoy our narrators, and through them to know the towns. Through the stories we can feel the pace of life, see changes taking place. We ask the reader to look with new eyes at the hills where the McCombie children gathered wildflowers, the rock walls built by the Italian gardeners, the spit which was once the only road into the towns, the stone fences built by Portuguese dairymen, the place where the drawbridge was raised to let houseboats and yachts into the lagoon, even the parking lot behind Main Street which was once open water. Old St. Hilary's, Lyford's Tower, the China Cabin, the Donahue Building are important landmarks in these towns; all of them might have been lost if our links to the past had not been strong enough to save them.

We see oral history as an ongoing project. We have been and will be asked why we didn't talk to some other people, why we chose these particular people to interview. We had to start somewhere, so we went to the oldest people in the community, and to those whose families went back to the earliest times. In transcribing and editing each interview we have tried to keep each personality intact, and to capture the speech patterns of each narrator. Some of the information given may be debatable, but it is reported as stated, in the words of the speaker.

When we began to think how these stories should be arranged in a book, we first thought of a chronological order; that had to be abandoned because each story ranges back and forth through time, and many overlap. We retreated to alphabetical order, with one exception: we placed Grace McCombie Wolfe's narrative first because her family came at the earliest date (the early 1860's), and her story, which is very detailed, gives a rich background for the others which follow.

—Shirley Mitchell
Tiburon, 1985

Acknowledgments

I am most grateful for the co-operation and trust of the twenty-two people who allowed me to interview them. They are old friends now, and I have been enriched by having known them.

Families and friends of those interviewed contributed valuable information and photographs which have helped to round out the histories; I am especially grateful to Ann and Howard Allen, Bettye and David Allen, LaVerne and Alfred Bernard, Audrey and Larry Coleman, Juliet Clark, Geraldine Davis, Betty and Aldo de Tomasi, Mary Souza Hedge, Diane Keaton, Dean and Scotty McLean, Priscilla Mitchell Miller, Karen Lamoree O'Connor, Dr. and Mrs. H. W. O'Grady, Dale Adams Sims, Jodie Smith and Ray Wolfe, Jr.

The sponsorship of the Landmarks Society has been essential to the project's completion.

My special thanks go to several people without whose help this book might never have seen completion:

Beverly Wright Bastian's constant support, encouragement and friendship have kept me going.

Philip Molten, a photographic wizard, performed wonders in copying old photographs.

Roger Felton lent his steady, guiding hand to the endeavor.

Louise Teather gave unselfishly of her time and historical knowledge.

Adair Heig contributed important editorial skills crucial to the book.

Joan Krivda and Ruthe Hamm, of the Landmarks Society staff, voluntarily gave extra time to help us meet our publication schedule.

And finally I thank my patient family and friends, whom I have put off repeatedly with the phrase, "After the book!"

—Shirley Mitchell

This book is affectionately dedicated
to all the old-timers of Tiburon and Belvedere

Table of Contents

Both Sides of the Track

The McCombie family dressed in their best for the christening of baby Christine in 1911. Father Alexander and mother Louise Heebner McCombie (holding the baby) stand with Harold and Percy. Kneeling in front are Grace (left), Horace and Ethel.

Grace McCombie Wolfe

1897–1984

Mrs. Wolfe was the granddaughter of one of the earliest settlers in Tiburon. Her grandparents came here in the 1860's, about twenty years before the arrival of the railroad, when the peninsula consisted wholly of cattle ranches with a few brick kilns in the coves on each side. She left Marin as a young girl in 1913, but her memories of life here are amazingly clear and detailed. At 78, her age at this interview in 1975, she was robust and lively, with a strong step and a fine wit and intelligence. Her manner made us feel we had been friends for years.

Mrs. Wolfe, when did you come to Tiburon?
I was conceived in Tiburon!

Then when did your family arrive?
Well, my grandmother, Justine Leukel Heebner, and grandfather, Karl August Heebner, were the nucleus in Tiburon. My grandmother came from Germany and my grandfather was Prussian. My grandmother at an early age went to Scotland to join her sister and there she met a Mr. Lewis and they were married. She saw the crown jewels, and Wales' sword was so big her husband could not lift it. Her husband was an American. They came across on a ship to I presume Boston.

Grandmother had a child by her first marriage. They set out for California and rode on one of the first trains across the Isthmus of Panama. Then up to San Francisco, with her first husband. Well, her husband one day went duck hunting and never returned. And by then she had three children; that was in the 1850's.

My grandfather Heebner had run away from his home in Prussia, joined an American ship in England, and eventually was plying up and down the coast from San Francisco to Tacoma, Washington. When he was in San Francisco he stopped at the boarding house where my grandmother was working to make a living for her children. They met and married in the late 1850's. Annie, the oldest of their children, was born in San Francisco, and then they moved over to just about where Hilarita Station was later built, where Reed School is now. At the foot of the little valley there was a dairy, and that is where my grandparents first lived, in the 1860's.

What was your grandfather's work?

After he left the ships, after he married, he began working in a brickyard. You know there were a number of brickyards on the Tiburon peninsula at that time.

Where were they located?

Well, there was one at Kozy Kove, which is where San Rafael Avenue and Tiburon Boulevard meet. And there was another one up near Del Mar, and another a bit north of the submarine depot, now Paradise Cove. My grandfather worked for awhile in both of those.

Kozy Kove is the name of the little house and the beach; the name is on the gate as you drive in. My aunt said the cove was named that when she bought it. The gate and cypress hedge separated the house from the railroad track. This is the little house on the right as you cross the bicycle path.

My grandfather was a kiln operator. When they built the McDonald Theatre in Oakland they sent him all over California to find the right clay. And when they tore down the McDonald Theatre I was here in Oakland and could have gone and got a brick from it but I didn't.

When did the brickyards close down in Tiburon?

Before the turn of the century. But my grandfather was still working in a brickyard when I was a little girl, up near San Rafael; he used to come home every weekend or just once a month. He had a fast little horse with a cart, the kind used in races, you know, one with a little seat, mostly wheels and a place for your feet. He would take that to work.

When your grandparents came to Tiburon where did they live?

In one of the brickyard's houses for employees. The little house on the creek was whitewashed inside and out; it was very crude, it did not have paper in it.

Your mother, Louise Heebner McCombie, was born in Tiburon?

My mother, yes, in 1874! She died last year, 1974, just a few days after her hundredth birthday. She was born in the house by the creek there in Tiburon. They were all born down by where the Reed School is now, where the dairy was at Hilarita. Hilarita was completely separate from Tiburon at that time; now it is all one. Actually that whole area to me is a double exposure now. I still recall very strongly the days when I was there, and there wasn't a mile of paving, everything was dirt road. You picked your way over the highest spots. I go over and see it as it is now, but in my mind it is still as it was.

You are most fortunate to be able to see it both ways!

Oh, I was thrilled to pieces, but I didn't appreciate it then! I thought we were terribly deprived to have to live there. We were a big family growing up on a farm, very poor and struggling.

Let's go back a few years. Your mother was born in Tiburon; now when does your father, Alexander McCombie, come on the scene?

Well, at about the age of eighteen my father was unhappy in England, so he left home. A half brother, Ed Carpenter, who lived in Tiburon, sent him the money to come out. He came out steerage; he was almost rolled overboard. And then he paid back the money to my Aunt Chrissie, my uncle's wife. She was a typical little Irish gal. He said he never did know how much it cost; when she finally said, "Well, you've paid for it," that was the end. He did various jobs as a kid; he was a bartender in Tiburon. I wish I could remember the story he tells about taking a rowboat with cases of beer over to Angel Island to the army, which was illegal. And how he hid on Angel Island with the beer. I should have written it down but I didn't.

You said his half-brother lived in Tiburon. What did this brother do?

Ed Carpenter was a machinist for the railroad. His house is still there, near Kozy Kove. You cross the bicycle path, and then there is Kozy Kove, and then you go around that sharp bend and immediately there is an old house set among the cypress trees. The second on the left, the white one. That is where Uncle Ed and Aunt Chrissie lived. And then Dad worked at the railroad as a rough carpenter until someone said he really ought to go into business for himself. I think he was getting $40 a month from the railroad. So he leased ten acres which is now Seafirth. And at that time it belonged to Eva Garcia, the illegitimate daughter of John Reed. And she had a guardian, Justo Vidal. That was the person to whom my father paid the rent, $100 a year! He paid it in gold pieces. The land had been just vacated by the Dupont Powder Works Company. There were a number of old buildings on the place and he remodeled them, one as a place for the family to live in. Then as the family grew he had to add on. Eventually, there were ten of us: Mom and Dad, Harold, me (Grace), Ethel, Alexander, Percy, Horace, Christine, and Allan.

How did your father meet your mother?

He met her at a St. Hilary's dance. At first they lived just across the creek from my grandmother, on the Lyford's side of the creek. That creek was the dividing line of the Reed and Lyford properties, the creek that empties into Richardson Bay at San Rafael Avenue. My folks paid rent to Hilarita Lyford, and my grandmother, across the creek, paid to Johnny Reed. My brother Harold was born at that house. And before he was born, when mother was expecting him — I think she was at the depot in Tiburon — she met Hilarita Lyford, who said to her, "If it is a girl will you name it for me?" Of course it was a boy. I wish she had named me Hilarita! I came next. But she didn't. I was born in that house, and when I was eighteen months old they moved to Seafirth. My Dad named our new place "Holly Farm" after the Toyon berries that grew on the hills around us. He had a stamp made; it was stamped on each and every egg that went to market!

Can we ask when you were born?

Oh, I don't mind at all, 1897! I'll be 78 in September, 1975. We didn't move right down on the beach. You know, Paradise Drive was always just called the Boulevard. Where the Boulevard goes by Seafirth it drops down, and there was a lovely home, on a little knoll, and we lived in that for awhile. And across the road and up a little was another lovely home, and when the powderworks was going full blast my Uncle Jake Olsen lived in that house and was a foreman over there. And my mother's older sister lived north in the next cove with her husband, Jim Wittusen. I have an article telling about Uncle Jim and Uncle Jake jumping ship, a Norwegian ship, and swimming back to San Francisco.

Your whole family on both sides were here then?

My father only had a half brother. My mother had a large family; there were about ten of them and most were around here. They were all born here, except that the first three that my grandmother had by her first marriage were born in San Francisco, and one of them died. And the other one, Kitty, was Uncle Jake's wife. All the time I was growing up my mother said that they were on a yacht and that the beam hit Kitty and she was killed. But when I got older my mother told me that Kitty had had an abortion and died. And she left three kids, and then Aunt Lizzie went over to take care of them and Uncle Jake married Aunt Lizzie and they had two more!

How many brothers and sisters did you have when you moved to Holly Farm?

I had an older brother Harold, and my sister Ethel was born just before we moved. It was a chicken ranch; we had a few cows and pigs. The chicken house was all the way down, you know that is a steep drop into Seafirth. Dad thought it was too much up and down the hill to the house, so he remodeled one of the powderworks buildings and made it into a house for us.

Where did he sell his eggs?

In Tiburon and Mill Valley.

Did he deliver the eggs?

As we got older we kids did. Horse and buggy mostly, sometimes a wagon. He'd trust us more with the buggy. He tied the crates on the front and back. And in the spring when he had a lot of fryers we'd separate them from the pullets and fatten up the fryers. We'd put them in great big crates, load them on the wagon and drive to Tiburon, right onto the ferry, and go into San Francisco and sell them to Wetmore Brothers, in the commission district in San Francisco, which at that time was near the Ferry Building, just right of Market Street; seems it was on Washington Street. When I was a girl the Ferry Building was a huge, magnificent edifice; it stood out against the skyline. When the ferryboats landed, people rushed about like bees in a swarm. That was always a treat, to go with Dad to the "City," to see those big Belgian horses go cloppity clop and hear the noise of the iron wheels rolling over the cobblestones. The street with the commission

An aerial photograph taken in the early 1920's shows the Tiburon hills, the lagoon, Corinthian Island, and Belvedere much as they were ten years earlier, when the McCombie children walked over the hills from Holly Farm to Belvedere School. A large hayfield, freshly mown, is just above the white barn at Hilarita Ranch. At the head of the spit is Kozy Kove, where the children stopped to visit their aunts and their grandmother.

houses was jammed with traffic, wagons all with a different direction in mind. Dad would back up against the platform in front of Wetmore Brothers and unload the coops of broilers and go inside, to get the papers to prove the transaction — the check to follow in due time. All the way home the air about us was filled with the aroma of apples and oranges coming from the boxes we would take home with us. We bought whatever could be used in a large family. The fruit was kept in a barrel in the barn or in a dark hallway and stored cautiously, a layer of fruit, a layer of straw, and so on.

I remember on one of these journeys to San Francisco, Dad thought he would treat us kids, or perhaps himself, to a Chinese dinner in Chinatown. It was two o'clock and too late for dinner. Dad probably was disappointed, but I can assure you I was delighted. I wasn't about to eat food cooked by a Chinaman, especially when I had been told they bury eggs in China until they are rotten before they eat them. All that we ever knew about the Chinese was that there were many in Belvedere and Tiburon, either working in the Belvedere homes or in the Tiburon laundry. In Chinatown we looked in the open doors as we passed and saw the pigtailed Chinese sprinkling the clothes by blowing a mouthful of water out of their mouths, standing and sweating over the steaming iron. We could feel the heat as we passed the open doors. To look into these places gave me an eerie feeling. And I do not remember ever seeing any Chinese women.

Sometimes when Dad went alone he would arrive home with a duffel bag full of bargains. One time his bag was full of shoes; it must have been a bankruptcy sale. I fell heir to a pair of high button shoes with pointed toes. I got them on but could not wear them until I broke them in. A hot wet towel laid over the toe helped stretch the leather and molded the shoe to my foot.

Did people from Tiburon and Belvedere come over to the ranch to buy fresh eggs or chickens?

No, but my mother used to make butter, and we kids used to deliver it. Everybody wanted butter from the ranch. Mother was very careful about getting all the buttermilk out so that it would stay sweet longer. About twice a week we kids would lug it over the hill and deliver it. I think they were a pound-and-a-half sizes, and they were round, the mold was round. We would deliver it right to the house. Every now and then she would send a couple of quarts of buttermilk; some of them really liked buttermilk. Mr. Carpenter, at Carpenter & Chapman's store, used to love it. He finally wanted to buy some, so we didn't always give it to the customers as my mother intended.

You'd give it to Mr. Chapman instead?

We'd sell it to him, and buy candy with the money!

Did the customers ever complain to your mother?

They didn't know about it! (laughter) That was just business.

Did you children always travel by horse and buggy?

Yes, we were reckless kids! We had a frisky little horse that used to shy at automobiles. If an automobile was coming from our rear we could always keep the horse on the road, but if we saw, in time, an automobile coming towards us we'd always turn the horse around so that it would pass us from the rear. Otherwise the horse would shy and sometimes go over the cliffs.

And then we used to sell milk to the coaling station. After school we'd put maybe two or three gallon cans in the buggy and drive down there. There was only one place wide enough to tie the horse off the road so that a car could go by. Then we'd climb down the steep trail, and the cook always had a lovely piece of cake or pie for us!

Often on Sunday people would come from San Francisco to see my Dad, so he stayed home. One morning he must have given the horse a little extra oats, and the horse was really feeling good. We were going to Sunday School, riding down the hill and laughing our heads off. The horse was just a-tearing along, galloping. And there were two gates at the bottom of the hill, right there at the old Reed School, where the cattle could go through. And of course we figured the horse would stop at the gates, but he didn't. He jumped right over, smashed the gate down. The seat flew out. (laughter) It's a wonder kids didn't get hurt more. We were so far away from the watchful eyes of our parents when we were little.

It sounds as if you were really put to work after school!

Oh, we had chores to do every day except Sunday. And Sunday's chores we had to do on Saturday!

Besides delivering eggs, chickens, butter and milk, what else did you do?

When the eggs were collected at night we had to wash them. And every year when the circus was in San Rafael, for about a month ahead of time, if we didn't do our chores, we couldn't go to the circus. We had to pull all the mustard out of the field, or we couldn't go. The mustard was so tall you couldn't find us and we had to pull it all out. I think my Dad enjoyed the circus more than we did!

It was a great day! In our best, we drove along the coast to San Rafael in the horse and buggy. Dad always bought popcorn and peanuts. I could not understand how he knew so many kids. Behind us, in front of us, at the sides of us, Dad would say, "Here Charlie, here George, have some peanuts." We always had seats where we could see the clowns, the trapeze artists, the lions, the beautiful girls on white horses in sparkling harness, red pompoms on their heads. The monkeys, the little dogs, and the enormous elephants! Dad laughed most at the clowns. And not everybody can boast of having seen Buffalo Bill. We did! He was on his beautiful white horse. On the trip home I can remember thinking, "Another year before the circus will return to San Rafael."

And when we had baby chicks we'd keep fifty in each little brooder. And when they got larger and were in pens they'd all crowd in a corner and smother if you were not careful. So one kid would have to stand in each corner and shoo them away until they learned to fly up on the roosts. And we would have to pick sacks and sacks of kale for the chickens, for their greens.

Oh, how I hated those chickens! Grain for the chickens came to Reed Station, I think from J.P. McNear in Petaluma. The station platform was as high as the wagon bed; if it hadn't been I would not have been able to do that job. The sacks held, I think, 100 pounds of grain, wheat, cracked corn, and sometimes barley for the horses or oats. I could catch hold of the two ears on the sack and drag them out of the station, across the platform, and into the wagon. We were never asked if we would do something or if we would like to do it. We were simply told to do this or that. We never thought of arguing. It was slow and monotonous driving the rutted, muddy roads home. It was fun to fiddle in the dust or mud with the whip. Or watch the wheel churn and struggle up out of one rut, hesitate, and drop down into the next.

You mentioned kale. Now what is kale?

It's like cabbage. We grew it just so the eggs would have yellow yolks. And my mother raised turkeys, too. Every Thanksgiving and Christmas we had to pluck turkeys. You'd get the feathers in your nose! Everybody wanted my mother's turkeys. Mom had a flourishing turkey business, but on a very small scale, maybe sixty birds. They brought in beautiful five, ten, and twenty-dollar gold pieces that she stashed away in a drawer in the parlor.

I wonder what Tiburon and Belvedere would have done without your parents' chicken ranch?

I don't know of any other in Tiburon. But Dad didn't get as good a value for his eggs there. So I used to drive to Mill Valley almost every Saturday. My brother Harold was older, but he was kind of a dreamer, and he'd come home and say he'd forgotten this and that. So I was the one. I took a list and did the shopping and went to the bank.

First I'd go to Mr. Braid's store and look at the San Francisco paper to get the price of eggs, ten or eleven cents a dozen. I'd deliver two or three cases with about thirty-six dozen to a case. I'd go in once a week, and Dad would go in the middle of the week. Dad would also make deliveries to the Blithedale Hotel, far up on the slopes of Mount Tamalpais. We kids loved this delivery; the cook always gave us a wonderful piece of cake. On one of these Saturdays Dad took me up to the top of Mount Tamalpais on the "Cog Wheel Railroad." And if there were still too many eggs and Braid couldn't handle them all we'd go to Sausalito, and the last resort was Tiburon.

Where was Tiburon getting eggs if not from you?

Petaluma, I guess, on the train. Besides the chickens there were hogs on the farm. To kill and dress a hog took the entire family. Dad lit a fire under a huge cauldron until the water was scalding hot. With a whack between the eyes to stun the beast, followed by a gushing stab in the throat, the hog was down. Dad had rigged a tripod over the cauldron. With a tackle we hoisted the hog up, lowered it nose down into scalding water. Hoist it out and here is where we kids got into it. We scraped all the bristles off. They came off easily enough except for certain spots, which Dad shaved with a razor. Now to gut it without smearing blood on the outside. Then we'd wipe the inside with a clean towel, no washing. Wrap it in clean flour sacks. We always had lots of flour sacks, even had "Sperry Flour" across the seat of our pants. Dad then took the beautifully butchered meat to market. We kept the heart and liver. Occasionally we kept half the hog. The sides were hung in the little smokehouse, under which was a tunnel to the edge of the beach in which he kept a fire smouldering with the best-smelling wood available, apple or oak, never laurel. After a time we had bacon. Dad also slaughtered the bull calves, skinned them, gutted them, and delivered them to Mill Valley. Again, we kept the heart and the liver — we had them for breakfast usually, a change from oatmeal.

Often in the autumn of the year Dad ordered a schooner-load of hay from J.P. McNear in Petaluma. For days we kept vigil over the bay near San Quentin. By the way, we often could hear the San Quentin band on a Sunday morning when the air was still or the breeze favorable. Sooner or later someone would sight the tiny sails of our schooner. It might take several days, depending on the wind, before its flat bottom slid up on our beach, not completely out of the water, just enough so that a plank could reach from ship to shore. We kids loved this. We were allowed to climb about the schooner stacked with bales of hay. With a team of horses, Dad unloaded it and stacked it in the barn. Harold helped. I don't remember wrestling with bales of hay myself.

Could you tell us about school, what you studied, who your teachers were?

Actually our school district was the first Reed School. And my brothers didn't get along very well with the teacher because she was elderly and had been my mother's teacher before — yes, my mother's teacher, Miss Hauss was her name. I don't remember much about her. Well, Dr. Scott, who lived in Belvedere, was awfully good to our family, and I guess Dad and Dr. Scott must have talked it over and they arranged it so we could go to a different school. At the Tiburon School they were all Catholic and Portuguese, which was never an issue, but it was a fact. As a youngster I used to think it was terrible that the Catholic kids got out of school early every Friday afternoon to go to catechism, and we'd have to stay in school.

So Dr. Scott arranged with the trustees for us to be transferred to the Belvedere School. We had three and a half miles to walk, over the hill from Seafirth. At Belvedere there was one teacher, Miss Edna White, who was really a jewel to us! She made a complete change in our educational life. She encouraged my brother to go to high school.

Sometimes my father would let us take the cart to school. And then after school we'd stop at the butcher's to pick up cracklins. Is that what they called it, cracklins? Anyway it's dried-out fat. They'd mold it into big squares and put a burlap sack around it. Dad would mix it up in the feed for the chickens. Once Miss White wanted to know if she could ride home with us, and then walk from our place back to her boarding house on Belvedere. We were humiliated to think we had to take her with that stinking cracklins. So, instead of putting it up front under our feet as we usually did, we tied it on the little step in the back. We didn't tie it too well, and we got nicely on the way when it was falling off and she was in the back scooping it up for us!

She probably enjoyed it.

Yes, but we were so ashamed.

What games did you play at school?

Recesses and lunch hours were fun at Belvedere with so many more kids than there were at Reed School. We chose up sides and played "Run Sheep Run" and "Tally Hi Ho," running up and over Belvedere Island, chasing or running away from the opposing team. The Island was a forest of trees with roads and trails. We had a long ladder which we used for sliding. Each rung had a kid on it as we flew down the dry grassy slope to the church.

We played baseball and prisoner's base. I loved baseball. I was supposed to go directly home, but how could I go right past the diamond and not put on a left-handed glove and play a few rounds? One day when I got home Dad had been in Tiburon and had seen me playing at the bottom of the hill, so

Dr. Florence Scott of Belvedere, with her nieces.

he went on home and left me to walk the three and a half miles.

Did you children feel a great class distinction between the people of Belvedere and Tiburon?

Oh, there was a difference! A very big difference! Two came from Tiburon along with us, Alfred Salkit and Thelma Fry. But there was a definite line between Belvedere and Tiburon!

Did the parents feel it as strongly as the children did?

I don't know how the parents felt; there was never any communication between them.

So you actually lived in separate worlds except when you were in school together?

Yes! That was Belvedere and this was Tiburon! Many of them had servants. Fred Boole came to our school, and the Boole family had a Chinese cook. Sometimes we would meet the cook on our walk and we were scared to death of him. We thought he would kill us and eat us. (laughter)

We used to walk to school over the hills, over the spit, now San Rafael Avenue, and on stormy days the water would wash over the spit, so we would have to go down the railroad tracks, then on to Main Street, over the drawbridge, along Beach Road and up to the school. My brother and I had to wear heavy shoes. The Belvedere School girls all had pretty patent leather shoes. And when they had to go to the blackboard their shoes went tap-tap-tap; my shoes went clump-clump-clump. I tried to walk lightly but it never helped.

My mother made my dresses, three gingham dresses a year. My dresses were washed, starched, and ironed for Sunday, to wear to church, and I wore the same dress to school for the rest of the week. Sometimes my mother would bake bread for the teacher.

Christmas was not really a happy time, especially after we were transferred to Belvedere School. It was hard to watch the Belvedere kids come back after Christmas and hear them count off twenty and thirty presents. We got one present, two at the most, plus a stocking filled with nuts, candy, and an orange in the toe. Usually there was a doll or a set of tiny porcelain doll dishes for me. Our tree was a Toyon berry branch nailed to the wall in our one big room, the living room, dining room, and kitchen all in one. Metal pinchers, like a tiny clothes pin, except they were tin, held a candle straight up, real candles! Dad sat directly in front, pipe in hand, and never took his eyes off the candles while they burned.

Christmas was the one night of the year we were eager to go to bed. Oh, I lost my love for old Saint Nick one year, the night I heard a crackle, crackle, well into the night when everything was pitch dark. I was so excited! Santa Claus was there and I heard him! But I was too frightened to go to the door and peek. On Christmas morning we ran to see what Santa brought. Well, what I had heard during the night was rats eating all the nuts in our stockings!

What did you wear to school in the winter when it was raining?

Our mother made our raincoats out of unbleached muslin and dipped them in linseed oil. We had sou'westers. We had to hike over the hill, I guess you'd call it Tiburon Hill, it landed us where my grandmother lived, then we'd walk the spit. San Rafael Avenue today. Then we'd come in right about where Kozy Kove is and from there we'd take the road to Belvedere. We always considered it about three and a half miles.

The Keils lived on the boulevard south of Paradise Cove. Occasionally their livery man exercising their beautiful span of black horses and the most elegant buggy, happened by our place just as we were leaving to cross the hill. He always gave us a ride to school. Later Mrs. Keil had a Ford. She met us early one morning just before the Spit. We piled in. Since the seat was full some sat on the floor. The Ford in that day had a front seat and back seat, but no doors. Of course, we older kids got the seat; Ethel had to sit on the floor. As Mrs. Keil turned the corner from near the Belvedere dumps to the Spit, Ethel rolled out, as the Ford was making the turn, onto the roadside!

How long did it take to walk to school? What time did you get up in the morning?

Oh, we'd leave before daylight. Sometimes we'd have an eerie feeling that things were quiet behind us, and we'd look back and see a coyote sneaking along. They would always give you the creeps, but they are not vicious animals. Cowardly.

At least you had someone to walk with you!

Well, my brother never wanted to walk with us sissies, he was always ahead of us. But we loitered. Dad would say, "you have to be home when the *Frisbie* goes behind Red Rock," which was four o'clock. The *General Frisbie* was a ferryboat that went from San Francisco to Vallejo. We'd see an anthill and we'd stop to feed the ants a few crumbs from our lunchbox. Or we'd go to my aunt's place, the Whitneys. They lived in a little house near Hilarita. Aunt Rosie had berries in her yard and would make jam, and we'd go there and have bread and jam. Or we played theatre on her bed, and put on her rouge and powder, which were considered vulgar! My Aunt Rosie and Uncle William had eleven kids.

And sometimes on our way home from school we'd walk to Hilarita by way of the railroad track. There never was an agent at the Hilarita Station. If there happened to be a box of apples in the station for someone at the dairy, we would break it open and help ourselves. We were always in some kind of mischief. Then we followed the creek out from Grandma's back door, and when we came to the stone fence, instead of carefully climbing over we'd push rocks off the top to make a gateway, thus providing an exit for the dairy cows. Next time we took that way home the dairymen would have patched it up again. But we just made another hole!

Did you ever swim in the lagoon?

Sometimes when it was very hot we'd stop on our way home from school and keep our pants on and we'd go swimming in front of Aunt Rosie's house. Once I slipped in the mud and cut my foot, and I didn't want my mother to know I had been swimming, so when I got home I put some pork leftovers on it. It's a wonder Ididn't get an infection! She never did find out.

What else did you do on your way home from school?

In the fall of the year we always detoured by way of Grandma's house. This was the time the sweet little red apples, called Grandpa's apples, were ripe. Grandma would go out to the shed and come to the door's edge and call out, "Scramble," let her full apron open and out the apples scattered across the floor for us kids to scurry after! Grandma was chatty and outgoing — very friendly and proud. Grandma had a stroke, and from that day until her death two and a half years later in 1911 she was confined to a wheelchair. Our aunts often wheeled her across the spit to meet us on our way home from school; then we took turns wheeling her home.

I think Grandma died in April. The first death in my life was my brother Alexander, who died in Children's Hospital. He was about five years old. We kids did not go to his funeral. So Grandma in her coffin was my first experience with death. Three of us older kids dressed in our best and were told we could go over to Hilarita and see Grandma. Instead of going over the hill on our usual trail, we took the road via Reed School, we knew where the pansies with the long stems grew. Each of us arrived with a handful of yellow pansies, but because it was a very warm day, the flowers were wilted and tired by the time we got there. I can see her coffin yet in the corner of her bedroom, just opposite the chair where she usually sat. We were brokenhearted.

I think what made us love Grandma Heebner dearly were the parties she had for her grandchildren. There'd be the Whitings, from Myrtle down, Sampson Olsen, the Creightons, even Gladys Harford from San Francisco, and the Cramer kids from Sausalito and us McCombies. In the spring of each year, while she was able, she, Aunt Theresa and Aunt Elvira set up planks covered with white tablecloths. It was spring; the trees were vibrant and fragrant. The flowers under the canopy of shrubs and trees were dainty and fragile.

Grandma always made sausages. There were jams, cookies, cakes. After we ate we played among the many little buildings. Around the gulch end of the house the creek was eroding slowly; soon the kitchen would extend over the creek and we would no longer be able to run clear around the house.

You said your grandmother was from Germany?

Yes. She told us with great pride of her happy life in Germany as a girl. But Grandma and Grandpa did not teach their children the German language. I think the children did not want to learn German. In those days you were not proud to speak a foreign language. Children did not want to be German, they wanted to be American.

Now this is getting ahead of my story, but after we left Marin County in 1913, World War I broke out in 1914. Letters came telling of Grandpa's silent grief. He never again saw his homeland after leaving it at the age of fourteen. He was pained by the news of German aggression and warfare and at the reflections on Kaiser Wilhelm. He felt all criticism of Germany was criticism of him, as if everybody were pointing a finger at him. Charles Whiting, my cousin, said, "When Grandpa saw me in uniform to go overseas, he was in tears." And when Harold left to fight with the United States soldiers, Grandpa said, "Does he have to go and fight my people?" Grandpa died at the age of 86, after the defeat of Germany and the exile of the Kaiser.

Grace, are there other memories of life at Seafirth?

Well, as a girl, I always wondered where the soldiers came from every spring. The Presidio, Angel Island, Fort Baker? Where did they bed down for the night? How far did they march? None of these questions were ever answered. But they did come marching from the south to the north on the boulevard above our house. We stood out in the field to watch them. We felt we should stand at attention and salute as they marched by. They were the defenders of our country. The cavalry and cannons brought up the rear. Sometimes we saw them practicing their maneuvers. Horace used to walk along the boulevard and gather empty rifle shells.

And how Dad knew, I don't know, but we hiked to the top of Beckman's High Hill to watch the "Great White Fleet" come through the Golden Gate in 1908. It seemed he even knew the hour it would steam through, four o'clock in the afternoon. This was Teddy Roosevelt's Peace Mission, Good Will Tour, around the world. Eight magnificent white battleships slithered through the Gate like huge proud swans. To add to our great joy, after the fleet had shown itself off to San Francisco, they dropped anchor for the night right outside our cove and home.

Did a vegetable man come to your door?

We grew all our own vegetables. What used to come around to our house were peddlers. You would see them coming down the road with their horse and buggy! Seafirth now is all trees, but at that time as you stood on the waterfront the hills to your right were all barren, and a road that went around and you could see somebody coming. We'd see a wagon coming and we'd say, "Here comes the peddler!" We kids would all be thrilled to pieces! And he'd open up his box — it would telescope out — and there would be buttons and pins and scissors. Mother would go out and look the things over, and we'd be all eyes! They'd come maybe twice a year.

And of course hobos were frequent, what with the railroad there. They would come walking by and want to do some work for a meal. Mother would let them chop some wood. They were not young. This was their profession! They didn't want to work. They went north in the summer and south in the winter.

We have heard that Tiburon's Main Street was a wild, rough, tough place.

Well, there were a lot of saloons on Main Street. We were never afraid as kids to go. My Uncle Jake would go down there with his launch and get plastered! And my aunt would finally have to go walking over the hill and along the boardwalk, and she'd look underneath the doors until she saw his shoes! Women were not allowed in the bars.

How did she get him out?

There were certain back ways in! (laughter) I know during Prohibition Manny Olsen's daughters — they all liked their liquor, the whole lot of them — used to laugh about giving the signal at the back doors to get into some of the bars!

And the stores in Tiburon! The butcher shop had huge carcasses hanging on hooks against the wall, sawdust an inch or two deep beneath your feet, and tremendous, thick square chopping blocks where the butcher cut up meat. Carpenter and Chapman's store was lined with bins from which they scooped up rolled oats, sugar, tea, coffee, beans, and just about everything else that now comes in packages. A bag was put on the scales, sugar or oatmeal in the scoop fluttered down slowly, then more slowly until the balance bar leveled off and the amount you wanted was weighed out. We always had a supply of dried salted codfish. They must have come from the codfish yard that was on the west shore of Belvedere. It might not sound like a delicacy, but believe me creamed codfish over boiled potatoes was one of my favorite dishes.

How did the 1906 earthquake affect your family?

Well, the house that we were living in had been a brickyard house, and it had a very high brick chimney in the kitchen. Well, that chimney fell and blocked our doorway. My Dad told us all to get under the beds. We did. When we went out in the yard the horses were all standing in a huddle on the hill! And my parents sent us to school that day — we were still at Reed School then — and every time there was a little quiver Miss Hauss would go to the doorway and call out to the men working on the trestle, "Say, did you feel that one?" She just about filled the doorway.

I was terribly worried; I was eight years old, and I thought the world was coming to an end. I wanted to be by my mother. The sky was all black from San Francisco burning. Whether we went to school the next day I don't know. But I do know we repeatedly went up to Tiburon Peak, then called Beckman's High Hill. We'd take our lunch up there and sit and watch the city burn and the cinder would come over.

It must have been awful to watch!

Yes! I'm scared to death of an earthquake, just petrified, I freeze!

Did any relatives come to stay from San Francisco?

Not relatives, but our little cove at Seafirth was a nice place for the Italian fishermen. Very often they would come in and stop at one end of the beach and leave a man out to hold the end of the net, and the boat would circle around to the other end of the beach and they'd haul in their fish. Often they'd give us a bucketful of fish and Dad would give them some eggs or a chicken or something.

And the morning of the earthquake they came over in droves! Every shelter that was available they filled. There were a couple of little houses at Seafirth and they moved in there. They made their own bread, you know. They'd make up the loaves the night before, and in the morning the wife got up early and put a clean dishtowel in the warm bed and put these loaves of bread in there to rise. We used to think that bread was so good! And we thought it was so funny because they had this big kettle of spaghetti in the middle of the table and they'd all eat from it!

How long did the Italians stay?

I don't remember; it couldn't have been terribly long. They would come and fish in herring season. There would be a mixture of flounder, pogies, and some kind of fish that were fat when they gave birth. They didn't lay eggs. And we kids would squeeze out the baby fish. Oh, I don't know what kids don't think of!

Did you ever go fishing?

Once or twice a year my Dad sent us to walk clear down to Tiburon to get baloney and cheese and French bread and then come back and make up a picnic. He'd borrow my uncle's rowboat, and we'd go down to where the submarine depot is and fish for rock cod. But my mother always got seasick. There was a lot of clam digging, anywhere on the beach when the tide was out. The best were longneck clams. You'd walk along the beach and they'd spit up at you.

Did you ever go to El Campo?

It was a picnic ground. Boats would come in the summer months from San Francisco every Sunday. And they would have dances and picnics. I particularly remember the bowling alley; it was right next to where my uncle lived. To this day I love to hear a bowling ball roll down the alley! It is imprinted in my memory. We could see the beautifully dressed ladies with puffed sleeves, full skirts and big picture hats dancing with their elegant men in the pavilion. We could see the strong men competing with the heavy mallet to see who could hit something to the highest spot on the poles. Sometimes they caught a greased pig for a prize or climbed a greased pole. The music went through me from my head to my toes! That was when I was about fifteen years old, just beginning to feel my oats! And we'd hear that dance music, you know, "Come on and hear, come on and hear, Alexander's Ragtime Band"! Oh, I used to look forward to the day when I would be old enough to go to the dances down there!

Did you ever go?

No! My Dad would never let us! They guarded us very carefully on those picnic days. And we'd go up on the roadside and watch the last ship leave and then we'd go tearing down there and browse around and find cakes that were left over. (laughter) My brothers said we even chewed gum that was stuck under the tables! Well, we are still alive!

The ferry slips at Tiburon as they appeared when Grace McCombie and her father drove onto the boat with crates of chickens to be sold in the produce district in San Francisco.

What else happened in the summer?

Dad rented camping space for the summer, first one camp, then two, to bachelors from San Francisco, usually tailors, and most of them Scandinavians. These bachelor groups put up huge army tents on the beach. The tents could accommodate six or eight men. As time went on more and more campers came, some with families, much to our delight. The space on the beach always belonged to the bachelors. There were pretty little spots leveled off under buckeye and laurel trees. Boxes were nailed to the heavy trunks of the trees as cupboards and left from year to year. The campers had stretched burlap tightly around the kitchen area to cut the nippy breeze and to give privacy. They always took this down in the fall. The moment the camps were dismantled in the fall we kids moved our playhouses into the abandoned campsite. Ethel and I would visit each other, going from one site to the other with our dolls and speaking in very sophisticated voices in our make-believe world.

Why did your father start renting his land?

To make extra money. Dad charged $10 for the season. An added jingle to the family pocket came from the sale of milk, cream, eggs, and chickens to the campers. The Swedish women had a coffee hour every afternoon, first at one camp, then another. Practically every day, we did not have mumps, measles, or some other malady, we were allowed to go swimming with the girls and ladies. The Carlson girls were our ages and the Johansens had a boy about Harold's age.

I remember our bathing hats were sort of like cooks' hats, with a band and a large circular piece of oilcloth gathered to fit the band. And, oh, our swim gear — from the feet up, we had long black stockings, with rubber sewed-on soles. The stockings went clear up under the elastic of a generous pair of bloomers. From the top tucked into the bloomers was a sort of sailor blouse. Over the bloomers from the waist down was a pleated or gathered skirt. All the ones I ever saw were dark in color. The finished product, if put on display, would make a dressmaker proud!

Some of the camps were set up as early as May, and the last taken down in October. During the school vacation the women and children usually stayed in camp, while husbands and fathers came over on the ferry from San Francisco on Friday evenings and returned on Sunday evenings. Together they hired a launch in Tiburon to bring them to our wharf, which extended out into the bay several hundred yards. The men would bring groceries with them and occasionally one would have brought his whiskey along for the weekend and would be a little tipsy.

Some campers would have violins under their arms, and another might have an accordion. On Saturday night the hay in the barn was swept into a corner and the floor was sprinkled with shaved wax. With two or three violins and an accordion we danced, mostly waltzes and two-steps, until perhaps midnight.

You were allowed to stay up that late?

Yes, I danced from the time I was about nine years old. I couldn't put my arm around my partner, but would just hold the two hands of some grown man. I particularly remember Mr. Emanuelson and Mr. Martin Vista — they were always watching out for our safety, morally and physically. They often cautioned other campers about using bad language in front of us.

The men went fishing, dug some clams and gathered some mussels. In the evening they played cards. The clams were hung in sacks on the pier to allow them to emit sand from within. For days before the Fourth of July driftwood and dried tree branches were gathered for a huge bonfire. On one occasion a pit was dug, rocks put in, and a fire kept burning until the rocks were very hot. At the right moment seaweed was placed over the rocks, then clams and ears of corn, again covered with seaweed, sacks over that and sand heaped over all. Even Dad entered into the fun and excitement, he went to Chinatown and came home with boxes full of firecrackers. Everything from sparklers to pinwheels to skyrockets that blasted far into the heavens over the bay!

On one occasion the campers hired Uncle Jake and his launch to take them across the bay to the lighthouse, The Brothers, near Richmond. I got to go along. I was fascinated to think a family lived on that tiny island. The two Stenmark girls had a little private school all their own. Their father operated the huge reflector lamps and signalled the foghorn for the safety of the ships in the north bay.

Oh, they included us a lot. Really and truly, when I think of it now, we kids must have been pests! But we had a good time.

You seemed to have a delightful time!

We didn't think so! We were just awful poor, we thought. But the kids today just do not have the opportunities we had.

Your social life revolved around your family, picnics and such?

Well, we didn't really have family picnics very often. And the only social life we had was Uncle Jake and Aunt Lizzie, who lived over in the other cove. We would go back and forth to visit over the hill. But in those days you washed on the washboard, and baked bread, and you canned hundreds of bottles. We didn't have a lot of leisure time. Sunday was a day of rest for my folks. And my grandmother and my mother's two sisters who never did marry would come over on a Sunday. We kids loved to sit and listen because they would go through all the gossip about the Reeds. They would chase us kids out and we knew it was something we weren't supposed to hear! And mother would never let us sew on a Sunday so that was the one day we would sneak our needles and our dolls and go out behind the barn and make doll clothes. A special treat on Sunday sometimes was for us to bring a block of ice and rock salt on our way home from Sunday School, and Mom would have made up a thin custard and gotten the ice cream freezer ready. Harold usually was the one who churned the ice cream, and the little ones got to lick the heavy paddle. A sack was put over the bucket and it was left to stand until supper time — that was gourmet eating.

Often in winter on a Sunday afternoon we walked the hills for miles gathering mushrooms. Sometimes we took the horse and buggy, with a washtub inside and each of us with a lard pail. We drove north to Mr. Ring's and the dairy nearby. We'd fan out over the hills and gather a tub full of mushrooms. The only safe ones we knew were the ones with little pink underfins. At home we'd peel them and soak them in salt water. Put a dime or a quarter in the frying pan with the butter. If the coin turned black they were not good and would poison us. We firmly believed that. The coin never disappointed us.

In the summer root beer extract and yeast was bought, the five-gallon crock cleaned, bottles cleaned with BB shots and bottles full of newly made root beer lined up under the kitchen cupboard. We couldn't always wait for it to set long enough for the yeast to do its job — sometimes the cork blew out and we got to divide a bottle early.

And Saturday night was always bath night, to get ready for Sunday School. Every bucket and kettle in the house was filled with water and placed over the stove to heat. We had our baths in the same tub that was used for the family washing two or three times a week. It stood in front of the open oven door for warmth and coziness. As we grew older and modesty set in, we older kids bathed in the same tub but in what we called the pantry. It was cold in there, and since as we got bigger we did not fit in the tub, we had to sit on the rim or kneel on the bottom of it. The stove really had a workout on Saturday, since it was also the day that nine or ten loaves and two pottery jars full of beans were all baked.

Sunday was always a day of rest. Of course the cows had to be fed and milked, the chickens and hogs fed. We always had a better dinner, in the middle of the day; a roast usually.

All three of us older kids got gold pins for attendance at Sunday school at St. Stephens's. We studied our catechism, were confirmed, and became full members of the church, partaking of communion.

I hate to tell this. But after we were confirmed Dad gave us ten cents each Sunday to put in the collection plate. Up to that time it had been five cents. Before church we went to the drugstore and bought five cents' worth of candy. As long as we put something in the collection plate, the church wouldn't know the difference.

Dad was very particular about Sunday School. We went to St. Stephen's in Belvedere. Dr. Scott meant an awful lot to our family, and that was her church. Of course it was also the Church of England which is my father's. Dr. Scott's two sisters Hazel and Sadie taught Sunday school. And her house was on the tiptop of Belvedere. And if Dad needed a prescription we'd have to walk up there to get it. She was the doctor for the whole peninsula! When we needed her we just got in the wagon and went over and picked her up and brought her over. She delivered all my mother's children. In fact three of them were down with typhoid pneumonia and she stayed all night with them one night and went through the crises. She never married; she was my youngest sister Christine's godmother.

There were three or four people who completely changed our lives. We might have been just borderline ghetto kids, you know, if it hadn't been for these people who were so good to us. One was Miss White, then Miss Durst, and even the principal up in Calaveras County, and a teacher up there who sent one of my brothers through the university, loaned him the money. And above all Dr. Scott. After I married, Dr. Scott had an office in San Francisco. My husband was in the service, and she offered me a job. And of course I was green from the country; I got married when my husband was in uniform.

I have intended to write to Children's Hospital to see if they have any information on Dr. Scott. It was unusual to have a woman doctor then. And I keep telling my grandson I just miss the family doctor. I belong to Kaiser. You could be just a number when you go in there. I hate Kaiser, but I have belonged for so long I just can't give it up. All my life I have preferred a woman doctor because of Dr. Scott. She diagnosed my brother's Hodgkin's Disease, which is cancer of the glands. She was a fine doctor.

When did your family actually leave the area?

In 1913. I had a brother Alexander who died of Hodgkin's Disease in 1905, and my mother was never happy after that. And my father kept looking to buy a place of his own. They had saved about $1,500. And he was forever going out to Livermore or someplace else. Finally he saw an ad for six hundred acres up in Calaveras County. He went up with a knapsack on his back and brought back a bunch of apples. That tickled us! And we moved up there, near San Andreas. My mother had never seen the place.

My brother Allen was born just six months before we left Marin County. In those days a new mother stayed in bed for ten days. Aunt Lizzie, who was more the midwife, came over daily from the Powder Works (El Campo) to take care of Mom and bathe the baby, but when Allen was born she no longer lived in El Campo so I was kept home from school to wash, iron, put up school lunches, and in general keep house.

A buyer had to be found for our chicken business. A Chinese man, his wife and, I think, five children did just that. In the short time that our two families lived there together, while we were preparing to move, May Chan, the wife, taught me to crochet. How my parents managed the move so well with seven children, cattle, dogs, chickens, turkeys, pigs, and horses will always remain a mystery to me.

Dad built a covered-wagon type top on his long iron-wheeled farm wagon. He negotiated with the railroad and rented half a freight car — it took planning! On the bottom went odd lengths of pipe that he knew he would need on the new cattle ranch in Calaveras County. Then odds and ends of lumber. The sewing machine, beds, dressers, chairs and tables went in the boxcar. Then the cattle, perhaps a half-dozen cows and calves. Then there was hay for their feed enroute. Our cousin George Whiting and my brother Harold rode along to water and feed them until they reached Valley Springs. The rest of us rode in the farm wagon by day and slept in it at night. Dad put in cleats halfway up to insert planks, sort of bunks, for sleeping. We traveled like gypsies for ten days to reach our new home near San Andreas, eating, sleeping, and cooking by the wayside. Two horses pulled the wagon and a colt was tied to the tailgate. The three horses that I was caring for pulled out the tailgate and went galloping down the road, tailgate in tow. It took some time to capture them. Then I had to hold them on a rope, which burned my hands each time the team started. I learned to let out a little rope each time they hoisted their heads.

In the years that followed, Dad acquired two more quarter sections, a total of 640 acres. We were land-poor. We were never able to surmount the lack of money for improvements and paying off the principal. We were always struggling.

My Dad was in no position financially to handle that big a project to begin with. We had Jersey cows down here, and when we got up there it was all beef stock. He just had disaster after disaster with his cows.

Anyway, one by one the kids left home. When I got old enough for San Andreas High School my Dad did not want to send me at all at first, but I protested and went to the principal to make arrangements for a correspondence course. And the principal said, "How would you like to work and earn your room

El Campo was a popular resort in 1912, when Grace McCombie and her brothers and sisters peeked into the bowling alley (building with sign) and watched the dancers in the pavilion. Picnic tables (far left) are shaded by immense buckeyes in bloom. (Below left) Grace McCombie Wolfe in 1973.

Main Street as Grace McCombie knew it when she came to deliver butter and sell buttermilk to Mr. Chapman in his store (left). Anderson's butcher shop was in the dark building, third from left. Kelley's General Merchandise (stepped facade with flagpole) and a gabled rooming house for railroad workers are farther down the street. In the background are houses on Mar West, overlooking the train yards. Wooden sidewalks and awnings and a dirt street complete this picture, from around 1900.

and board?" I worked for a family while I went to high school.

A couple of teachers kept urging my older brother to go to the university. One teacher was a Stanford graduate, a marvelous person. And she made arrangements for my brother to work on a chicken farm in Palo Alto. He never had a penny's help from home. He worked his way through Stanford, and he served in World War I and came back and got his law degree.

Thus we left Holly Farm, El Campo, Marin County, in August 1913. It was a good life that took me years to appreciate. In spite of all my griping I must have loved my formative years, else why would I have remembered so much and in such detail?"

Marion Parker Allen in 1969.

Marion Parker Allen

1890–1981

Marion and Lemuel Allen, who ran the only grocery store in Belvedere during the 1920's and 1930's, were transplanted New Englanders. When we interviewed Mrs. Allen in 1974 at The Redwoods in Mill Valley, she had just sold the Belvedere house she had lived in for sixty years. In her eighties she was spry and full of life; the air was alive with her humor, spirit, and her strong Boston accent.

Mrs. Allen, when did you come to Belvedere?

Mr. Allen and I came for our first visit in 1915, the year of the San Francisco Fair. We had been married three years and had just purchased a lovely house, 250 years old, in Reading, Massachusetts, my home town. Oh, how I hated to leave it, even though I was going on the wonderful trip to California. Our funds were limited, but we had added to them by going without dessert for a year. The trip by train was worth the denial.

We came here to Belvedere to visit Mr. Allen's uncle, Mr. John W. Pew, one of the very first people in Belvedere. He was the first mayor of Belvedere, and the first commodore of the Corinthian Yacht Club. He owned the Union Codfishery, and we stayed there in a little apartment upstairs. Mr. Allen's brother, Chip Allen, was manager of the codfishery, and he also had a room there. We came out to stay one month and stayed six. We loved living at the codfishery. Every night we could take the boat, a little sloop, and go across the bay to see the fair. From the waterfront, where the bandstand was, we could watch the fireworks. We would anchor, and on a moonlit night it was simply gorgeous. A wonderful fair, from April to December, 1915.

The sloop was owned by the Union Fish Company. That boat was used to go and get the mail over in Sausalito. When Mr. Allen and I first came out, they rowed over to Sausalito every day. Mr. Allen would row over and back. One time I lost my pocketbook late at night. We had to go, rain or shine, with nothing but an umbrella over us. That went on for years.

How old was Mr. Pew when he first came to Belvedere?

Uncle John was fourteen years old when he came to California without a nickel in his pocket. He came around the Horn. He went off to Sacramento, where he made his money in mining. He was a millionaire. There were really three or four millionaires who owned Belvedere at its start. But you would never know that Uncle John was, he was not the type to air it at all. He then came to Belvedere and bought the fishery with another gentleman. Uncle John lived in a hotel in the City, but had a summer home in Belvedere. You know, Belvedere in the early days had only about twenty or thirty houses. They were the summer homes of wealthy San Franciscans.

Uncle John — he was known to everyone as Uncle John — bought the Pagoda House, which was the second or third house in Belvedere; it was lovely. Chip Allen bought the house from Uncle John. Lemuel and I lived there with Chip while our house (130 Bella Vista) was being restored, about two years. Yes, it took some years to restore it; we weren't in any hurry. Ours was about the fourth oldest house in Belvedere, built in 1890. It was in fine shape, but it had no foundation, just little stilts held it up. There was a lovely rock base. We dug out and added a room down below and shingled the house.

We bought our house in the 1920's from Judge Haven. We paid $9,500 for it, and $2,000 for the extra lot of land.

What was it like living with the men at the fishery?

When we lived at the fishery we watched the men who worked there. They were funny old characters. They would go to San Francisco and spend all their money on booze. Coming back from San Francisco they were the funniest looking things you ever saw. They could hardly walk down the steep grade to the fishery. It was an awfully rugged path from the top of the road, nothing but stones. It was the only way over the hill to Tiburon. They fell many times when they came down the path. The men lived right at the fishery, or on the boats. There was a sleeping area and an eating place where a Chinaboy did the cooking. This same cook would bring our meals right to our rooms — that was living in style!

At times the ships were anchored in Richardson Bay. There were three ships that went back and forth constantly to the Bering Sea. The *Balclutha,* now at Fishermen's Wharf in San Francisco, was one of them; she was then called the *Star of Alaska.*

The codfish was dried on big racks and packed in little wooden boxes. It was shipped everywhere. If you have ever had codfish balls, this is what you would use. When Mr. Harry Allen took over the codfishery in 1937, there had been a fire, so he had it torn down. He built a road and later built fine houses along it, on what is now Westshore Road.

Oh, we loved Belvedere so much we decided to stay. Mr. Allen had asthma, and the weather here helped him wonderfully, so we decided to go home and sell our house. Oh, my, did the tears roll down my cheeks. I'll never forget it. We left our families behind, and our lovely old house. It was not easy to do.

When we came back we bought our house from Judge Haven, the original owner, who was from Berkeley. We lived in it up to last year — fifty years — until I sold it in 1973. To this day the "Cod of Massachusetts" is atop the flagpole in the yard. Our house is still in perfect condition. We kept it up.

What was Mr. Allen's business in Massachusetts?

When we were in Massachusetts, Lemuel had a drug store. But here we had the only little store in Belvedere, the Belvedere Grocery. In the building the Land Company is now in, on Beach Road. We were the only store for about fifteen years. No one but us. We sold out after fifteen years and played hookey for the rest of our lives.

At first Lem delivered groceries himself. We ended up with quite a bit of help. That little store grew and grew. We put in drugs; Tiburon had no drug store then. Our supplies came from San Francisco by ferry, and by the big truck; United Grocers came around. They also delivered to Mill Valley. Our customers were the wealthy San Franciscans who came in summer. Then later people didn't all go back to the City in winter months; some stayed. We were kept busy.

Did you work full-time in your store?

I worked sometimes but not always. The whole time we were in the store we had Dolores Coleman working for us. She was the handsomest little Irish girl you ever saw. Oh, she was just a beauty! We really had a good time. We laughed from the time we opened the store in the morning until we closed it. And people loved to come in. They'd sit around and have an ice cream. Little children would come in

Top: The sloop Union, *about 1915.*
Below: The Union Codfishery.

and ask for a cone — we had a soda fountain. We'd say, "Go get the cone," and we'd stand back and they'd pile it up as high as they could pile it. All for a nickel! They were cunning little children. We made a much better soda in Massachusetts than they did out here because we used milk and out here they used water to make sodas. We didn't do that; we used cream and a little bit of soda water. Really, it was most delicious; it was more like Mr. Blum's at 75 cents, but we only got fifteen cents.

Was the Belvedere Hotel across the street from you then?

It was just being torn down; there was only a little bit left of it when we were there. They tell me Saturday nights there were wonderful. Dinner and dancing, really classy. There were some very handsome people in Belvedere, like Mrs. Masterson, and some others who were just beautiful. The hotel was once the place to go.

There wasn't much to do in Tiburon in the early days. There were lots of saloons. Sam the bootlegger supplied everybody for a long time. He had a wonderful wife.

What was Tiburon's Main Street like in those days?

Tiburon was a quaint town. Billy Beyries' store there had a wooden awning, really old-fashioned. Mr. Chapman had it first, but he died and Billy and his sons took it over. Now, we all had a good time together. We all had one customer, a real tightwad, who would call all the different stores. One morning I answered the phone and she asked, "How much is catsup?" "Fifteen cents." A few minutes later Chapman called me up and asked, "How much is catsup?" The next call was Harvey, from Anderson's butcher shop. "She ordered two frankfurters today, she must be having a party!"

The people in Belvedere were very kind to me. We made a lot of friends through our store. Our store was friendly. After fifteen years we just decided to close the store. We sold everything off to all our customers. In three days we had all our money; we wanted cash. Miss Huntington would have bought the whole darn store if we had let her. She was such a nice customer. Mr. Lathrop was there too. They all took advantage of our sale, so we cleaned it right straight out. No one ever went back into the grocery business there.

Did you own the space the store was in?

No, we were renting our store space from Harry Allen. Our store was on the corner, Miss Livsey down the way in the post office, and the telephone office next to her.

Miss Livsey was the postmistress, a funny little English woman, if there ever was one. Polly Parrot was always on her shoulder. If she didn't like you she'd stick Polly in the little square where you'd pick up your mail. Polly would nip at you. Miss Livsey was a funny little character, but a fine lady.

Do you remember any of the characters who lived in Belvedere then?

Let me tell you a little about Smitty. He lived in a boat down on west shore for years. He had to move when they began to build that road. He used to come in every afternoon to buy his groceries. He used to write beautifully. He wouldn't let any of us girls wait on him; he would take his note either to Mr. Allen or Wally for his order. He would go to the City at 4 p.m. on the bus; he was a model. He was out in the sun all the time; that was before people went sunbathing. He never wore anything but his little shorts, and he had a beautifully tanned body. That was how he got the job modeling. He also would bring a check from England and ask us to cash it for him. He was a funny man. You'd ask how he was and he'd say, "Absolutely!" That was about all he'd say. He hardly talked.

There was another funny character, Johnny. He and his mother had one of the first houses on Corinthian Island. He'd come and work for you, mow your lawn. We always called him Johnny Vonnie.

And there was Rose Verrall, the Goat Lady. She was wonderful; when she died she left her land to the town. Her goats meant more to her than anything else. She would walk to Mill Valley. We'd offer her a ride, but she wanted to walk. When she came into the store, she would say, "A quart of milk," and turn around and leave. Not a friendly person. Every week she'd walk to Mill Valley to have a good piece of pie. I remember going to Mill Valley one day, to the restaurant, and the woman said, "Oh, you can't sit there." "What's wrong?" I asked. "Oh, the old lady's coming. She comes over from Belvedere." I stayed; she came. It was Rose Verrall. That's where she went every week to have her pie.

Did you belong to the Belvedere Golf and Country Club?

Some of the women belonged; it didn't have many members. Helen Camp really boosted it and kept it going. Helen was a wonderful golfer. She made all the fun. If we had clam chowder she usually made it. Some people came from Mill Valley to play there. You could go there for luncheons or cards or dominoes. And they had a great big dining room; it was a lovely place. Later it became a private home; they haven't changed it much.

We've heard that the ferry would toot for the women on the island.

Yes, they would blow the whistle for the women on the hill when the ferry was coming. People were waiting at home for the "coach." The coaches were all open air; there would be about ten people in one little two-seated coach. They'd sit on each other's laps. The fare was fifteen cents at first, all around the island for fifteen cents, think of it! It really was fun; you couldn't help laughing. In the morning they would come and take you to the boat. You'd worry and wonder if they'd be there on time but they always were. You never missed a boat.

When Bill Barr ran the bus you could go anywhere on the island for ten cents. He was a funny old character — jovial, kind-hearted. When the fare went up to fifteen cents people nearly died. Then it went up to twenty-five cents. Of course his old wagon almost fell apart every time you went around a corner, but he got you to the boat every time, it never failed. The ferries had wooden seats and were cold as thunder at 11:00 at night. There was no heat at all. The men could get doughnuts in the morning. The husband would give their wives five dollars to go on the ferries and they had no change on the bus, so they used to stop in our store to get change. The last ferry to run at night left San Francisco at 11:00. Oh, it was cold. You had to walk home; it was a long walk.

Did you ever use the trains?

We went on the train, up the line, mainly for picnics and outings, toward San Rafael. And there were picnic grounds galore along the way that everybody went to. The train went way off up to Eureka, the line did. At times we went up to Ukiah which wasn't too far.

We have read that people on these Sunday outings would be singing and passing beer around.

Oh, yes, some of that happened. There were two or three cars and those people would run ahead and get in the front cars. It was quite a lively thing to go on those trips. To be honest, it was like a party.

Did you know any of the Italian gardeners?

I'd like to talk about them. We only had four Italian gardeners in all who took such good care of all the gardens on the Island. The Island was simply beautiful because they loved their gardens. Louie Soldavini was a boy when I came. He would come into the store and sit and listen to any word anyone said, until he learned the language. His father Vincent was one of the original gardeners. He knew just what to do about gardening and everyone wanted him. He and his lovely wife came into the store often and talked with me. The Italian gardeners were fine people. They loved to garden. They did something that isn't done any more: they got every one of their plants from seed. What made the gardens so lovely was, they made you a great big box of zinnias and then one perhaps of petunias. He'd take a dozen plants from me and a dozen from the other's box and then bring something back, so everybody would have a beautiful flower garden.

The gardeners had great pride in seeing the gardens grow. They loved flowers. I remember Charlie saying, "Come upstairs, Missie Allen, come up and see you yellow flowa," and I would go up and there would be a dahlia, perhaps, as big as a hat.

Most of the gardeners lived in Tiburon. There were only about four and they took care of all those gardens for $2.50 for a Saturday afternoon. Ten dollars a month it cost us to have our gardens taken care of. That was all it cost for thirty years. Then it got to where I paid seven dollars an hour last year. What made the lovely gardens was raising plants from seed in those big boxes. They would come and water them and watch them and we didn't have to do a thing. Any plants left over they would put in the parks. There were three little parks, one in front of our store and another on top of the hill back of Blandings. The gardeners worked hard; they killed themselves working so hard. My Charlie went home to Italy and he was gone in a few months, dead. Charlie and Harry Pariani were the two who started the gardeners coming here. They were good men!

Top: Belvedere Grocery in the Land Company Building; Lemuel Allen in the 1930's.
Below: Dolores Coleman behind the counter.

Did you know Mr. Blanding?

Mr. Blanding had his estate in Belvedere at that time. He was one of the first to come and live here. He would come into my store once in awhile. His help came more often than Mr. Blanding. He lived in the Fairmont Hotel in San Francisco, but he still had his meals sent over from Belvedere every day. The cook would make his dinner and take it over by boat. He was very eccentric, you know. Mr. Allen and I went over to see him at the hotel; he later died there. He only came to Belvedere about once a year.

Were there many Chinese cooks in Belvedere?

In my day most of the people had a Chinese cook. In my house off the kitchen was a Chinaman's bedroom, and off that was his bathroom. Almost everybody on Belvedere had a Chinaboy. They would come in our store about six or eight when they were going to the City on their days off, and they'd say, "Missy Allen, lend me two dollars." I'd say, "What you do?" "I make more money, I make more money, I pay tomorrow!"

And sure enough, they'd go to Chinatown and gamble with the two dollars and pay us back. They were nice, the Chinese cooks were. There were quite a lot of them on the Island.

And I remember the Chinaman who used to go around with fresh fruit and the pole on his shoulder to carry things. He came over from San Francisco with fresh fruit and vegetables every day. We didn't want to interfere with his business, so we didn't sell vegetables, but he would leave a head of lettuce or some carrots in case people forgot. He went around every day to the top of the hill. Then later there was a Chinaman who went around with a wagon.

Do you recall the Night in Venice?

I only saw it once. Oh, it was just wonderful; everybody had an open house, and we hung Japanese lanterns from the trees. People decorated very much. You went from one house to another. Some had drinks and lemonade. There was a band out on a boat and the music drifted up the hill. The yacht clubs were lit up; they were very popular places to go. All the arks had Japanese lanterns too. Oh, it was something to see!

Do you know why the arks disappeared from Belvedere Cove?

After a while the arks in the cove started to go, some just sank down in the water after a while. They just gradually disappeared. The last one belonged to Clarence Dobie. He was a relative of Mr. Allen's back four or eleven degrees. He was practically the first person to have an ark. When the 1906 fire destroyed San Francisco, Uncle John, Aunt Clara and Clarence Dobie's mother and his brother Charlie, the writer, all came and lived on Clarence's ark. Charlie wrote a crackerjack book on San Francisco, "San Francisco A Pageant."

Clarence's ark was one of the first ones in the cove, and the last one to leave; it was towed away on a Sunday, as the bells rang and tears rolled down people's cheeks. It was sad to see the last ark go. The cove was empty without them.

Winifred Bridge in 1914.

Winifred Bridge Allen

1893–1976

Winifred Allen's family, the Bridges, began summering in Keil Cove in the 1880's; their first house in Belvedere still stands on Beach Road. Her husband, Harry Allen, bought the Belvedere Land Company in the 1930's, after completing the development of Seacliff in San Francisco. Winnie's great enthusiasm for art, horticulture, and education shines through her words in this interview, taken in February, 1975. She was a vibrant, extremely articulate person, with a remarkable memory and strong ideas.

Mrs. Allen, we would like to hear your stories about growing up in Belvedere, your memories of your childhood.

Well, I'll have to start with the Bridges, my mother and father. My mother's mother was English, and her stepfather was very British. They owned a ranch in the Napa Valley, a vineyard. The girls had spent most of their lives there, so in 1888 he decided to sell the vineyard and take his wife and step daughters to England to meet relatives. Both girls kept diaries, which we have; they are very interesting. And then when they returned they went to San Francisco to live.

My grandmother, my mother's mother, had a distant cousin, Mrs. Bridge, who had four very pleasant sons about the same ages as the girls. So they decided to have the girls meet the boys, and they said, "Why don't we rent for a month in the summer a cottage on the back of the Tiburon hills, overlooking Keil Cove." And so they did. The young people, after they met, decided it would be a good idea to own a rowboat, so they could row from the ferry in Tiburon around to Keil Cove. They called it the *Commodore.* They had sailor suits made with insignia on the front. And each one of the family had a place on the crew. The boat had three sets of oars, so they all fitted very well. They became such good friends, before the month was up they were engaged. Two brothers proposed to the two sisters, and then the third brother married a first cousin of theirs. So it was a very interesting and close corporation.

My mother and father, even before they were married, rowed around Belvedere Island, and they so loved it that they decided they would live in no other place. And so when the Belvedere Land Company was formed in 1890 or 91, they bought one of the first twenty lots put on the market. Their lot went from Beach Road down to the beach. They built their house in 1891, and it is still there. My brother and I were both born there. We loved that house and lived in it until just before the earthquake. To live in Belvedere all year round was almost impossible; the winters were quite cold, and there were only wood fireplaces and coal and wood furnaces. The roads weren't surfaced then, just dirt roads, and they were watered by a watering cart with salt water to keep the dust down.

So that was the first house I remember, and I loved it. We played on the beach and made rafts and had a small sailboat as well as a motorboat. The Harmons lived across the road — she was Mr. Keith's only daughter — and the two Harmon girls had a canoe and we kept it for many years. I still have a canoe and love it; it is at the little cabana that the family has on Beach Road. I love a sailboat, you can go so much farther — but just for on the bay a canoe is a lovely thing to have. You are close to the water and you have to sit up very straight. It is good for you.

Did your family have a Chinese cook at this time?

No, a Chinese cook, no. We had a great many Scandinavian girls. There was a Chinese cook in the Holmes house; Mr. and Mrs. Holmes built this house (334 Golden Gate Avenue) in about 1905. My mother and father built the house at 340 Golden Gate Avenue in the same year. That was our second home in Belvedere; we sold the first to Dr. Stillman, who sold it to Marion Huntington. She had it until just a few years ago and sold it to the Mannings. Miss Huntington loved it. She brought it up to its present good condition. She added on one wing because she adopted an English boy and an Irish girl, because a maiden lady in America was not allowed to adopt a child, they are supposed to have a balanced home. So she brought them back here and she lived every summer in Belvedere. She built another wharf and float which the children loved. In fact the daughter grew up and bought a lot on Westshore, she loved it so.

Can you tell us about your schooldays in Belvedere?

There were two grammar schools. The first one was a one-room schoolhouse; all the benches were joined together, the front of one desk came down and was the seat of the next, and the whole row, about twelve seats, was all joined together. I would say that room held about twenty children. And then the larger school was built about 1900. It had a bell and a belfry, and two rooms that opened with two great doors to make one room. Many times, for music and singing, the wide doors were opened.

Miss Florence Boynton was the principal; she was a very handsome unmarried woman, and she was beloved by every parent and every child. And the two rooms then held about twenty pupils each, and Miss Boynton had an assistant teacher whom she guided. And the authority she had — the unconscious knowledge of psychology! When the room would get busier and noisier, Miss Boynton would take the long pointer and open the front window of the huge clock, and just with the pointer push the big hand a fraction of a fraction of a minute — and there was absolute silence. And she knew how to do it gently, without any discipline. She lived out on Belvedere Street in San Francisco, and crossed the bay catching the 8:20 ferryboat from the ferry building, and then walked up from Tiburon to the school. She loved her work, and it had the most beautiful dignity. It was a fulfillment of her great, courageous desire to impart her knowledge and her art to children.

Our report cards were not just ordinary report cards. They were in her beautiful printing. They were for a year, and each month was a page. On the outside was written some proverb, some quotation from the philosophers, that was appropriate to that child. I think mine was "Men die, books never." Each child's report card was a work of art.

She taught us how to do things with our hands. Each Christmas we made Indian baskets for our mothers and wastepaper baskets for our fathers. We started right from the beginning and we created these things. They were supposed to be a complete surprise for our parents. And her keen interest in Oriental art was handed down to us. And when a composition won a prize she printed the whole composition on parchment paper. I have one, in fact two, that I've treasured, and I have five or six beautiful report cards, each page done on beautiful paper.

When we would go for the four winter months to live in the Oliver Hotel in San Francisco — four

Top: The cottage where the Bridge family spent summers in the 1880's, overlooking Keil Cove. Below: May Bridge (right), Carrie Bridge (center) and Kate Safford (left) with "four very pleasant" cousins, also named Bridge. Note the sailing costumes with insignia.

or five families lived in the same hotel — the children would never dream of going to a city school. We would catch the same ferryboat as Miss Boynton from the ferry building. We ran down Pine Street, through old Chinatown, right down to the ferry building. I will never forget my first view of branches of this great Chinese magnolia — one is in blossom right now in the garden — on the bare branch come those great crimson and striped blossoms, and there's not a sign of a leaf. They come out at New Year's time, as well as masses and masses of China lilies that are always kept back just so they'll be in full bloom at the opening night of Chinese New Year. And the fragrance of firecrackers! The streets would be covered, gutters would be full of red Chinese paper and the fragrance for a week would be the smoldering gunpowder, and the half-burnt firecrackers.

And people would say, "Do you let your little girl run down through Chinatown?" But we weren't afraid. We heard about opium dens and tong wars, but we were something different, we were on our way to school. We ran down the hill and loved it.

Miss Boynton led the singing every morning, and we sang for perhaps twenty minutes. There was no piano in the school, but she had a lovely little flute like whistle that she blew to start the singing. She had a tuning fork, but this whistle was hers and hers alone. And then she would lead the singing; it was a lovely way to start the day.

We all took our lunches. We each took a low Chinese basket with a strap around it, and we strapped our books on the way home. The boys ate their lunch just anywhere, but the girls — there were about eight or ten of us — had our own special oak tree for our own tree house. We ate our lunch up in the tree, and we saved the string; the string was our telephone wire for the oak trees. When we climbed into that tree we were in a world apart, and we loved it. I imagine there's no other class that had a special oak tree all for themselves. It was a part of Belvedere, and very wonderful.

And all the classes were together in one room?

There were three classes that Miss Boynton taught all the way through from first grade to eighth grade. The first one had just two in it; the next had four, and Sommers Peterson and Arthur Bridge were members of that. I was in the third. Miss Boynton would plan so that one of the grades in the same room with four other grades would be doing their silent reading work or their memory work while she was paying attention to the others. Of course it was the great era of blackboards. We would prepare our work, and then step up and write it on the blackboard. English, grammar, arithmetic. There was no feeling of confusion. We learned to concentrate no matter what was going on around us. It's one of the things that eastern peoples can do. We live amidst so many hundreds of people, so many noises and distractions, it's wise to be able to build a conscious retreat for yourself.

Miss Boynton had a sympathetic feeling with each child, but she didn't treat them differently. Her discipline was gentle. She was so respected and so loved, we felt as though she was giving us the treasures of the world, the treasures of knowledge. We memorized great parts of "The Vision of Sir Launfal," and to this day, when I'm taking a long walk, those beautiful passages of poetry flow through my mind. I feel there's a great advantage to memory work. It not only teaches you mental discipline, but you have treasures that nothing can take from you. I think the children of today haven't any idea of the charm of learning. Many of the classics that they're given to read are deleted or boiled down. They haven't the stamina to go through a full volume of Dickens. We had all the American poets, and Wordsworth and Tennyson. We were allowed to dramatize stories. Of course we were amateurish, but when you live a story you never forget it. If you dramatize the stories of the Bible you not only get the most majestic language in the world, but you live the characters, you know what they went through; you learn the lesson of their experience. Miss Boynton was very wise to have the children memorize the classics of those days. Her influence has held through the years. There isn't one child who had Miss Boynton for a teacher who doesn't think lovingly of her as an ideal.

What were the children like?

Most of the children had hobbies. One collected stones, another tops, another jacks. Arthur collected cigar bands. It was the great era of cigars. And he would insist on staying outside the lower Market Street saloons, and he would place me, his very little sister, at the edge of the gutter, and say, "Now you watch and collect as many as you can of a certain kind, and I'll slip in under the swinging doors in the saloon and find the treasured ones in the sawdust." I never got any compensation for that.

Arthur was brilliant. He was bossy; he pulled hair. It was the age of braids, and the inkwells on the school desks always were full of ink, and the pigtails would be dipped into the inkwells behind you, and you never knew until your mother scolded you after you got home, and the end of the braids had smeared ink on the back of your middy blouse.

And what did Miss Boynton do about such behavior?

Well, we did have corporal punishment. There was a strap, out in the anteroom where we hung up our coats and hats. Johnny Meenan and George Irwin were the two really strenuous boys. They would fist-fight, and Miss Boynton would punish them. She would make them stay in the anteroom and then, if she felt that they should be strapped, she would have one go out, and there was this heavy silence in the classroom. We would hear her say, "Put out your hand, John." And John would put it out, and then he would pull it back again, and then Bang! would come the strap, and we would hear him say, "Oh, Miss Boynton, I made a mistake, I'll never do it again."

And the parents appreciated what she did; they treasured her influence on our lives. And Miss Boynton's influence is in every way a living thing. No one will ever, ever forget her.

She left in 1906 after our class graduated, and went to Tokyo with the Howells family, where she taught English in the schools, and then she had many private pupils in the embassies and among the royalty of Japan. She became a great friend of Mrs. Mitsui the elder, and then she met the Matsukata family. Mrs. Matsukata had been through college on the east coast, but her husband's family was very conservative in its old Japanese dress, habits of thinking, and government of the family, and so Mrs. Matsukata, being a good Japanese wife and mother, had to bring her children up in that style. But they loved Miss Boynton, and they invited her to live in a house in their garden, to direct the education of their five children. And Miss Boynton did. When the war came every American was sent away from Japan, but one of the Matsukata daughers came with her to live in San Francisco. She lived with Miss Boynton several years after she left Japan. Miss Boynton hated to leave Japan and the friends she had made there. It was a sad ending to her life. She gave her whole life to teaching, first in Belvedere and then in Tokyo.

During the war the small house that Miss Boynton lived in was bombed, and nothing was left of it. Recently the Matsukata family have built a fine international school in Tokyo, called the Nishimashi School, because that was the street that Miss Boynton's house was on. The school is a kind of living memorial to Miss Boynton, and we all love to support it in our own way.

Can you tell us about the ferryboats you rode to school?

We rode either the *Ukiah* or the *James Donahue,* which was the single-ender. The *Donahue* was something wonderful. All the interior was painted white, with carved and gilded moldings. And the seats were red plush. There was a little walkway back to the great paddle-wheels on each side, and beside the paddle-wheels were large chests full of life-preservers. It wasn't very long before the Belvedere children found they could lift up the lids of these chests and hide their books there, and their candy, and other things that didn't go to school with them. And then on the return journey we would rush out and lift up the lids and settle down on top of the life-preservers. It was our own private refuge, and it was great fun.

We had the pleasure of watching the vegetable Chinaman pack his two huge baskets on a pole that went across his shoulders. That was the vegetable and fruit supply for all of Belvedere. And on Monday mornings if we didn't have any fruit for our lunches, we were each given five cents, and we would stop the vegetable Chinaman and he would lift a tray, first of the heavy vegetables, and then the light ones below, and then down at the bottom the fruit. He'd let us choose which we wanted, an apple or orange or banana. Stopping on the way to school to choose fruit was great fun. It seemed to give a special flavor to our picnic lunches.

Can you tell us about Miss Livsey?

Oh, Miss Livsey! I remember her very well. First there was a little post office in back of the Belve-

Top: Belvedere School pupils in 1902, with the beloved Miss Boynton second from left. Winifred Bridge is directly below right edge of flag. Below: Belvedere eighth-grade graduating class, 1905. From left: Kate Peterson, Edith Harmon, Edith Hooper, Henry Heyneman, Winifred Bridge, Walter Heyneman, Minnie Harmon, Helena Howells.

dere Hotel, then it moved to the building where the Belvedere Land Company had its offices. It was a room maybe eight feet wide and fifteen or twenty feet long. She stood at a little window with bars across it, and you asked for your mail there. The mail came in twice a day. Miss Livsey had a parrot. It sat for many, many years on her shoulder, and they grew to look alike. When it spoke to you, you weren't sure whether it had been Miss Livsey or the parrot.

She didn't open your letters, but she did read your postcards, and she slipped magazines out of their wrappers before you came to call for them. And in the winter if you were on a trip or living in San Francisco you gave Miss Livsey permission to open them up and read them, and she did. When the boys in the first world war would write home, the postcards would say,"Dear Miss Livsey and Mom." They knew she would read it anyway, and they would sign their names and give their regards to her. She knew everything — who was going to get married, who was engaged. She knew the news before anyone else did. Oh, she kept secrets very well.

Everything was hand-cancelled at that time. She held the cancellation stamp in one hand and the letter in the other. First she'd stamp the inkpad, then the letter. Bang! Bang! The people who rented the upstairs always asked when they had company to please stamp more quietly.

Miss Livsey was related to Lotta Crabtree. After Lotta died, it was discovered that Miss Livsey had received some sort of inheritance, in money, enough to make it worth while to go back east to claim it. So the great excitement in Belvedere was Miss Livsey's going back to claim her inheritance. She did. And she came back and it didn't spoil her, she didn't change, she lived very much as she had. She was a very small, erect person, and she always dressed in a very mannish way. Everyone loved and teased Miss Livsey. She was English, and how she was related to Lotta Crabtree no one ever knew. I have forgotten where she lived in Belvedere; it must have been close to the Post Office, for she had long hours. I don't know how many years she was postmistress. She was a character. We enjoyed her; she was part of Belvedere.

We are curious about the beautiful Belvedere gardens and the Italian gardeners.

Three families came from Italy: the de Tomasi family, the Salvadini family, and the Harry Pariani family. Harry Pariani married an Italian girl and they had two daughters. He took care of about four gardens and he would come early in the morning. You could always tell he was in the garden by the fragrance of his long black cigars. They didn't always light and burn, but he always had at least part of one in his mouth. He talked very loud. He worked also for my sister, who lived next door. When he came early my sister used to say, "Now, you mustn't have arguments with Harry Pariani before seven o'clock in the morning!" Harry Pariani loved the two gardens. This was one of his first gardens, and he worked in this garden the thirty years the Holmeses had it and the thirty years we had it. He worked until the middle of World War II. So many people had lost their gardeners and they would plead with Harry Pariani to "get up an hour earlier and give us that extra hour. We can't let it die!" He really worked himself to death.

Most of the gardeners lived in the arks anchored down on the edge of the lagoon. Originally there were 32 arks. They would be towed into the lagoon through the drawbridge each fall. First they stayed on the railroad side, then the railroad wanted to build the road, and there was a strike, so they asked them to go over to the Belvedere side of the lagoon. They moved to the Belvedere side, along what is now San Rafael avenue. There was a large accumulation of them. Gradually they filled in a little and a little more and planted, and eventually they even had chicken coops out back. They had vegetable gardens and sometimes because it was the edge of the saltwater the vegetables would be salty.

The Italian gardeners built all the rock walls on Belvedere Island. They would go up the roads to the Tiburon hills, collect rocks of usable sizes, and bring them home to Belvedere on carts. Then they would pile them along the road until they used them. Harry Pariani's greatest wall was the one across the road, at the top of Golden Gate Avenue, which is about three blocks long. It has never cracked, it has never sunk, it has never done anything. It took him months to build it. They did have helpers that they trained, younger sons or cousins, who came over after.

Harry Pariani was a wonderful gardener. He was a loyal, good friend to me. He loved Harry Allen and he loved me too, but he never would admit it. After

Harry Allen drained the lagoon, all the arks had to go. Harry Pariani loved his ark. A couple of the other gardeners had their arks moved up on the hill, two or three of them. Harry bought a lot from the Belvedere Land Company on the end of Acacia Avenue, and when he decided he was beyond living in an ark he asked Albert Farr, who had designed the town hall and the Belvedere Land Company Building and the shingled houses across Beach Road, to design him a good house which was not to cost more than eight thousand dollars. Mr. Farr did, and Harry loved it and planted some very good permanent plants around it. He loved to bring new plants to Belvedere; how he got them I don't know. Many of those plants we love dearly. One is that big Chinese lemon by my gate. And persimmons. And there was one mistake Harry felt Mr. Farr made in his house: at the head of his bed was a drain pipe and Harry could hear the first drop of rain coming down right at the head of his bed. It always woke him in the middle of the night.

Harry Pariani came over as a young man. I don't know whether he was married and brought Rosy over, but at least the two daughters grew up in Belvedere and married. Harry began working in this garden when he was in his twenties. So his whole life was devoted to the gardens. The de Tomasi's were as important a family, and there was Louie Soldavini, who still works for the town. His father brought him over, so he grew up in Belvedere.

How did the lagoon get filled in?

The railroad needed a road, a highway, alongside their tracks coming into Tiburon. They asked permission of the Belvedere Land Company, and also of the two yacht clubs, to pump mud from the cove into the lagoon to build a roadbed. They were to pump only enough dirt for that road. But when they began pumping they found it was so expensive to contain all that loose, liquid mud, that they just let it slurp all over the beautiful lagoon and filled it up. That was one of the worst bay fills in the history of this bay. Belvedere was joined to Tiburon, and lost its identity as an island. This was in the 1920's.

In winter the lagoon was filled a few feet deep with drainage water. You have no idea how it poured down these hills. Then in March it was mud. Then most of it dried in the summertime, turned into fine pulverized salt dust, which covered everything.

Harry Allen took over the Belvedere Land Company in 1936; he bought it from the second generation of those who formed it. Almost two-thirds of Belvedere was still empty when Harry took it over. He re-designed the lots. He put Golden Gate Avenue right through the golf club down to the northern tip. He created Crest Road, at the top of the island. He then made the lots so they were different shapes and had more road exposure, which was very wise.

Then he thought, here this beautiful inland sea once existed. And he longed to get water back into the lagoon. So he hired several engineers. He took two years and $200,000 as a beginning, and fleets of dredging trucks. And he moved every inch of mud in the lagoon, and made peninsulas. He let every member of the family name the peninsulas. I named the two northern ones, Leeward Road, and Windward. And then he had a little bit of mud left over, which he plopped up in the other end, and gave his wife a little island. But I had to give it up when the Lagoon Owners' Association was formed.

Then he waited six years for the peninsulas to drain and dry, before he could lay out the lots. You couldn't build on them for six years. And I would row out to my little island and put in sacks of earth, and plant trees. It was only a spot for meditation; the Orientals teach us to meditate under three kinds of foliage, the pine, the plum, and the bamboo. And so the pine, the plum, and the bamboo, I think, are still there.

There were many adventures to making an inland sea. First of all, Harry made a very deep exit for water at the northern tip. And then he installed great iron gates that opened to let the water out when it needed to be drained, thoroughly flushed out, and then, when the water comes in, they wait for the very highest tide to fill the lagoon with fresh ocean water. But there were unforeseen problems. One was that as the peninsulas dried, they cracked as a cake does in an oven when it dries too fast. And in those cracks came salt-water mosquitoes. Never heard of before. So Harry had to take a hill down from the top of Belvedere and put a skim coat of good earth, a frosting, which filled up the cracks and there were no more salt-water mosquitoes.

Then widgin grass grew very fast, because a lot of fresh water had come in, drained from the hills. That was conquered. Then one day a frantic mother phoned Harry and said, "You promised the children

The Belvedere bus, although horseless, is almost identical to the horse-drawn earlier model, with three steps up at the back, canvas curtains that rolled up, and a driver, presumably F.M. Ballard, in a duster coat. Building in back is not identified.

could swim here and you've let stingrays come in!" During construction they had pulled up all the ugly stake fences that had once protected the clam and oyster beds in the bay. That permitted the stingrays to come in with the high tide, into the lagoon. And how to get rid of them? Harry phoned every maritime museum and college professor who knew anything about stingrays, but nobody could tell him how to get rid of them. At last a professor down at Scripps said, "Mr. Allen, how long has the water been in the lagoon?" And Harry told him a few months. "Do you know if there are any bivalves in the lagoon?" "I don't think there are any yet." "Fine, just go to sleep and rest well. Those stingrays have nothing to live on. They'll die of starvation." And they did. And then Harry put taller stakes at the entrance, so no stingrays could come in with the high tide.

Do you recall the Belvedere Hotel?

The Belvedere Hotel was not noted for its architecture. I don't know who the architect was. It was a very large building and it spread over quite a bit of both the beach and Beach Road, just exactly where the San Francisco Yacht Club is now. It had a wharf and a float. Downstairs one of its front rooms was large, and was used for dances and public gatherings.

Can you remember dancing there as a young girl?

Well, most of the dances we had were in our own homes. We had a pianola, where you have rolls and pump with your feet, and that was the music. I don't remember any phonographs. Mr. Keith — the Harmons — bought the property right on the corner of Golden Gate and Pine. And they also built the only tennis court, on top of the hill, and then below the tennis court, which was on the level of Golden Gate Avenue, Mr. Keith built a home for his sister, Miss Keith. She lived upstairs and the downstairs was a room that was given over to fun! We had a pianola there, and that's where a number of the dances were held. Not great big parties — about twenty children or so. There was a separate entrance, and we were allowed to do anything we wanted down there. We made chocolate or punch for our informal parties.

And the grownups had the dances and parties down at the hotel. The one party I remember most clearly was a Halloween dance. They were all supposed to dress as witches. There were three huge kettles which they stirred, and quoted from Hamlet (Macbeth?) as they brewed the witches' brew. We were allowed to see the decorations but we weren't allowed to come. Then of course there were many yacht club parties.

At the time of the San Francisco fire people were asked to leave San Francisco and go to friends or relatives or hotels, and they came over to the Belvedere Hotel. Many people such as the Arthur Pages and the Hellmans stayed there first, I think, and then bought lots and built houses in Belvedere.

Was the Belvedere Hotel very luxurious?

No, I wouldn't say so. People just lived in summer clothes; it was much fuller in summer than in winter. The bus that met almost every boat came up on the island, so it would stop and deliver people and their suitcases to the Belvedere Hotel. You ate all your meals at the hotel; there were no restaurants at all in Tiburon, so you ate at the hotel.

In Tiburon first came the butcher shop, Mr. Anderson's, Harvey's father. They built the first house around the corner in Lyford's Cove, and we used to call it Butchertown, because the butcher owned the house. On Main Street in Tiburon the shopkeepers would throw lots of things into the lagoon, out their back doors, so when you came walking along Main Street there were lots of smells. There was one grocery store, Chapman's, and that stayed a long time. Between Chapman's and Anderson's was a saloon, next to Chapman's was a place you could get a drink, and then another and another. There were a lot of saloons because of the workers on the railroad. They had to have their refreshment. Now whether they ever got sandwiches made at any of the places I don't know.

The people who stayed at the Belvedere Hotel did not go into Tiburon. No, they did not, no, they did not! There used to be quite a difference of feeling between Belvedere and Tiburon. Tiburon had its own school, about as old as the Belvedere grammar school, but we felt we were a little bit apart. We don't any more. That's all changed since Tiburon has been developed so beautifully.

But I think then the buses backed right up close to where you came off the ferryboat on the wharf. The mothers with long skirts, hats, and capes were

A stroller rests on Golden Gate Avenue, Belvedere, looking northward, in the 1920's.

always allowed to ride. The gentlemen let them take their seats. The buses were open; they just had canvas that you rolled down. And of course the Barn; you remember where the Barn was? Right where Barn Road is — they only took it down a few years ago. There were three steps to go up into the bus and in the winter when the horses were tired and it was dark, the gentlemen would step down and help push the bus up a steep place. One of those places was on the way up to Acacia Avenue. And it was a lot of fun.

There was hay on the bottom of the bus, because people came in with mud on their feet in the winter time. You bought a ticket for one dollar, for I don't know how many rides. The driver punched your ticket when you got on the bus. The seats were shiny hard black oil cloth and they were very cold. And the children, if they could walk, had to walk from Tiburon home. We had long black stockings, and if we went to the theater in San Francisco we carried our silk stockings in our purse and then on the boat we would put them on. We had to take a very early boat to reach San Francisco in time for the plays — I guess the plays were at eight o'clock. They were not very often. We also went to plays on Saturday afternoons. That was terribly exciting.

As a child did you go out to dinner with your family in San Francisco?

No, we had our entertainment at home. But when we had a birthday party we were given a choice between having a party at home with a cake or going to Ocean Beach, out beyond Sutro's, or to the playground in Golden Gate Park, which had donkey rides and a merry-go-round. You invited six or eight children, and the mothers came along, and you took your own cake. It was exciting!

I have some pictures of birthday parties at the beach. And we were allowed to go wading if there was no surf. We would take off our shoes and stockings and tie them to a bush so we knew where they were. It was a long trip because first you walked to Tiburon, then you took the ferry, then you took a car as far as Presidio Avenue, then you got on a little railroad train that went all the way around to the Cliff House. Then you walked a ways down. And there was a large chalet on the beach just built for picnics and parties. You could make coffee or tea or chocolate there.

And I do remember El Campo perfectly. It was a local picnic area in Tiburon. The man Crowley, who had the tugs, owned the underwater lots, and he ran tugs and boats to El Campo on summer Sundays. They had dancing there on a platform, and refreshment. But we liked to go to Paradise Cove, adjoining El Campo, where there was a great anchorage for yachts and everyone went up on weekends and anchored their boats, took their own food, and spent the night on their boats. And we would row ashore. We did that until the last World War came and they used the cove for the Net Depot. You couldn't land there any more. But now of course you can because we all thought it would be a good place, when the government was through with it, to have a park. So now you just leave your car up near the road and walk down. But the beach is just as lovely. They put in a lot of good lawn, but I think perhaps there could be more native trees; they put in more city trees. Perhaps they will change them. It is still a good place, but not a great many boats go there. More boats now go to Ayala Cove, on Angel Island. I think as time goes on they will permit anchorage on the east side of Angel Island, which is a good climate too, and out of the wind.

Can you tell us about the arks?

There was a large ark colony in Belvedere Cove. Each ark had its own rowboat. On the back of each ark was a davet to pull up the rowboat. The back side of each ark had a large barrel for fresh water. One ark, the most beautiful of them all, was built around a courtyard. It was shingled. It had many, many plants, and was very fancy. They had a pipe run out from shore that came up for their water supply, so they had to anchor in the same place every year.

When Harry dredged the lagoon he gave me an ark, the *Mermaid*. It was on land for years and years. That is one of the reasons they named the Ark Apartments, because there were about five arks where the apartments are today on Beach Road. I gave the *Mermaid* to the town for young people to use as a conference room; it is near the Recreation Center (Tiburon Peninsula Club). Then another one was very good, it was on the other side of the *Mermaid*. I had it put on a barge and sent over to San Francisco, to the wharf at the foot of Hyde Street. They promised to put a plaque on it to say it had come

Top: Harry Allen with his children (from left) David, Elizabeth, and Howard, around 1930. Below: Winifred and Harry Allen rowing at the San Francisco Yacht Club, 1960's.

from Belvedere and who had sent it, because it was very expensive to have it towed over and lifted up onto the wharf. They have kept it perfectly. They wanted to use the whole thing for an office. I said no, they could use the back two rooms, they could use the kitchen for an office. But the two front rooms, one was a living room and had a corner stove in it, and the next two were bedrooms with bunks in them — they were to be furnished, and I gave some furnishings, just as though there were ark-dwellers still living in them. I think they have kept it up very well.

People owned their own arks in the Cove. And they were there in the Cove for many years. The last one was owned by Mr. Dobie and his brother. Mr. Dobie was a writer. It was in the Cove for around fifty years, winter and summer, it was never towed in . Not many of us were anchored for that many years.

It was a great event when the drawbridge was lifted and the arks were towed in and stayed the winter time in the lagoon. And when spring came they would be towed out again and they would put down moorings. The owners all had their own special places they enjoyed. They would only really use the arks in summertime.

You said the Dobies' ark was towed out of the Cove. Do you know where it went?

No. But one went almost to Keil Cove, almost on the Keil property — whose that was I don't know. One was pulled up on Corinthian Island and kept in perfect condition. I think Mrs. Dakin bought it. She used to write a great deal and so I gave her, for one year, my apartment down at the codfishery.

Can you tell us about the codfishery?

You see the codfishery was one of the very first buildings on Belvedere. Up to two hundred men worked there. In May the two- or three-masted ships would be towed to the Gate and the sails would go up and they would sail up to the Bering Sea. Sometimes they wouldn't see each other until they got back to Belvedere again. It was a very successful business. The men would come from San Francisco and work at the codfishery after a boat would come in from the Bering Sea. Then the whole hull of the ship would be full of fish that were cleaned and in salt. The fish were unloaded and put into large redwood tanks, in brine. Finally the men would spread them out to dry in racks, and turn the halves. Then they took the flesh off the bones and packed it in strips in little wooden boxes, and ship them mostly to South America and Mexico. You see people who need fish on Fridays, a great many of them lived in Mexico and a great many of them not near the water, but they had to have dried fish and so that was where this codfish was shipped, in little wooden one-pound boxes. You slid the top off, this way. You can't find codfish now. Codfish from Canada, on the East Coast, used to come in little one-pound boxes, but I have not been able to find that for years now, three or four or five years.

How did the codfishery get its food and supplies?

On a boat; the *UNIFCO,* Union Codfishery Company, was the name of the boat. It was a motor boat with a mast. They would bring half steers, and I mean enormous amounts of meat for the men, and tubs of butter, and they had great tables laid with oilcloth. I have some of the dishes the men used for their meals. I still have some of the Swedish white enamel with a blue edge that was not made in America, it is very, very good. I have two pitchers and little sauce bowls that came from the codfishery. They were their everyday dishes. I used them on our sailboats when we went on long trips; they were easy to wash, easier than the heavy crockery that used to come with a sailboat.

There were three bunkhouses where the workers at the codfishery slept, and they ate in a large room under one bunkhouse. There were not two hundred men every month of the year, but when the work was heavy there were. The cook stood over this enormous stove. And in front of the sink where he scraped the dishes, there was a trap door that went down to the beach below. He would stamp the trap door with one foot and all the scraps went down to the beach. Underneath, on the beach, was a pen with pigs. It made a terrible smell. Howard Allen and Evan Pugh, when they were little boys, when the codfishery was still a going concern, would sharpen bamboo poles and then in the evening when the pigs were eating, the skunks would come down to eat what the pigs had left, and Howard and Evan would prod those skunks and pigs with the bamboo poles and then run!

Top: Codfish ready for packing. Below: Codfishery apartments, 1950's.

And then the owners of the codfishery decided they would can some salmon. They would bring salmon down from the Bering Sea too. It was a big mistake. To can things you have to use heated gas and heat the cans. So they put in gas, and there was a gas leak the first season they started to can salmon. Then there was a fire, early in the morning, and the building where they were canning burned; it was a terrific fire.

Now the rule was, that any building in Belvedere, on the beach, if it was more than half burned it would have to be demolished, they couldn't use it any more. And so that is why Harry Allen bought the codfishery, all those buildings. There were no other buildings on the west side when he came over to take over the Belvedere Land Company.

Oh, I forgot to tell you, the cook was so tired of the men that he built himself a little cabin. He put up a gangplank to the bank and he could pull it up when he got to his own little room. Seldon Giles painted a number of pictures of the codfishery, and one of them shows this little building with the gangplank. The picture is down at my cabana at Belvedere Cove. I paid rent on the cabana for years, because they took away my codfishery and they took away my ark and so they said you can have this little cabin, and that is where I keep my canoe.

But anyway I gradually fixed up and remodeled the different buildings at the codfishery, and used them for guest houses when friends came over. And then during the war when there was such a need for housing for the workers at the war plant in Sausalito — you know they built Liberty Ships there at the shipyards — we rented them at the time, I think there were six or seven that we had remodeled. And the workers went over by motorboat to Sausalito. One of the men had his own motorboat and he took them all over.

But after that there was one large building which had held the salt for the brine. They mixed the brine and ran it by pipe to the large redwood tanks where they kept the fish until they dried them. The downstairs was just a large empty space that a boat builder had once used. Upstairs were bunks where the men had slept all along each wall. When we remodeled we whitewashed them all, tons of whitewash, to clean them up. On the inside of the bunkboards were many addresses, some those of the fancy ladies who lived along the waterfront in San Francisco, and so we didn't wash those out. We left those. We took most of the bunks out and left only a few. This last building at the codfishery was made into two beautiful apartments. Howard owned the northern one and I owned the southern one. We cut out windows and made a porch on each. It was a very warm place because it got the last rays of the western sun.

Mr. Rivers took charge of that building for us. And his wife, who weighed, I think, at least 250 pounds, couldn't walk up the steps and over the hill to Tiburon. And so she fished most of the time. I can see her fishing now! She would even catch eels, which I didn't know until she told me. And she would take an eel and hold it with a pair of pliers, and then with another pair of pliers she would peel off the eel skin just as you would peel off a rubber glove.

When the herring came in people would scoop them up with baskets, pickle them and smoke them. I remember an artist drawing a picture of a smoked herring that was a beautiful copper color. They would catch it, they would smoke it, and then they would paint it. They learned to live on many things there. Mrs. Rivers would walk at low tide, from the codfishery all round the north point of Belvedere to Tiburon. And if someone was driving to the west side of the island they would take her and she would walk down from Belvedere Avenue down the trail to the codfishery.

I have given several mementos that I had collected down at the codfishery to the Maritime Museum — fish awls, and those hand-blown glass balls. I had a hundred or so, because when the men went north, I asked one of them if he would collect a sack full for me and he did.

Oh, these are good memories!

The Shamrock Club on Beach Road, Belvedere Cove, was the clubhouse of the railroad workers' union. The picture is undated, but is probably from the 1890's. The ornate little house, with ridge spindles, rolled canvas awnings, and shamrocks at each roof corner, is bedecked with flags and greenery. The house now stands at One Laurel Avenue, across from Belvedere City Hall.

Harvey Anderson on Main Street, 1926.

Harvey Anderson

1906–1979

At the time of this interview in April, 1975, Harvey Anderson was a large, raw-boned man with a booming voice and a very friendly manner, very quick to laugh — his eyes always dancing, looking for fun. And he was a great story teller. He loved an audience; we could tell he had told most of these stories before with great pleasure. Small-town life always suited him perfectly, yet he traveled all over the world after his retirement. He was a fixture in Tiburon, known by everyone in both towns, and mentioned by almost everyone we interviewed.

Harvey, when did your family come to Tiburon?

My father, H.D. Anderson, came to Tiburon in 1898 from San Francisco, where he had been working for the Bacciocco California Meat Company of San Francisco. He was originally from Brooklyn. He had heard that Victor Beyries had a meat market for sale in Tiburon. My father was the only butcher in town; he bought his meat from the California Meat Company. He sold out in 1938 to Bennett, the station agent.

My mother was from London; she arrived in San Francisco when she was thirteen. Her father worked in San Francisco until he made enough money to send for his family. There were three girls and two boys, times were tough, so marry the girls off! My mother married a gripman, had two girls, and then the marriage ended. She came to Belvedere as a housekeeper. The girls went to the Belvedere School.

How did your parents meet?

My mother did a lot of the ordering for the families she worked for on Belvedere so she and my father got to know one another. And in 1906 I was practically born right in the butcher shop. My father went to the barn, where the Tiburon Vintners is now, to get the horse and wagon, and on to Belvedere to pick up Dr. Florence Scott, who lived with her sister Elizabeth on Golden Gate Avenue. A woman doctor in those days was an oddity. Then he went back to the butcher shop to pick up a spring scale to weigh the new arrival. My mother was five feet tall and weighed about 115 pounds. The doctor had told her to eat enough for two. Well, I weighed in at twelve pounds. I have two sisters; one lives in San Rafael.

(Looking at an old postcard of Lyford Cove) Is this the house you grew up in?

Oh, yeah! This one, the large brown house across the street from the water. This was called Anderson's Beach. But there were no houses there at all. My grandfather lived here too. He came here after my dad did, from Connecticut, where he was a ship's carpenter. He was married to a Moody — Moody was the founder of Hartford Life in Hartford, Connecticut. You see, my great-grandfather went out to Arizona and married a squaw, and he was ostracized. So he said, "the hell with you," and went down to New York and that is where my grandfather was born. Then my grandfather went to Connecticut, and he finally came out here.

Did he build his house too?

Well, my dad won $1,200 in the Louisiana lottery and two weeks later my grandfather won $1,200! With that money he built the house!

Which other houses were built then?

Mrs. Brentin's, of course Mantegani's, Mrs. Ross's, Hooper's, the Randolph place — in fact Ronnie's widow still lives there.

We had a vegetable man come around and deliver to us. There were two brothers, their names weren't Mike and Ike, but they looked so much alike we dubbed them that. Mike and Ike, they look alike! A Chinaman used to come around in a horse and wagon. And an Italian fella came around. As kids we'd hide alongside of the bank when he came around the stone tower, that was a sharp turn in the road, see, he'd be driving his wagon and we'd run up from behind and get the peaches and apples. Before he got all the way around the corner we were back out of sight again!

Who were your friends?

Well, the Whitings and the Creightons and the Clements, all kids that lived around the area, mostly boys.

What other kind of trouble did you get into?

Oh, we would go down under the railroad docks and strip the copper sheeting off the pilings and sell it to the junkman. The railroad put copper sheeting around to keep the worms from destroying the pilings.

When your father had his butcher shop on Main Street, what else was there? Was the Tiburon Hotel still open?

Yes, Mrs. Carpenter ran the hotel and restaurant. Some of the railroad workers lived there. Next door was Billy Burke's saloon, then Anderson's Butcher Shop, then Forrester's Hall, J.H. Kelley Groceries, the Time Card Saloon, Harry Adams' Grocery and Barbershop — he gave me my first haircut. He had a hard time of it!

We kids used to steal from him. We'd ask for five cents' worth of potatoes, he'd go to the back, and while he was gone we'd reach around the counter and fill our pockets with candy. Next was Norby's saloon. The last two buildings housed the railroad workers. Captain White lived in the end building. Around the corner were rooming houses for more railroad workers. This was before the 1921 fire.

Was there a fire department in Tiburon then?

The railroad was the only fire department. Did you know the railroad burnt down? All but two of the buildings. The buildings had all been brick red. After the fire the new ones were brought down from Willits, all the yellow buildings. The railroad furnished some housing for the workers below Mar West. The only one of those buildings left standing is the storage room; now it houses some architects. The road, left of Main Street, ran as far as the icehouse. The railroad delivered the ice to the icehouse, and it was stored there and then delivered to customers. The meat market ice box is still in the Surprise Shop; they just took off the door. We took a few hundred pounds of ice.

The only building on the water side was the McNeil Building, a saloon and living quarters. Sam McDonough's son Milt still runs the boat to Angel Island. Main Street changed after the fire. They rebuilt the same ten-foot wooden sidewalk and wooden awnings on the north side, and they decided to widen the street so they made the cement sidewalk as it is now on the water side. Then people built up the water side.

There was a barber shop down there with a wooden barber pole out front. The sign outside read "Baseball NWP vs. —," the barber wrote on it what team was going to be playing the next Sunday. That was the Tiburon team, the Northwestern Pacific. They played every Sunday. Everybody went out

Left: Mr. and Mrs. H.D. Anderson pose on the running board of their flivver.
Right: Harvey, circa 1912.

there on a Sunday afternoon. The ballfield was right behind Main Street after the lagoon was filled in. The original baseball field was out there where the tennis courts are now at Judge Field, the Tiburon Peninsula Club. Then it went closer to town and then it went over to where Safeway is now, and then it went back out to Judge Field.

(Still looking at pictures of Main Street). At the end of the street was the drugstore, Ed and Arnold, they had bought it from George Morrison and his wife. See, Arnold and Ed were chief pharmacists in the war, and right after the war they bought in. Arnold still owns the Corinthian Pharmacy on the Belvedere Boardwalk.

It must have been nice before the street was built up on the water side.

There was nothing but two wharves on the beach side, until you got down to the eastern end of the street.

What kind of business was run on the piers?

There were just the two piers, one for Kelley's grocery store and the other for Carpenter and Chapman. And they had floats out there off the beach for the yachts. The yachts would have to anchor out there — there were no berths — and then people would row in on their skiffs to get the groceries and booze to go out on the bay for the weekend. And the yachtsmen used to run their yachts up on the beach at high tide and run a line from the top of the mast to each wharf and when the tide went out they'd lower the boat to one side and scrape and paint the bottom of it and pull it over and do the other side of it and they'd wait for high tide to launch it again. There was just this galvanized iron building, where the Dock Restaurant is now, it finally got to be Williamson's garage. And previous to that it was Kashow's place and he leased it to Dick Williamson, who ran a garage there for a long time. Then he sold it to Korto or Grant and finally Zelinsky bought the whole bit. He tore the old dock down and built the Dock Restaurant.

Can you tell us anything about Miss Livsey?

Oh yes. She was the postmistress of Belvedere. Before we had the rural delivery, the butcher would deliver the mail up on Belvedere, we got a dollar a month. We had two meat deliveries going out every day to eighteen or twenty customers up on Belvedere Island. Well, we'd stop and get the mail from Miss Livsey and deliver it to the houses along the route. She lived over the post office and Mrs. Erhenfelt took over from her.

We would stop in and pick up the mail until Bill Barr muscled in and took it away from the butcher shop boys. He used to go to Belvedere pret'near every time the *Marin* would come in; he was running a taxi service and so could give them better service than we could.

Right in the corner of the Belvedere Land Company building was originally a drugstore — Dr. Marson. And upstairs, above the drugstore, was Dr. Florence Scott's office. She turned it into a hospital when the flu epidemic hit in 1918.That epidemic took over six million lives in the United States — more than we lost in three wars. And my sister was one of the nurses up there. She was an RN at Children's Hospital in 1912. Dr. Scott lived with her sister up on Golden Gate Avenue, at the top of the hill. Elizabeth, her sister, used to teach at the Sunday school when I was going there. The church is now the city hall; they moved it down the hill onto San Rafael Avenue.

Do you remember anything about the Belvedere Hotel?

I was there a couple of times. My mother and dad and I went up there for dinner.

Was it a fashionable place?

Oh, it was a fancy house! I don't mean that there were call girls there, but you know, these men would come over every week with a different wife. It was all very convenient.

Were the Lemuel Allens in Belvedere yet?

Lem and Marion came here when his brother took over the superintendency of the Union Fish Company on the other side of Belvedere. They made a grocery store out of the drug store in Belvedere.

We have heard that Main Street was rough and tough. Is it true?

I didn't get all these lines from age! These are not age wrinkles. But, oh, you made it as tough as you liked; you could always find a taker. The sailors coming off the carriers and the codfish sailors, they were

Top: Anderson's Beach, 1907. The largest house (center) is Andersons'; left, second Anderson house; small white house belonged to McNamara. Mary Brennan's house, lower right. Below: Harvey, second from left, and fellow caddies at the Belvedere Golf Course.

pretty crude in spots. But when you got to know them you'd get along with them. It's the same with any people; you've got to live with them to know them.

Did Tiburon have any police service?

Just the sheriff's office in San Rafael; it'd take them a week to get here. But we didn't need any help; we took care of ourselves. Hell, if a couple of guys wanted to argue, let 'em get out and argue. We didn't bother 'em. Like in prohibition, when Sheriff Keating was in office, I wouldn't say it was him, but if they were going to raid Tiburon, why, someone would call and say "We're going to come down and knock you over. It's time you paid your taxes." So the bootleggers would hide all the booze and have a pint right there on the bar so they could find it, so they would confiscate the pint and Sam Vella would have to go before Judge Helmore in Sausalito. This one time I went over with him, and Sam goes up to the Judge, who used to be over here at Sam's two or three times a week lapping up the booze himself. And he'd say, "Good morning, Vella, how are ya?" Sam would say "Fine, Judge!" The Judge would say, "Fine, five dollars." Sam would pay right there, that was all, and then he'd come back home. His place was never closed.

Was Sam the only one who was doing this?

Oh, no, no, no, no! There were four bootleggers who sold whiskey on Main Street, and every Italian in the neighborhood sold wine that they made, a dollar, dollar and a half a gallon.

Did you ever help with the winemaking?

I made wine for myself with the Simontacchi's, just across the street from Reed School. There was a dairy there, and Simontacchi lived in the arks there on the lagoon. This fella Jack Barch who worked at the coaling station and I would buy a ton and Simontacchi would buy two tons of grapes. A ton made about one hundred fifty gallons of wine.

Who else lived in the arks along the east shore of the lagoon?

Baterinis, Arbinis, Simontacchis, Souzas. The Souzas operated the ranch where Reed School is. They were Portuguese, the rest were Italians. They were all related in some way. They were pret'near all cousins. Most of them came here to work on the railroad to begin with. Then the railroad strike came along so they went into gardening.

We had a Christmas storm in 1921 that knocked the sea wall down and the arks broke loose and blew over onto the spit, the north end of the lagoon. And along "Wop Alley," the flats where the Italians lived in Belvedere below San Rafael Avenue. As far back as I can remember there were arks along "Dago Flats." They were not all arks; there were some buildings and a very few homes. Like the Fletch house, that was the first one, then the Zucchi's, and Carlo de Tomasi's, those were houses. Then Paul Stevens, Soldavini's, Lee Rivers, Charles de Tomasi, Harry Pariani, Coleman, Compagna, Reed, Oldfield, Avila, Joe Rose, Mrs. Murray, Hilton, the plumber, Greenwood, Malini, and Conziani — they were all arks. They ran up to where the golf links used to start. A nine-hole golf course ran right out to the north point of Belvedere.

What was along Beach Road?

Well, there was the wood yard, and before that it was the blacksmith and in the back was "Charlie Laundry." And in back of Charlie Pon was the jail. Belvedere had a police department and a town marshall; Belvedere was incorporated, Tiburon was not. A fellow named Duncan Kennedy almost drowned in the Belvedere jail. He had been put in jail, he was one of the town drunks, to keep him out of trouble. We had a storm and the jail flooded, and "Charlie Laundry" went in and rescued him just in time.

What was it like here during the Depression?

We had a box in each grocery store and in the butcher shop, and if someone felt like it he could put in an extra can of beans or something, whatever he could. We had men coming through, going south in winter or north in summer. There was one we'd always ask when he came through, "Well, how are things up north?" "Oh, they're slowing down, have to go down south now." I kicked him out of the butcher shop once for telling me not to give him any more of that god damn lamb stew. I told him he wasn't very hungry. We had a little club here called the Tiburoners. We generally took care of our own pretty well, and we still do.

The Corinthians baseball team represented Tiburon and Belvedere in 1913. Back row, from left: Harry Baker, Ray O'Connell, Carl Fennema, Francis McMullin, (unidentified), Douglas Wosser (pitcher and best hitter), Oscar Schilling. Front row: Charles McNeill, (unidentified), "Botchie," the catcher, and George Wosser.

Geraldine Coleman Halverson and Louise Coleman Averill, 1940.

Louise Coleman Averill

1883–1979

Geraldine Coleman Halverson

1919–1985

At the time of this interview in September, 1975, Mrs. Averill was 92, and her daughter Jerry was 56. The love and humor and mutual respect which had sustained them through hard times formed an almost visible bond between them. They thoroughly enjoyed each other's company; bursts of spontaneous talk and great rolls of laughter emanated from them as they reminded each other of events in their past. At the end of the session we felt we had witnessed something rare and very precious.

Can you start out by telling us what brought you to the Tiburon-Belvedere area?

Mother: That was sixty-six years ago on the ninth of this month, September, 1909, that I came to Tiburon. My husband was working on the railroad at the time, the Northwestern Pacific. That was Mr.Coleman, my first husband's name was Coleman.

Daughter: My name was Coleman.

Mother: We lived—

Daughter: It was in the arks, right by where Hilarita is now, where the station was then. My mother had eight living children; two were born before we came here.

There were eight children, and you all lived on an ark?

Mother: Yes, we lived on a small ark rented from Mrs. Mahone— that's where the twins were born. Then we moved to the side of the hill in Belvedere, where she (Mrs. Halverson) was born. The house is still there in Belvedere. I have only two daughters. All the rest are boys.

Daughter: It has been remodeled — the second house on the left, north of the police station. It faces San Rafael Avenue.

Mother: Belvedere Avenue, that was what they called it.

Daughter: It's San Rafael Avenue now!

Mother: Now, yes. And then we moved down to the ark in Belvedere. It was a nice big place. We had a garage alongside. But we had to get out of there on account of Harry B. Allen!

Daughter: That ark was on the lagoon.

Mother: The building of the new lagoon took care of all those places. And we had to get out of there! Mrs. Scott owned that ark.

Was she related to Dr. Scott?

Mother: No!

Daughter: Dr. Scott delivered all of us. (laughter)

Mother: Yes, she was our doctor. None of the kids were registered, not one of them. Because she never made no record of anything. You had a hard time getting papers, you know, for different things. She never registered any of them. But she was a good person.

Was it unusual to have a woman doctor at that time?

Mother: Oh, yes. There was Dr. Marson, he had a drugstore on the corner there at the Land Company building.

Daughter: But for your deliveries you wanted to have Dr. Scott!

Mother: Oh, yes, she was the only one who did it, yes.

Let's go back to your first ark in Tiburon. Did you have indoor plumbing?

Mother: We had three rooms. We had no running water then. Oh, we had one faucet in the house, but no bathroom. We had coal oil lamps, you know. If you wanted to take a bath you had to get in a big tub in front of the stove and fill it with water! We had a woodstove, everything was wood.

Daughter: I remember when they piped the gas into Belvedere from Tiburon. I was twelve years old. PG&E coming in and everybody going out to buy gas stoves.

How did you get from your Tiburon ark to Main Street in Tiburon?

Mother: Oh, I walked! I walked to town down along the railroad tracks. I put one baby in the buggy and two alongside me. Of course there was nothing but a grocery store there — you couldn't buy any clothes there.

What would you do for clothing?

Mother: Well, we would have to go to San Rafael. The little train stopped right there above the arks, the arks were right beside the tracks. It stopped at the Hilarita Station and we got on and rode to San Rafael.

Were most of your neighbors railroad people?

Mother: Oh, yes, all railroad people. My husband came first to this ark and then he sent for me.

Did you know Mary Bernard Silva?

Mother: Yes, they lived farther up the tracks, above the Hilarita Station. We then moved up to the Tiburon hill, we rented from Mrs. Pauline.

Do you recall the winemaking days?

Daughter: Oh, definitely! On the arks in Belvedere all the Italians made wine. My brothers used to help; all the kids from around the neighborhood were called in to help. They'd have the kids wash their feet good. And then the kids would crush the grapes in big vats. Great trucks full of grapes would come down from Asti, and the little kids would get excited and try to grab the grapes off the truck. The vats were inside big sheds they had built right alongside their houses. They treated you to grapes afterward if you came to help. I remember my brothers washing their feet and rolling their pants up above their knees and going in to crush grapes. They thought it was a lot of fun.

Where did they store the wine?

Daughter: In their own sheds. There were no cellars.

Mother: The Italians, they put the wine down in the hull of their arks. They had a door that went down underneath; it was cool and damp. It smelled really marvelous.

The Italians always had vegetables in their gardens. They'd put the tomatoes to the front of the yard until the kids started stealing them, and then they moved them farther back, close to the house. Oh, they were the greatest people! Really when you think back, it was a great little town —— a "Little Italy," right there on San Rafael Avenue.

Was your family affected by the 1924 railroad strike?

Daughter: No, my father was working for the government at that time. But a lot of new people came to town, mostly from Pocatello, Idaho. Remember that strike, Mom?

Mother: Yes. They were striking for more pay. A lot of men came in and worked at the time; they were called scabs. Jerry's stepfather, Mr. Averill, lost thirty years' work there; he never got a pension because he went out on strike. So many lost everything because they wouldn't work during the strike.

Daughter: There was a lot of resentment in the town then. No one socialized with the scabs.

Mother: I remember a lot of the railroad workers used to come to work from Sausalito. I used to see them come up the road. A lot of Sausalito people depended on the Tiburon railroad for work. At five o'clock at night there was nothing but a parade of cars along San Rafael Avenue, a long line of cars heading out of Tiburon back to Sausalito.

And there was a big fire in Tiburon that one year, that wiped out Adams' store and a little bar. He had a bar there in a tent, right on the beach. Right next to Sam Vella.

Daughter: Sam Vella had a tent too, right where his place is now. And I remember a green shack, until he built what he has now.

Were you allowed on Main Street as children?

Daughter: Yes, I had to go to the butcher all the time.

Mother: I guess you have talked to Harvey Anderson about his father's butcher shop? He was the only butcher shop. Harvey was just a young kid then. Mr. Anderson was a nice person. He always gave the children wieners. He'd make them sing a song, like "When the Moon Comes Over the Mountain." And he'd smile and hold that wiener in his hand until they finished the song. Nowdays whenever I see his son, Harvey, I sing that song.

Daughter: I was down at the Corner Market about a year ago and a hippie-type woman and her little boy were at the meat counter. The butcher tried to give the little boy a wiener and she said, "Is there something wrong with it?" Oh, how we have changed.

Did you think of Main Street as a rough and ready place?

Mother: Tiburon! Oh, Brother! I should say! Drunks! If you went out at night that's all there was. It was enough to scare you to death.

Daughter: I remember where the old barber shop was on the corner, where Rooney's is now. They had a bench out in front, and all these Irishmen, my father and Tim Reilly, they'd meet every night at that bench. They called themselves the Sunshine Club.

Mother: Whee! Sunshine all right! (laughter)

Daughter: We used to kid them and ask, "Is it the Sunshine or the Moonshine Club?"

Mother: Tiburon did not have a fire department; the railroad was the town's fire department. The town burned down one time when we were living in Belvedere. We couldn't hear it that night and when Mr. Coleman went to work he found none of the town standing.

Daughter: It depended on how the wind was blowing if you could hear it or not.

Mother: In Belvedere they had only one drug store, in the corner of the Land Company building, a Dr. Marson. And Dr. Florence Scott had her offices upstairs. And across the street was the Belvedere Hotel. My boys used to go swimming there. And the Payne house was next door, the Keatons.

Daughter: And farther down the beach was the old Tropic Bird, where Vic Pariani was born. Oh, every time we walked by there with Vic he would say, "That's where I was born!" There were mostly old boats along there. The old China Cabin was painted green.

Mother: I used to work down at the Belvedere Hotel. I used to help with the cooking. It was the best place around to eat. Mrs. Payne would sometimes have dinner parties there and I'd help serve the tables.

Daughter: After it was torn down there was just a big wharf for a long time, and my brothers used to swim off of it. It was a long time before the yacht club came. When the hotel was running it was just a summer place. The Mailliard family and all those people were just there in the summer.

Mother: I wasn't down there much. I used to send the kids down there to get the mail. Miss Livsey, the postmistress, used to give those kids the devil. Boy, I didn't blame her.

Daughter: Oh, yes, we kids used to make a racket outside while we were waiting for the mail. She'd get behind her window and say, "Too much noise! No mail!" And then she'd close the window on you, Bang! Then she'd put the parrot there, which was the meanest thing in the world, just to get you. We were all scared to death of it because it would bite. There was a park across the street and all the kids would play there and get into fights. We were supposed to wait quietly in line. We had to call out our name to her. Oh, she was a funny little old lady with her glasses down to here.

Left: Belvedere School. Right: Bill Barr's school bus.

Opposite page: Belvedere School kindergarten class, 1923. Above: the same class in 1930; front row, from left: Evan Pugh, Larry Coleman, John Simontacchi, Ronald Entwhistle, R. Harrison. Second row: Alice Ehrenfeldt, Madeline McLean, (next two unidentified), Martha Beyries, Mary Jane Jordan, Alice Place, Juanita Stevens. Third row: Mrs. McCurty, (unidentified), Mary Alice Donzel, (unidentified), Eileen Ehrenfeldt, Jean Reed, Vera Brooks, Dorothy Taylor. Top row: Al Coleman, Babe Campagna, Harry Wong, Chong Quan, (unidentified), Jake Wosser, Scotty McLean.

Larry Coleman, Jerry's brother, recalls: "Harry Wong was houseboy for the Crocker family. We never asked the Chinese boys where they came from; they were just part of our class. Crocker was always buying new cars, and Harry was allowed to drive them. He would pile his friends in and we would go driving. He drove as fast as the car would go until he saw the police, and then he'd slam on the brakes. It was a big Packard. Chong Quan worked for Britton Rey. Bill Barr's bus had five doors on the curb side, each opening to one seat, all the way across. Barr turned the next-to-last seat around so the boys could play a card game called 'Pedro.' I think that's the only reason we went to school."

Mother: Oh, she was a terror, Miss Livsey, but I don't blame her. Then later she lived over in Sausalito at the Alta Mira Hotel. She retired there. She liked her Black and White, that was the whiskey she liked. Her tastes were good. She would come to Belvedere to dine with her sister who lived on Acacia Avenue.

I used to see Miss Livsey over here in Sausalito — we had to move to Sausalito because we couldn't find a place in Tiburon or Belvedere after we had to move out of the ark on the Lagoon. Thirty years in Tiburon and then I had to get out! We couldn't find anything. And when we had to tear the ark down people came and wanted to buy the door or the windows, but they wouldn't give you nothing for it, so Mr. Averill just had to tear it down. We just tore it down and sold the doors and windows. No one would pay us for the ark. This is when Mr. Allen came in and built up the lagoon, and everybody had to get out of there, everyone all along San Rafael Avenue. We did not own the land we were on. We had to pay ground rent to the Land Company. We had to take our ark and move it off the land or tear it down.

Daughter: See, my stepdad owned two beautiful lots over on Paradise Drive, and he wanted to move the old ark over there, but they couldn't get the ark past the old castle; the ark was too wide. It was a nice ark, just like a house. We had extended it, modernized it and everything. Then he sold the lots for such a price — six hundred dollars, can you imagine?

Mother: Where that willow tree still is in Belvedere, near the firehouse, that was our front yard. Mr. What's-his-name told me he was trying to keep it alive. It looks pretty good. I was by it about three years ago. I had two willows in the front yard and we had to cut one down. It's nice to know that one is still there. Yes, we had a nice little place there. It had a fence around it and lots of flowers, everything like a house. No vegetables, just flowers. With so many children I couldn't be bothered with taking care of vegetables too. I have a picture of the little place. I also have a picture of us in front of the railroad station in Tiburon. In it are my three oldest boys and my oldest daughter. It's at the the old ferry slip, where the ferry would come in every day.

Were you going to take the ferry to San Francisco that day?

Mother: No, I was just out for a walk; my sister was with me. I didn't go out much when the children were small. I was tired; I couldn't go out much. Not with eight children! My oldest was born in my home town of Irvington, in Alameda County. It was called Washington's Corner then; they changed it to Irvington, and now it is Fremont. And my second son was born in San Francisco. I came to Tiburon with two boys. I came to live in San Francisco after the earthquake when some things were still down. Their father, Mr. Coleman, worked with the Iron Works. Now they call it Bethlehem Steel; years ago it was the Union Iron Works. We lived in San Francisco. Then he got a job with the railroad in Tiburon; he was a laborer. Then after the strike he worked out at the coaling station — then it was called California City — on Paradise Drive. He was working out there when he passed away. All my children are Colemans, from my first marriage. I was widowed for two years when I married Mr. Averill. He was a widower.

When we talked with Marion Allen she spoke highly of your daughter, Dolores.

Mother: Oh, yes, she worked for the Allens at their grocery store. She was Mrs. Allen's favorite. She worked as a clerk at the store and when the Allens would go away they would have her run the store for them. Dolores still keeps in contact with Mrs. Allen. Dolores is now up in Healdsburg.

Did your children have jobs in the community?

Mother: When they got home from school they would go around Belvedere and sweep walks and pick up leaves, things like that. They made a little pin money. And they used to caddy at the golf links in Belvedere. Oh, times have changed; it certainly is different over there. I loved living over there better than I do here in Sausalito. I liked the climate better in Tiburon and Belvedere. We had to move. We had to come over here. I lost my second husband over here. And my son Pat died here when he was thirty-four. My husband once worked at the codfishery after the strike; so did my son Pat.

Daughter: They had to slice the fish and dry it, fish that were brought down from Alaska on the big sailing ships . They put the fish out on big drying racks. We would go down that hill sometimes. When things were so tough the men got their meals over there. They didn't get paid much, but at least that made it less a burden on the family.

Mother: Some of the men working there had families but most were drifters.

Daughter: My brother, Pat, made a trip up on one of the schooners when he was seventeen. That trip took three months. And he came back starving, but he was pretty smart; he made sure he signed on in the galley so he would get something to eat. Mom, do you remember that time we went out to the point of Belvedere to watch the ships sail out the Gate? And you know it was the *Balclutha,* which was then called *Star of Alaska.* Oh, to watch the ships sail out the gate — that was a most beautiful sight! And when the ships came back from Alaska they'd anchor out in Richardson Bay and then row the men in to the dock. Pat was glad to be back. He was the only kid from Belvedere that I know of that went out on the ships. He was just daring. He just wanted to go.

Mother: But he hated it. He was hungry the whole time and didn't make any money. They paid so little. Oh, there were lots of drunks that worked on the ships. When the ships were in you'd see them lying in the roads. They'd get drunk in Tiburon and have to lie down on the roads or the paths on their way back over Belvedere to the ships. They'd drink down at Sam's and not be able to make it back.

Daughter: And we used to go over the hill to the old fish yard; we knew the cook there. And he used to make us sandwiches of good fresh bread. Oh, they were good!

Were you worried about your son shipping out?

Mother: Oh, he wanted to go. I just had to let him go.

Daughter: He was a rough and tumble type.

Mother: He worked in Tiburon for years, at Sam Vella's. He was a bartender. After that he got sick and passed away — oh, that was long, long ago. He was just a young kid when he went to work for Sam.

Could you tell us about prohibition?

Mother: Oh, yeah! Moonshine! A lot of moonshine! Your father used to go buy it and take it out to the fellows at the shipyards. That stuff was HOT! They had to dilute it with water to be able to drink it. It was awful!

Daughter: I can remember, my sister and I were talking about it, it was like things you see in the movies now. Those men in the cars coming in here to Tiburon in black hats — it had to be the FBI, looking for the stuff, and before you knew it somebody'd be knocked over. The Italians were making stuff called grappa. That was fifty cents a pint, violent stuff! It wasn't wine. It was like a whiskey but not a good whiskey.

Did you drink it?

Mother: No, but I saw it. To tell the truth I never took a drink in my life when my first husband was alive. But when I married Mr. Averill I went out to parties in the City with friends and they said, "Louise, you have to have a drink to participate." Well, that is when I started to have a highball. If I go to dinner now I will take a little wine.

Women were not allowed in the saloons then?

Mother: No, not very much. If they did it was to get their husbands out.

Daughter: Women stayed home in those days, you know. The women had it easy. Look at all the running the women have to do for their children today — drive them here, drive them there. The women just stayed home with the children. They did the baking, they did all their own bread, they did everything.

Mother: It was a long way downtown to Tiburon to lug it all home. And you couldn't buy bread in the store anyway. You just made everything at home. My mother used to send me sacks of peas and grains and fruit. I'd cook it for my bunch of kids. I'd can fruit every summer. And we got our milk at the Reed dairy, at Hilarita, at the big barn.

Daughter: The other dairy was at Del Mar, where Del Mar School is today. We bought raw milk, right from the dairy, and in those days you didn't think you could get anything from it.

Mother: And remember, Jerry, when Joe Titus used to row over in the rowboat to the dairy to work and get the milk? He was my nephew who lived with me for a long time when we lived in Belvedere. He worked for Bettancourt over there milking cows.

Oh, everything has changed so! Not what life used to be. All my kids were strong when they were born. Now they are all raised and married, all working and they got kids! Do you know my son,

Larry Coleman? He is the only one who lives in Tiburon.

Daughter: You know the arks that are along Ark Row now? Well, those people used to work for Mare Island. When they closed up the old coaling station they all went to work at Mare Island. There were lots of ark groups: the Italian gardeners, the railroad people, some dairy people, the Mare Island people. When the coaling station closed it became the Naval Net Depot.

We've heard the name California City. It was never a real city, was it?

Daughter: No, it was just a little area out there by Paradise Park, right about where the coaling station was.

Mother: Yes, that is what we called California City years ago. Your father was a watchman out there. He worked nights. He used to walk over the hills to work.

Daughter: When I was young a group of us girls used to sleep out in the hills in Tiburon. No one would bother us. We'd go out there on the beach and build big bonfires and cook, and in the morning we'd hike back.

Did you buy vegetables from the man who came around door to door?

Mother: Oh yes. The Chinese vegetable man came by for years in Belvedere. But not at the other ark in Tiburon.

Daughter: When Bert was little and the Chinese vegetable man came he had these hanging baskets on poles across his shoulders. Well, Bert would cry because oh, what terrible things people used to say to their kids! Like, "If you don't watch out the Chinaman is going to take you away in the basket!" And the little kids would be scared to death and run in the house when they saw the Chinaman coming. My poor brothers.

Mother: And remember there used to be a Chinese settlement out where they had their shrimp boats, out at China Camp, up by San Rafael. They'd come around with baskets of shrimp and fish. I'd be out washing on the "Irish Piano" — that is what we called the washboard. The Chinamen would come around and I'd tell the kids to be good or the Chinamen would take them. Oh, did they start crying!

Daughter: And remember the fish man that came around on Fridays, always blowing the horn on his little truck?

Mother: Oh, yes, always blowing the horn!

Daughter: I can tell you my father had many a job when he lived in Belvedere. He also delivered coal and ice for Mr. Weeks, in a wagon with two horses that they used to call Jack and Nig. They used to cut the ice for you, as many pounds as you wanted. We didn't have freezers. And I can remember the kids teasing us: "Old Mr. Coleman! He is the iceman!"

Mother: Yes, the kids used to call out "Here comes the iceman!" And they'd try to get ice out of the back of the wagon. At one time the mail was delivered up on the Island and everyone else had to go to the post office to get their mail. I think Bill Barr delivered the mail up on the hill.

Daughter: Bill Barr's bus is how we got to high school. We loved it because he had an old bus and it was always breaking down. More times than not we had to get out and walk home. We called it Bill Barr's Old Green Streak. He took us to and from school. We had to pay two dollars and fifty cents for the month.

Mother: And Jerry was always late, running around saying "Here comes Barr, here comes Barr!" She wore black ties with her middy and the tie was always in her hand, and I was always telling her not to forget her lunch as she was running out the door. You'd think she was having a stroke just to get out the door in the morning to go off to school. Oh, Good Night, just to think of it again makes me laugh! She was never on time. He never left without them, always blowing on the horn to make sure they heard him.

Daughter: And we used to tease the daylights out of him, old Bill Barr. Poor old Bill Barr! He was a big old fat man who everyone took advantage of. But he didn't seem to mind; he never left. Then when the older boys were able to drive he would let them take the bus to school. And then we'd be worse than ever. We'd climb out the back window and up onto the top of the bus, onto the rack. Oh, all the things we used to do — the girls too, in their uniforms.

When we were in school in Mill Valley we'd be asked where we were from, and if you said Tiburon they'd say, "Oh, that dump way over there!"

Mrs. Averill stands on the porch of her ark, across from the old firehouse on the road below San Rafael Avenue in Belvedere, 1939.

Top: Jason, the Chinese produce vendor, later used a horse and wagon, and finally a truck. Below: A train steams north near Hilarita with plenty of wood for the boiler, around 1900.

Now if you say you are from Tiburon they say, "Oh, Really!"

Tamalpais was a union high school, and there were only two high schools in the county. Everybody had to come down to Tam from Kentfield and Ross, and if you did that you were in, but not if you came from that dump, Tiburon.

And Billy Barr used to run his bus out of Tiburon on Friday nights and take you to the movies, to the theater over in Mill Valley. You got in for a nickel. You didn't have to pay him; he just did it.

Was your family affected during the Depression?

Daughter: Oh, definitely. I had graduated from high school. Boy, did I know there was nowhere to work! There was nothing for me to do but take care of children. So I left Belvedere and moved in with a family in Mill Valley. They are still my very best friends; they live in San Diego now. I went everywhere with the family — New York, everywhere.

Mother: It was hard those years, real hard.

Daughter: Those were terrible years. It was terrible getting work, so all the girls around here did the same thing, go to work for families. You had to bring in money for the family or else. Everything was cut back — work at the railroad, everything.

Mother: You know, after they took the trains out of Tiburon, Tiburon went dead. That ruined the town; nothing there now. I went down there the other day. I think it is awful, just walking down the street, how it has changed. All those new stores. As I walked by the old stores I thought "Beyries used to be there; Anderson's butcher shop used to be there." It is just awful now. No real character.

Do you remember when Mr. Musso's bakery came to town?

Daughter: Gosh, I can't! It's like he was a fixture there, like his bakery was always there, it's been so long. He was not there in the early days, though. It was first a boarding house on that corner, for the railroad men. Later there was another boarding house on Main Street, run by the Hunts. They were the only black family in Tiburon. They were just wonderful people. Mr. and Mrs. Hunt also ran a restaurant. Percy and Hayward were their sons; they went to school with us over in Belvedere. They were just the finest family, and they ran a wonderful restaurant, mostly for railroad men. The railroad men lived in the boarding house. And then there was the Fleming Rooming House, where Tiburon Vintners is. The served regular old home-cooked meals, with separate tables.

What was the price of a meal?

Daughter: Oh, Gosh, I don't know. But what you could get then for fifty cents was fabulous.

How much did it cost to feed your family of ten?

Mother: Oh, I don't remember that. We used to run up a bill at the grocery store and pay up at the end of the month, on payday. And we had to pay rent on the ark.

Daughter: Yes, we had to pay thirty dollars a month. That was a lot of money then, though. I used to walk all the way over to Burke's; he was the landlord. He lived in Tiburon. He owned the place on San Rafael Avenue. I remember that thirty dollars was a lot of money to carry in your hand!

Did people use banks as we do today?

Mother: Banks? No, no banks then. People used to go to the grocery store to cash their checks.

Daughter: We charged at Beyries' Grocery Store, and Bum Beyries would do the delivering. To help bring in more money my mother went to work as custodian of the Belvedere School. She got about thirty dollars a month.

Mother: I later got fifty dollars a month. I had to give it up when I was with child. And then we moved to Sausalito. I'd go up to the school and make a fire in the furnace in the morning before the school opened, before the teacher got there. One time the basement got full of water and I had to walk in it. The big heater warmed the three rooms upstairs. I had to clean up and clean the waste baskets and wash the windows. There was not much money at that time. All my kids went to Belvedere School.

Here is a picture of our house with the little picket fence and the willow tree in front and the garage. It nearly broke my heart when we had to tear it down and move, it really did. When we were there we had no lights — we had kerosene lamps. We had no conveniences. We had a porch out back and I would put the dirty laundry out there to do and the seagulls would come and try to carry it off. There are electrics in town now; years ago they did not

Union Codfishery on the west shore of Belvedere. The schooner Sequoia *at the dock; schooner* Galilee *and barkentine* Fremont *at anchor, the sloop* Union *approaching from Sausalito. Pat Coleman sailed on ships like these to Alaska's Bering Sea.*

have any. We didn't have running water and we went down to the lagoon and just threw our garbage into it. Everything went out into the bay.

Daughter: They'd kill you now if you did that.

Mother: Oh, it was a quiet town, but I was used to it.

Daughter: And the kids didn't get into any bad mischief when you think of it. Everybody knew how to operate a boat and swim. I guess we all learned how to swim down at the beach in Belvedere Cove. It was just In You Went. And one of my friends used to have a rowboat, and we'd row at night in the lagoon. Oh, I'd like to do that now!

Do you recall the Night in Venice?

Mother: Oh, yes, down in Belvedere Cove.

Daughter: We used to have Chinese lanterns; we'd put them up on the ark. And then we went down to the street dances at night. The boats were all decorated. Oh, it was beautiful!

We have heard people refer to arks and houseboats. Was there a difference?

Daughter: To us the houseboats were those that were really in the water, anchored in the water. They used to move those around. There were a lot of them at one time. They used to bring them into the lagoon in the wintertime. They'd open the drawbridge and let them through.

Mother: The kids used to go swimming down there at the bridge. The water used to come through there, you know.

Daughter: I remember my brothers diving off the top of the bridge. I'd go down to watch them swim there.

People enjoy the beauty of Tiburon and Belvedere now. How was it in your eyes then?

Daughter: Oh, now it is nothing! Nothing! It is a shame what has happened. It was so beautiful then!

Mother: Up on the hill around old St. Hilary's Church there was nothing but cow pasture. Just cows. The Bradley family lived right next to the school and the church was right up the hill. Mrs. Bradley was always entertaining at her house after church affairs. That was all we had as entertainment. We only had one mass on Sunday. The boat had to come over from Sausalito to bring us the priest. And the kids in Belvedere would race the kids in Tiburon to see who would carry the priest's bag up the hill for him. Those poor old priests would have to walk; the cars — few that we had — would never offer them a ride.

And if you wanted to go to church in Sausalito it took you all day. We had to get on a boat in Tiburon and go all the way to San Francisco and then back to Sausalito, and that would take all day. They did not have lots of ferries running at the time.

Daughter: But later they had the little *Marin,* and that ferry took you right to Sausalito.

Mother: And one time I wanted to go visit my sister in Sausalito, and I had all the kids with me. When we got on the boat to go back I noticed I was missing Pat. I got so excited! I threw the baby on the seat with the other kids and went looking for Pat. Well, he had followed the crowd onto the other ferryboat. We were going back to Belvedere and the boat he got on was going to San Francisco. It was a wonder I found him before the boats left. I thought we were going to lose him! Oh, Lordy, Lordy! I said never again would I go off with that gang of kids! It was a chore.

Daughter: It was an interesting little town , I think, with all the stories behind it.

Mother: Yes, a nice little town. It was just a one-horse town, but a nice little town.

Marie Louise and Richard Bates, 1983.

Marie Louise Sutton Bates

1925–

Mrs. Bates' grandfather was one of the founders of the Belvedere Land Company, which bought, developed and named the island in the late 1880's. The sale by the Reed family was possible only after more than thirty years of litigation, ending with a decision by the U.S. Supreme Court that the land was attached by the spit to the Tiburon peninsula, and thus was not a true island (all islands in the Bay were U.S. Government property). Israel Kashow lived on the island from 1855 to 1885. Toni Bates, as she is known to her friends, is a vigorous, energetic woman whose manner is direct and friendly. Her speech is thoughtful and precise, showing her care for accuracy. The interview took place in August, 1985.

Toni, how did your mother's father, Edgar M. Wilson, acquire Belvedere Island?

Family hearsay is that he went down the spit (later San Rafael Avenue) and told Israel Kashow that he and Alexander Forbes, his father-in-law, had purchased the island. Why my grandfather was not shot no one in the family knows, because as the story goes, Kashow was well armed and told my grandfather, "If you take one more step I will shoot you!" But he survived the day. He was an attorney with his office in the Mills Building in San Francisco, and he finally took this issue to the Supreme Court of the United States. He claimed that this land was not an island because it was attached by the spit to the Tiburon peninsula, and he won the case.

When and how did Edgar M. Wilson first come to San Francisco?

He was born in Bloomingburg, Ohio, in 1855. His father was a preacher and an abolitionist. Their family home was used as part of the underground railroad. His father went off to war as a chaplain in the Union Army and came home with "preacher's cough," which was tuberculosis. They closed up the house completely, doors, windows, everything; everybody was to be sick in there together, that is what was done. Well, the two little boys, Edgar and his brother, could not stand to be cooped up in the house; they got to run outdoors, and did not contract t.b. The entire family died except these two boys. They were sent off to live with a cousin, who raised them.

My grandfather went to Worcester College in Ohio, and then read law with an uncle, a judge in Chicago. One winter when he was in his twenties he became very seriously ill, so he took a train to

California to recuperate. So he started his law practice in San Francisco, but he had no clients. He got down to twenty-five cents in his pocket on a Sunday morning. So he bought a cup of coffee and a doughnut with the first five cents, and he went went to church — he was a Presbyterian — to share his remaining twenty cents with the good Lord.

While he was at church somebody in the parish invited him for lunch and somebody invited him for tea and somebody else invited him for supper, so that took care of eating for that day. He went down to his office the next morning, thinking he was really at the end. All of a sudden a man came racing in with a very important matter that had to be worked out with the Southern Pacific Railroad. And from then on he never had to look for another nickel. He always told us when we were children, "the Lord will provide! If you divide with the Lord, he will provide!" He ended up one of the top attorneys for the Santa Fe Railroad.

How did he and your grandmother, Alice Maud Forbes, meet?

Through business he was doing with Alexander Forbes. Alexander Forbes came to San Francisco in 1849 and became a merchant. He invested in a lot of Marin County and California property. Now I think Alexander Forbes was a friend of Thomas B. Valentine, and Forbes had money invested in Belvedere before it was incorporated. Valentine also had invested a lot in California land. Forbes had land in Corte Madera, Fairfax, and half of San Rafael.

Your grandparents married and were living in San Francisco. How did he become interested in buying Belvedere Island?

Through Alexander Forbes, his father-in-law. So grandfather bought Belvedere Island and the Belvedere Land Company was incorporated May 15, 1890. Thomas B. Valentine, president, and Edgar M. Wilson, Curtis H. Lindley, George Bargate, and Charles Forbes signed the legal document of incorporation, which I still have. In 1892 the board purchased 2,500 trees and 1,000 more the next year, so soon the island was no longer barren hills. They advertised "Villa Sites" on the Belvedere Peninsula.

Corinthian Island in 1892 was known as Valentine Island and in 1907 the Corinthian Island Company was incorporated. The stockholders of the Belvedere Land Company on October 2,1906 were Edgar M. Wilson owning 1259 shares, Sophia C. Livery 5 shares, C.J. Rey 196 shares, George T. Ruddock 439 shares, and William Hoffrohneider 91 shares. The family story was that grandfather named the island Belvedere because it meant "beautiful view."

After grandfather bought Belvedere he built his house in 1891 and moved in in 1892. He called his house the "Chalet"; he had it copied from a Swiss music box. He had the pick of the island at that time to build on. The lot he chose went all the way down to the water. But his favorite spot, his real lot, was on the top of the island, which you have probably heard people refer to as "Wilson's Lot." We spent a lot of time playing and picnicking there. That is where he was going to build his real home. And my grandmother always said, "over my dead body! I'm not going to to be stuck in Belvedere all year long!" She wanted to be in the city and have a little bit of fun. So he just held it and held it, hoping one day that he would be able to convince her. He never was able to, and then she died. He decided not to build another house. He had a bad heart; my mother and uncle were very concerned about him. They wanted to get him out of there so that he might survive a little longer. So in 1935 they sold the whole thing, the house to Dr. Frederick Bost and the Land Company to Harry Allen. Before they sold, grandfather used to walk all around the island checking everything that was still going on; he still felt it was his island. He died in 1938.

When did your mother, Maud Lane Wilson Sutton, first come to Belvedere?

Her parents built the house when she was three years old in 1892. And from then on she was here every summer. Mother said that one of the houseboats in the cove was owned by the Orpheum Theatre, and the performers would come over on weekends for a little rest and relaxation. And as children mother and her friends, Anita Mailliard and some other girls of the island, would row around the cove and watch them do their acrobatics and juggling tricks. I think mother must have been around ten or twelve then. She was born in 1889. And I can remember her saying, of that same period, very often when it was a quiet night in the summer grandmother would row from the point of

Top: Edgar M. Wilson and daughter Maud in 1898. Below: On an outing, May 13, 1904, (from left) Dorothy ?, Ward and Tom Mailliard, Carl ?, Page Mailliard, Ralston White, Forbes Wilson, Marion Mailliard, with Anita Mailliard and Maud Wilson behind driver.

Belvedere over to Tiburon to pick up grandfather when he got off the ferry.

My grandfather told stories about commuting by ferry. He always walked around the outer decks during the trip. So he said he walked all the way to the city and back. One time someone asked him, "Mr. Wilson, why don't you ever come in and sit down?" And he answered, "Well, because when I come in and sit down everyone wants free legal advice. When I am outside walking, if they can weather the storm and take the cold, then they deserve free advice!"

How was your grandfather's family affected by the earthquake of 1906?

Somehow my grandfather got a wagon with a horse, and he went around the streets in their neighborhood in San Francisco and all their friends brought out their valuables — family pictures, silverware, jewelry — and they'd flag him down, and he'd say, "I'm on my way to Belvedere. I'll take your things with me." He had some kind of special pass so he could get onto the ferry. So he brought all those things over here. And mother said the rest of that summer was most entertaining because all of a sudden someone would arrive on the doorstep and say, "Excuse me, Mr. Wilson, did I give you great-grandmother in a gold frame?" And they'd wander into the living room and say, "Oh, there's grandma!" But the treasure of all is this little letter that was mailed to my mother. The only paper my grandfather could find in a hurry to write on was an envelope. This letter was written April 19,1906:

> Miss Maud Wilson, in care of the J. C. Kirkpatricks in Pleasanton.
>
> Dear Maud,
> We are all well and are at the ferry building and are awaiting the 12:15 for Belvedere. We are glad to get out of this and we are glad that you and Mrs. Kirkpatrick and family are away from here. Please ask Mrs. Kirkpatrick to allow us to trespass on her good nature and to keep you a little longer as we do not know yet where we will find shelter. We hear that the Belvedere cottage is knocked out, and we hope to get to the Hotel Belvedere, if not then the Hotel Rafael. And if not that then grandma's cottage in San Rafael. All wires are down so could not send you word earlier and this is the first opportunity to send a letter. We heard the country is all safe so we conclude that you and friends are also. Please express our sympathy to Mrs. Kirkpatrick on the loss of the Palace Hotel, tell her that really those have been most fortunate who have escaped with their lives. Poor Frisco! You young people cannot live long enough to see her fully recover from this blow! With much love and thanking God it is not worse, Papa.

The family was relieved to find the house intact when they arrived in Belvedere. Also in the family records is a certificate stating the following: "This is to certify that the chimneys of E.M. Wilson's house have been inspected and condemned. D.A. McLean, Inspector. April 26,1906."

There is also a telegram from a relative in London asking "Are you safe?" The telegram was sent on the 24th of April and it was not received until the 10th of May. It had to be first sent to Los Angeles, not directly to San Francisco.

You said your grandfather was a Presbyterian. Where did the family go to church?

Yes, he was. But my grandmother was an Episcopalian and there was no Episcopal Church in Belvedere, so she thought, then we had better start one. She started it in somebody's living room. She and Mrs. Hellman, who was the sister of Mrs. Mailliard, and a couple other good ladies would meet, and then they would have a bake sale, and if they would make all of, say, two dollars, they were tickled to death. I think they used to meet in the old church that is now the city hall, when it was up on the hill. Then later they had a church on Acacia Avenue. Whoever the minister was did Sausalito and Belvedere because it was a mission. And the service had to fit in with the ferry schedule so he could get back to Sausalito, poor fellow. My mother was always impressed with him because he encouraged the children to come to church and bring their tennis rackets, bring their bathing clothes, or whatever and leave them on the back pew and partake of the service. And mother always said this was marvelous, as you walked into church and there were all these tennis rackets and heaven knows what all, riding gear and everything else, on the back pew! That mission was turned into a church in the mid fifties. I was a member of the altar guild then, and then they built the St. Stephen's Church we have today.

Top: Ferryboat commuters disembark at Tiburon. Below: The Marin *carried passengers to Sausalito for transfer to San Francisco.*

When these women started the church did they name it St. Stephen's?

Yes, I should say they did with the permission of the Bishop. It was St. Stephens even as a mission. St. Stephen was the martyr who was stoned to death, and we celebrate his birthday the day after Christmas.

Where did your mother go to school?

In San Francisco. She commuted in the fall and spring months while they were still summering in Belvedere. She went to Miss Murison's School for Girls.

Did your father's family also live here?

Yes, the Sutton family. But they did not come to Belvedere until 1915.

Your grandfather owned a sailboat with Mr. Page?

Yes, that was my Grandfather Sutton.

Did they belong to the Corinthian Yacht Club?

I'm not sure. I think it was Mr. Page who was the member, and it could have been the San Francisco Club.

Was your grandfather Sutton a golfer like your father?

No. My father was the only golfer. After we built this house my Uncle Forbes came to visit us. As he started up the driveway he said, "For Heaven's sakes, Marie Louise, you're right smack in the middle of the Matterhorn!" "The Matterhorn" was a steep section of the old golf course. And sure enough when we dug out the back bank we found golf balls. We also found Indian artifacts, a mortar and pestles, right here in the hill.

Did your mother tell you about her early life in Belvedere?

Parents were very strict then, and mother told us many stories of the way her parents disciplined her. When you were in San Francisco you had to be thoroughly chaperoned at all times, at the theatre, at the opera. Even when she was engaged there had to be a chaperon.

But her parents seemed to care very little when they came to Belvedere. She and Anita Mailliard used to have a pony cart, and they would hitch up the pony and gallop off to San Rafael or Mill Valley by themselves, with no chaperon. And another one of their favorite occupations, with all the other boys and girls, was to get together on a moonlit night and canoe out into the bay and paddle around Belvedere and wait for the high tide at the spit and then paddle over the spit into the lagoon and back into the cove, back to Beach Road. No chaperon in sight! When she went back to the city, on went the long white kid gloves and there were the chaperons. My mother had the most marvelous sense of humor. Everything had to be very correct, but, boy, she sure could tell you some stories.

Where did they keep their pony and cart?

Across from the old Mailliard house on Bella Vista Avenue, on the hill side of the road. Or they kept them at Mr. Blanding's coach house on the west side of the island, because they were all such great friends. They probably only kept the pony there in the summer and put it out to pasture the rest of the year.

Did you grow up on the island, Toni?

Yes, in the summer months. I was brought here as a tiny baby. My grandfather never changed his routine after my grandmother died; he still continued coming over every year for the summer. And he brought his son, Forbes, who was not married, and a housekeeper, and our family would come and spend the summer with him here.

Then you did not go to Belvedere School?

No, I went to Miss Burke's in San Francisco.

Can you give your earliest recollections of Belvedere?

I remember being very seriously injured when I was about six. To this day I carry the scar. The milkman delivered the milk in bottles. I decide to play milkman that day, and carry the milkbottles across a concrete platform to the kitchen. I tripped and fell on one of the bottles. The maid saw the blood pumping and wrapped my wrist in a dishcloth. My parents were away, so the maid got me up to the Mailliard house, Aunt Lizzie's; she called over to San Francisco, and I had to be dressed in proper clothes and wait for the *Marin* to come in at one o'clock to have the doctor look at it. So down the hill to the *Marin,* over to Sausalito, then on to San Francisco, then on a streetcar ride to the doctor's. This took hours; it is very clear in my memory. There was no doctor here in Belvedere then. Dr. Scott, who used to take care of my mother, was gone.

Where else did you go on the island?

I would walk down to Allen's Grocery Store, but only with my sister — I think they were afraid I would fall over one of the cliffs. And down there was also Miss Livsey and her wonderful parrot that I just adored. She let me play with it.

Somewhere in the family papers must be Miss Livsey's will, for my grandfather was her attorney. And I think she left the residue of her estate to him to dispose of for her. Now I don't know if he just gave it to the city of Belvedere or if he gave it to start the library — he was to give it to whatever cause he felt could use it.

I remember my grandfather paying us a penny for every hundred slugs and snails we would bring to him in a big bag. Barbara and I would spend our morning out collecting slugs and snails, and then we could walk down to the grocery store to buy a lollipop. I always remember the Allens with great warmth because they were always so dear to the children.

Did you ever venture over to Tiburon?

No, that was just not the place one went. Because of the drinking of the men. It was not really discussed; you just didn't go there, you just didn't do those things.

I remember the Italian gardeners, very warm friendly men who lived in the arks along San Rafael Avenue, and the happy time they always had. Whenever you went by there was always singing and gaiety.

Did your mother ever mention the Nights in Venice to you?

Oh, what wonderful parties they had! They invited lots of people from San Francisco. But I remember as a child I was thrilled by all those lanterns, it was like living in fairyland, all the lights. One time my parents had a very large dinner party and everyone was out on the porch looking at all the lights. The whole cove was decorated with lights and there were fireworks going off. I kept coming down and being shooed back to bed until finally they gave in and I got out on the porch and watched everything!

Anything else you can tell us?

There was the Chinese vegetable man with his funny old truck chugging up Beach Road with the big slanted bins on the side. And him honking the horn as he came up the hill and the maid going out and telling him exactly what she wanted. I think he came about three times a week. And then they would phone and food would be delivered to the house, probably Beyries' or Chapman's. As I told you earlier we were never allowed to go into Tiburon.

Can you describe the ferryboats?

Oh, I remember wonderful things about them! Like the *Marin,* I remember that well, because it was narrow and sleek and small, and you knew everybody on it and everybody knew you.The pathway to the *Marin* went past our house, so that we knew every man who rode it. I can remember the men running past and people calling out their windows, "Hurry, hurry up, it's going!" And the men thundering down, knowing that the *Marin* would not leave without them! Because those on the boat knew how many were coming and they counted noses. Oh, I do remember that well. It would go to Tiburon first, and then it would come to Belvedere, in the morning, and my father and uncle would still be having coffee. The maid would come and say, "Mr. Sutton, Mr. Forbes, it is time to get going, here she comes!" And they would finish their coffee and grab whatever they needed and down the lane they went!

And of course I loved the big ferries because they had those marvelous big machines with claws that came down and picked up a bubble gum or a toy of some sort, when you worked the handle for a penny. That was great fun. But there was a big difference between the passenger ferries and the car ferries. There were so many more people on the passenger ferries. The car ferries were always great fun because usually if it was a cold morning everybody had to jump out and crank their cars up so we could all chug off in Sausalito.

Lucille Graham Boole, 1982.

Lucille Graham Boole

1896–1983

Mrs. Boole lived in Belvedere for more than sixty years, and she kept in memory stories of her husband's family even before her own arrival. Until her retirement, she worked as an administrator of social services at UC Medical Center in San Francisco. During this interview in July, 1975, she served us tea with a graceful, steady hand in her handsome living room. Small in stature, she nevertheless seemed to have great reserves of strength. Her manner was calm, dignified, proper, and her speech very precise and cultivated.

Mrs. Boole, could you tell us why and when you came to Belvedere?

I came to Belvedere in July, 1920, when I was married to Fred Boole, the son of people who had lived here for a long, long time. My father-in-law, Fred W. Boole, had been one of a group of gay young bachelors who had arks out in Belvedere Cove around 1890. They used to come over on weekends. Mr. Boole fell in love with Belvedere and bought a house here in 1892 or 1893. Then in 1896 he married Dee Beck. The day they were married they came to Belvedere. Then in 1897 my husband was born here.

Their house burned in 1902. In those days Belvedere was largely a summer colony, but that winter the Booles had not gone to town. So in January of 1902 the old Chinese cook was down in the basement stoking the furnace and stuffed too much excelsior in and the house caught fire. Mrs. Boole early in the morning in her dressing gown took up her young son and what silverware she could save and went to the Hendry house on Madrona Avenue.

The next house they bought was built in the early 1890's by two brothers, Neil and Dan McLean. Not many people knew of Neil because he moved to San Francisco, but he was a fine builder and fine workman.

In those days there were many Chinese here in help. And they all knew each other well and would gather at each other's houses and play wild games of fantan. The Chinese congregated in the house below us, then called the Matton house.

Did your Chinese cook have a family, or was he single?

Well, most of them had families in China. Their

conditions of employment were very different from what we would consider adequate or proper now. It worked well for them at that time. That is why so many houses in Belvedere were built with the living room upstairs and the dining room and kitchen downstairs. And there was a cubicle of some kind with a toilet for the Chinaboy. But when the Chinaboy wanted a bath he would have to go to San Francisco to a Chinese bathhouse. There were no private baths for Chinese in those days. The Pagoda House, which was owned by Mr. Pew and his wife, had quarters for the Chinese downstairs. So did Boole's house and the Hendry house, and many others. The later houses had proper bathrooms for the Chinese help.

Who trained the Chinese servants to cook western food?

If you took a boy you could train him in your ways, but he would always have his own notions. But then if you got an experienced cook he would have his own very different way of doing things. The Boole family had just two Chinese cooks over a period of forty years or more. The Chinese cook that Mrs. Boole had when she was married came with her as a bride. Her family could not stand the thought of her coming to Belvedere all by herself, so they sent their faithful old Sam to take care of her. Sam stayed with Mother Dee Boole until he got ready to die and then he went back to China. Then they got Sing, an experienced cook, who stayed with them for thirty years. By this time they also had a house in San Francisco so he travelled back and forth with them. In San Francisco they had proper facilities for him.

What business was your father-in-law in?

He was an insurance broker. He commuted by ferryboat. In those early days the ferry ran directly to Tiburon.

There were many tales of gaiety in Belvedere in the 1890's and early 1900's. I have vivid descriptions from Miss Elizabeth Sullivan and Miss Sophie Sullivan. Mrs. Sullivan and her four daughters used to come from Sacramento and spend the summers here, to get away from the Sacramento heat. And they used to stay at the Belvedere Hotel and also in the Farr Cottages.

Did they give you an account of their stay at the hotel?

Oh, yes, it was very gay, a very nice place. The hotel was still standing when I came to Belvedere but it was closed and very badly run down and a year or two later it burned. But in its prime it was supposed to be a very nice place to stay.

Mrs. Sullivan bought and remodeled the Hendry house and lived there with her four daughters who were all maiden ladies. Miss Elizabeth, who was really a beautiful woman, said that around the turn of the century every evening in the summer the girls would get in rowboats and row over to meet the men when they came in on the ferryboat, and then they would row them from ark to ark to ark, and it was gay, but fun!

Of course, the main travel in those days in Belvedere was horse and buggy. There were four horses to pull the little bus up and down the hill because in the rainy season the roads were so muddy they needed the extra horsepower. The horse and buggy days continued until after the earthquake of 1906; Mr. Boole hired a team of horses and took the family on a two-day expedition to see the great earthquake fault over at Olema, where the earth opened up.

Where was the family when the earthquake hit?

My husband, who was nine, was in Belvedere with his aunt, and his parents were down in Los Angeles. They heard reports that Belvedere had sunk into the depths of the ocean. They couldn't get any word, so they got back to San Francisco as fast as they could. Mr. Boole bustled around the waterfront and paid an outrageous amount of money to get somebody to row them across the bay. They found that Aunt Lizzy and Fred had hardly noticed there was an earthquake. Belvedere felt the eathquake very slightly if at all.

What market did you use?

There were very good markets in Tiburon. Mr. Chapman had a market on Main Street, and then later his brother-in-law, Billy Beyries, pulled out and opened a market of his own. Mrs. Chapman and Mrs. Beyries were sisters. The Kelley brothers had a grocery too. Anderson's Meat Market was excellent. After the earthquake, when so many of the Belvedere people did not know where they stood

Top: G.E. Holmes (left) with Fred and Dee Boole, Paradise Cove, 1900. Below: Women rowing, Corinthian, 1900; Lucille Boole, 1920.

financially, Mr. Anderson said he would carry his old customers as long as he could. As a matter of fact the Belvedere men found they were much better off than they had thought they might be. That was the spirit that prevailed.

Of course, I never went down to market. My first days here I didn't have access to a car, so every morning I would telephone my order for meat and staples. And the Chinese vegetable man came to the door with fruits and vegetables, so life was really simple. The L.D. McLean Company, one of the fine old grocery firms of San Francisco, would send a man or woman over and they would go from house to house to take your order. They would deliver to you on Friday mornings. So we had access to that sort of gourmet thing through the L.D. McLean Company. So there was no need to go to Tiburon. Besides the markets the only other thing there were saloons!

Did you ever meet Mr. Pew or Mr. Blanding?

I met Mr. Pew once; he died shortly thereafter. He was the first mayor of Belvedere, and the commodore of the Corinthian Yacht Club. He was a New Englander.

And Mr. Blanding could be a very friendly, kindly man and then he could be very dignified and withdrawn. He lived in great elegance and luxury out on the point. Blanding's Point! He had his big white house with his bedroom, a reception room, and a kitchen. Then he had his library and organ in a separate house. His two sisters had a home just down the slope a bit. Then way down at the water's edge was his boathouse on the east side. And on the west side was his gardener's cottage, and beyond that what had originally been the great stables which were converted into garages. He lived on all this property.

He was one of the biggest taxpayers, I suppose, besides the Belvedere land Company. And he paid his taxes in full the minute he got the bill so the city could have full use of the funds. Every once in awhile he would invite us to a musical and we would go up Sunday afternoon to the organ and library house. The organ room was a great long rectangle with the organ at one end of the room and the chairs lined up precisely along the walls in rows facing each other. Refreshments would be served after the concert, very formal. He lived in Belvedere all summer and in winter he went to the Fairmont Hotel in the city. His butler took food over to him, little packages of cakes and cookies, all winter long.

Did the Belvedere people socialize with the Tiburon people?

No, there was not much socializing. By and large the people in Tiburon were the railroad employees and their families. At times I think it was a little strained, but not always.

Did you know Miss Livsey, the postmistress?

Now my mother-in-law, Dee Boole, told me Miss Sophia Livsey was the daughter of the people who lived up on Golden Gate Avenue, they lived nicely and there were two daughters. Mr. Livsey died or his business failed and he left the family in straitened circumstances, and it became necessary for the girls to earn a little money. In those days no true lady worked in an office or did commercial work, so Miss Livsey chose to get this little job in the Belvedere post office. It paid very little money but she lived in dignity on it. She was really a very interesting woman. She knew every good book dealer in England. She was slender and had a rather prominent nose; her parrot and she were similar in profile. She always wore very prim and proper clothes, a collar up around her neck long after ladies stopped wearing collars, skirts that almost touched the ground. So in some ways she remained in the past, but was very much in the future in her reading. She had firm likes and dislikes. I think she rather liked me because I liked books too. She would pass on to me her book catalogues. She could be very gracious and dignified, and very humorous!

Can you tell us about the Italian gardeners?

Oh, yes, they were wonderful! The senior Booles had one and I had one all the years. They lived in little arks that had been pulled up and put on shore and converted into very nice homes. There was a little colony along the lagoon, where San Rafael Avenue runs now.

They were wonderful gardeners! Among the best perhaps was Harry Pariani; he was supposed to be the most knowledgeable. But I had Charlie. Later when Mr. Harry Allen bought the Belvedere Land Company property and did away with the arks the Parianis and the two Charlies built nice little houses

Belvedere Cove in the early 1890's. The Keil beach house (left center) was later expanded. Wooden stairs wind down from Beach Road to boat docks. The first Belvedere Hotel occupied the pair of cottages to the right of center; one of these cottages is thought to have been built by Israel Kashow, who claimed the island from 1855–1885. They were removed when the new hotel was built in 1898. Further right, the Shamrock Club, home of the railroad workers' union, sports a striped roof and flagpole. This building stands today at One Laurel Avenue. The arks are at their summer anchorage, with rowboats tied alongside. Among the typical flat-roofed models is the famous Nautilus *(right center), which James McNeil built out of four old horsedrawn streetcars.*

for themselves on Acacia. They were really devoted to their gardens. Everything was planted from seed, so when the seeds were put out, Charlie would raise the gunnysack every morning and look in and water it a little bit. He would always say, "I will pass through your garden." And on his way home he'd stop to water whatever might need it. After a windstorm he would always come up to see what had happened in the garden — very personal, very personal!

Did you ever participate in the Nights in Venice?

Oh, yes! Everybody was supposed to decorate, so there were lots and lots of lights strung up in the gardens and across the fronts of houses. One year Rose Parker organized a group of singers who were towed around the lagoon on a barge singing Neapolitan songs. The boats were all decorated with lanterns. There was an atmosphere of gaiety. It was an event to emphasize that we lived almost surrounded by water in Belvedere and the charm of the life on the water with all the boats. Of course, during prohibition whatever liquor there was was bootleg. One of the reliable bootleggers was Sam Vella.

Were you and your husband members of the Belvedere Golf and Country Club?

Yes. The golf club was a simple little shingled building with a tennis court and a nine-hole golf course, evidently a fiendishly difficult course with all the hills. Every once in a while they would have a dance or put on a play or an extravaganza of sorts. There were lots of skits — that was very amusing. It was a private club, you paid your dues. You could play bridge and have tea in the afternoons. Miss Sophie Sullivan was in charge of the catering service. There was always a couple who looked after the club. The man would tend to the gardens and the wife to the household affairs. The course itself was one no experts liked to play on because it was not tournament quality. It was just a pleasant little club used mostly by Belvedere people and some people from San Francisco and Mill Valley.

Can you tell us about politics in Belvedere?

My father-in-law had been one of the early mayors of Belvedere and then in turn my husband was mayor two separate terms.

What were the issues of the day?

Oh, everything was an issue! The closing of the drawbridge, which would cut off the flow of water from the lagoon into Belvedere Cove, that was very much an issue. Some people were very strongly opposed and some strongly in favor of it. After blocking the flow of the tides, Belvedere Cove began to silt up fairly soon and they had to dredge it and still do. And here in the lagoon without the flow of the tides grasses started to grow. Yes, the lagoon was an issue and still is an issue today!

Did you go to San Francisco very often?

Oh, a great deal, all my activities were in San Francisco. And to get to the ferryboat you either walked down the lane that led to the steamer *Marin* landing or you called Bill Barr's taxi to take you over to Tiburon to the boat landing. When I first came you got ten rides for a dollar, because the city of Belvedere subsidized Bill Barr. The price went to twenty-five cents a ride after the city stopped the subsidy. Occasionally when you were hurrying for the boat you would find the drawbridge up! Then Bill Barr would have to turn around and go all around back along San Rafael Avenue and down into Tiburon on what is now Tiburon Boulevard. But somehow you always made it. The ferries had big wooden seats, really very comfortable. You could sit indoors or out. The steamer Marin ran all day to Sausalito; from there you changed to a bigger ferry that took you to the Ferry Building in San Francisco. Twice a day the big boats ran from San Francisco to Tiburon — they had to keep their licenses — one in the morning and one in the evening, mostly carrying freight. And you could take your automobile on the *Eureka.*

And on Sundays you could hear the church bells from Angel Island, which was then an immigration station, the so-called Ellis Island of the West. Even after I came here, all immigrants from the Orient were taken to Angel Island first before they were allowed to move over to San Francisco. The immigration station was later moved to San Francisco. The children of the people who were stationed on the island came over to Belvedere School on the little Angel Island boat. And you could always hear reveille in the mornings and taps in the evenings.

Belvedere Island, looking north, sometime after the Belvedere Hotel was built in 1898. Arks line the shore of the lagoon near Hilarita Dairy (center right).

The Edward A. Creighton family at home on Paradise Drive, 1918. (From left) Estelle, Edward, Mother holding Robert, Father, Lorel, with Carol and Allan sitting in front.

Carol Creighton Ericson

1914–

Carol Ericson is a sharp, quick, humorous woman, very open and direct, with short-cropped hair and sparkling eyes. Long active in the Landmarks Society, she has a well-formed historical perspective; at this interview in 1975 she knew what she wanted to talk about. Her family, the Creightons, came to Tiburon early, and her father was chief engineer on the ferry Cazadero. Her narrative is especially valuable in giving a sense of what Tiburon was like in the 1920's, when she was growing up.

Carol, can you tell us how your family came to Tiburon?

Oh, yes. My mother and father were both natives of San Francisco, so the Tiburon peninsula was not new to them. My mother used to talk about coming over with the Sisters of Mercy on picnics. They would walk from the ferry slip two miles to Glen Cove, which we know now as Keil Cove.

My father's name was Edward A. Creighton, and my mother was Loretta Ryder Creighton. My father's family came from Ireland, from the town of Creighton. We have a record of Terence Creighton getting a license to be an engineer on San Francisco Bay in 1863. My mother's father came as a volunteer from New York in the 1840's, during the Mexican War. After he was mustered out of the army, he came back to California in 1852.

My parents were married in San Francisco in 1905. My father was working on the ferry boats as a marine engineer. They came as bride and groom to Belvedere, and lived in one of the Land Company cottages on Beach Road. These were owned by the Belvedere Hotel then, and were rented out in October, after the summer season. They're called the Farr cottages now.

Well, in April, 1906, the earthquake came while they were living in those cottages. A lot of people from the City came to stay, so my mother always said that the first year of her marriage was chaotic, with people sleeping on the floor. It must have been just awful.

Where did your parents move after the Land Company cottage?

When the lease ran out on the cottage they moved up the street to the corner of Laurel and Acacia, in

Belvedere. That house still stands. Then they moved over to Tiburon on Mar West, in the house the Vellas live in now. In fact my brother Edward was born in that house in 1909, with the help of a midwife. My oldest sister was born in the Belvedere cottage with Dr. Florence Scott attending. When the main ferry station was changed to Sausalito, the whole family had to move there. I was born in Sausalito in 1914. It must have been a big burden; my eldest sister was only seven, and I was child number five!

Before then, my parents had already purchased a piece of land in Tiburon, at 2203 Paradise Drive in Lyford's Cove, because they really loved it over there. They bought the land from Dr. Lyford. The house was built in 1914. Next door was Mr. Glass. Bud Glass still lives in that house on Paradise Drive. On the other side was Bert Hooper. Harvey Anderson's house was there, and Mrs. Brennan lived at the bottom of the hill on Solano and Mar East. Across the street was the Trollson House. There were in all only about fifteen houses in Lyford's Cove then. All the rest was bare, with no trees.

Did you all buy the land from Dr. Lyford?

No, Lyford's property was always in litigation. Hugh Boyle, one of the Lyfords' heirs, was given that section of Tiburon as part of his inheritance. So my father made subsequent purchases from Hugh Boyle. Boyle was kind of a sharpie himself. Every once in awhile he'd come and ask my father if he'd like to buy the lot next door, which my father owned! He couldn't keep track of his property.

Hugh was quite a ladies' man. Ida. M. Boyle was one of his wives. She received a big quantity of lots in Lyford's Cove in the divorce settlement. So she used to sit down there in the stone tower on Sunday and try to sell you a lot for $50 or $75. She must be turning over in her grave now!

There was an arch over the road at the tower. There was never a gate in that arch. I don't want you to write that there was. The gate was about 100 yards down towards town — a square iron gate.

When I was young, our neighbor Mr. Glass had a soda water concession in the tower on Sundays. My younger brother Bob and I used to help him. Mr. Glass kept the soda water in a big washtub full of cold water, and used to sell it for ten cents a bottle. Numerous hikers came over on the ferries, and they would walk up from the ferry slip, have a bottle of soda water, head out to El Campo on Paradise Drive, and buy another bottle when they came back. That was his Sunday business!

A lot of the German societies would come over in groups from San Francisco, and the Sierra Club too, I think. They were all very pleasant people, singing and enjoying everything.

Where did Mr. Glass get his soda water?

From the Mason Distillery in Sausalito. They later went into the making of whiskey as well. They brought the soda water to Mr. Glass in their truck once a week, and my brother and I would each get a free bottle for carrying the cartons and helping out on Sundays.

Did you and your neighbors design your own homes and have them built?

Now that is a very good question, because I have seen our house all over California, one in Ukiah, one in Eureka, one in Petaluma. You bought your plans from a magazine for $25. My brother, Allan, has the plans for our house. It was built by a contractor, Mr. Campbell. There was always a big discussion in our house because the beams that held up the first floor were 40' long and the plans said they should be 38'. Mr. Campbell would not cut them off. The house was completed in June, 1914.

Sausalito, where we had been living, was a pretty grown-up city, but in Tiburon the roads were just dirt. There were a lot of dairies. The cows came right down by the house. The cows worried my mother to death because she was not used to them. She said that when I was out in the yard in the baby buggy the cows would come down and lick my head. She used to tell me that. She was afraid to do anything about the cows.

Was your father still working on the ferries at this time?

Yes. In those days my father worked 24 hours on, 48 hours off. When we moved to Tiburon, he had to take the ferry to Sausalito to get to work. The railroad, NWP, ran a special launch at 5:30 a.m. to get the workers over to Sausalito in time for the first ferryboat at 6:30. The engineer and the captain kept sleeping quarters on the boat, and would stay there if they were on the last shift.

My father put in forty-five years of service there.

Forty-five years on the boats! He was a very energetic, robust man who did all the work around the house, painting, building the fences.

How early would your mother get up to feed that big family?

Goodness knows! I always remember my mother sleeping in! I was the last child, and by the time I got ready to go to grammar school, she had had enough of it. The eldest one had to see that everyone had their breakfasts. Shredded wheat and oranges. That's all we ever had. You could get shredded wheat out of a box for yourself, you know. My mother stayed in bed until all of us left for school. She had made up our lunches the night before and set them out in bags on the table. She got very smart!

Could you tell us a little about your school days?

I went to the old Tiburon school. It was a two-story building, but the upper floor was never used. They built for expansion and expansion never came. The furnace was in the basement, and it smoked like the devil! In the two downstairs rooms the first through fourth grades were on the left side and the fifth through eighth on the right, with big stairs in the middle. The school looked right down on the lagoon. I remember it was a big challenge to see who could throw a rock from the school yard and hit some of the houseboats below. I could never do it!

When I started first grade I was six and a half. Being number five I had already looked at all the textbooks. The same ones, they never changed them. I didn't have any trouble at all with schooling. I had for one of my teachers Miriam Grbac; she was just out of Normal School at the time. I had Miss Du Foue, who still lives in San Rafael. Then came Margaret Smith, then Mabel C. Bean. She was there when I was in the eighth grade and she truly did not understand me.

School was very uninteresting. It wasn't at all exciting like it is now. We had no science. We had art, if you wanted to call it art, on Friday afternoons, while the boys were doing manual training in the basement. There was no library. However, we had to diagram sentences backwards and forwards, and I can still do it. I taught my daughter how. I know the multiplication tables very well, all the combinations of fractions, what the fractions are in decimal. That was the type of thing they taught you. Everything by rote. But it didn't hurt me.

Were there many pupils in the school?

In the fifth to eighth grades, 22 to 25 kids were in the room with one teacher. First thing in the morning, we saluted the flag outside the building, then marched into the room to the "Stars and Stripes Forever," played on the wind-up phonograph. I still feel like I'm marching when I hear that! Then we sang songs from the California State textbook of songs. I can still recite "Old Black Joe," Flow Gently Sweet Afton," Oh, Susanna," and all those old cornball ones that no one else knows. I loved to sing. My mother put a stop to that because I sang so flat. That's what I enjoy about going to church now, I can sing so loud in church! I love that.

Then all four grades had arithmetic. Then we'd have spelling. She'd say "The word for the fifth grade is 'catch,' " and so on. Then we passed our papers around and corrected them on the honor system. Then we had geography and history and writing. I still have a sixth-grade composition I wrote on the history of Tiburon. You should have seen the spelling on it! How we happened to write on the history of Tiburon I don't know. That assignment didn't fit with Mabel C. Bean, who was so uptight. I guess she was a good teacher. She was strict. She used to wallop the boys with a twenty-inch ruler. Mabel C. Bean's husband was killed on the last day of World War I.

The girls would not get walloped?

No! She punished me by giving me a P in Deportment. It was written in red ink on the report card, and was the worst you could get. My mother would say, "Now Carol, what is this all about?" I'd have to explain what happened. I got a P in Deportment once for calling one of the girls in school a wop! Another time I got one for laughing at the wrong time during a Christmas party.

What did you wear to school?

I was the rough and tough type, more like my brothers than my sisters. My sisters were always cooking and sewing. I didn't want any of that! I had my own baseball mitt and bat. I had shoes with brass toes! We took the ferry to Sausalito to buy those shoes from Jacob & Krug. My mother made my dresses, and being number five, I got a lot hand-me-downs!

How did you get to school? What was your route?

We walked straight up what is now Solano Street, over the hill to Centro West. The streets were just cowpaths then. Going to church at Old St. Hilary's we went along a cowpath called Vistazo West. One time going into the church my mother tripped on the step. She turned to me and said, "I'm glad I fell into the church and not out!"

Can you tell us about Main Street?

My mother never allowed us there. We were not allowed to go down except to get the mail. The postmistress, I remember, was one of the Wosser girls. She married Joe Souza, from the dairy. When there got to be six of us in the family, the postmistress got so mad at the Creighton family calling for the mail that she said we had to get a box. We had box 122 for more years than I can remember.

Then Mrs. Chapman, whose husband owned the grocery store that had the post office in it, took over. The post office was always part of the grocery store. And the grocery stores were in all different places; they moved around. There was Chapman's, Beyrie's, and Mantegani's. Fires periodically wiped everything out.

My mother was more lenient with the boys, but the girls just didn't go to Main Street, just as we didn't go to Belvedere to swim at the drawbridge where a lot of the other children went. We always swam at Anderson's Beach. The Kirchers and the Bradleys would come too, and it was really very pleasant.

I can still remember when people from the arks rowed to Main Street. There was a dock at the back of the store and you tied up your boat and came in and got your groceries.

Why didn't your mother want you to go to Main Street?

Tiburon's Main Street was, I guess, about as wild as you could get. Even before my parents moved here, my father talked about the good times they had on Main Street in Tiburon. They used to have dances and big parties. The man who ran the Sonoma Hotel, I remember, was Mr. Narbie, an Irishman. It was a regular old saloon with sawdust on the floor, oh, quite the thing! Later on there were many different saloons on Main Street. It was just restaurants and saloons and that's all — and the grocery store and the butcher shop.

It must have been pretty lively before 1900. You had the yacht people coming over on the weekends. They were a very hard drinking, exuberant group of men! You see, no women were involved in the yacht clubs in those days. And there was never any police protection, none at all! We finally got one sheriff from Marin County that I remember, Sheriff Selmar. The bootleggers in town would be advised that Selmar was going to make a run through Tiburon. You can ask Harvey Anderson how they disposed of the liquor at those times, how they put it overboard, or under trap doors. It was really terrible! You could come to Tiburon and do whatever you damned pleased!

When the codfishery boats would come in, all hell would break loose on Main Street. These men would rush off the boats, come over the Belvedere Hill down to the bars. Let's be honest — there must have been some loose women down there. Someone tried to say there had been a house of prostitution in the top of the Donahue Building, but that wasn't true at all. That floor was always used as living space by the railroad workers. So that story should be dropped.

Even in Belvedere up until the 30's there was an ark across from the San Francisco Yacht Club that was just used to service the yachtsmen. That is one thing that is definite. Both Tiburon and Belvedere had loose women.

Oh, and somebody should just write a chapter on baseball in Tiburon! It was The Thing! All the big companies in San Francisco had their own teams and they'd come over to Tiburon early on Sunday to warm up for the game on Sunday afternoon. There was a Yellow Cab team from the city and all the Southern Pacific shops in San Francisco had teams. Everybody went! That is, everybody but my mother, who said that at least baseball gave her time to read the Sunday papers in peace.

There was fighting, betting, and drinking at the baseball game. But it was a lot of fun! You just didn't miss that!

Did the Belvedere people come to the games?

Yes, some did!

Waldo and Jack Ericson in 1914, about the time they threw the family silverware out the window of their ark into the lagoon.

Where did you shop for your groceries?

We had them delivered. Chapman's store rang up their customers every day and asked them what they wanted. They would call you! My mother never knew what was in season because she never went downtown. My poor mother! The groceries were delivered by truck. My brother Allan worked in the grocery store and drove the grocery truck, so I used to go down to the stone tower — that's as far as I was allowed to go — and wait for him to come to Lyford's Cove and then help him deliver his groceries. He liked that. A vegetable man would come around, too, once a week, selling apples and oranges and things. There was also the Railroad Express Man with a Model A Ford. You paid him to deliver goods and groceries that came in on the ferry. At one time we ordered our staples once a month from the city, and my father would go down and bring them up to the house in a wheelbarrow. If I was good I got to ride in it down to the ferryslip!

The Costa brothers delivered our milk. They were still delivering it in 1941 when my father retired. The first thing he did was light into the milkmen for leaving the gate open. He told the milkman not to darken the door again if he could not close the gate. Here he is, first day of retirement, attacking the man who had been serving us for years and years! So the man just said, "All right, you put your milk box out by the road. I'm not coming up here anymore." Oh, after all those years.

We also had laundry service. The only advice my mother gave me when we got married was, "Carol, never wash sheets!" Isn't that something. Never wash sheets. The laundry was put out in a bundle on the back porch once a week and the sheets were sent out to San Rafael or Sausalito. My mother had a thing about sheets.

We have heard that a lot of Italian families made their own wine. Did your family ever do that?

No. My nother never allowed us to drink. I do remember the winemaking very well. In the fall each one of the Italian families along Mar West Road, the Mantegani, Milani, Polacchi, Locati, and Bertoli families all got grapes trucked in from Sonoma. It was Prohibition, but it was allowed because they were Italian and it was part of their tradition. They all helped each other make the wine. They dumped the seeds and skins down the bank and made a big stink. I can remember it so well! And Mantegani made a Hell of a lot of money selling wine during Prohibition.

Wasn't there a major strike at the railroad yard in the 1920's?

Yes, there was a national railroad strike in 1924. It made a big difference to Tiburon, because strikebreakers from other parts of the country were hired by the NWP to take over the jobs of the local people. They brought over a ferryboat for the strikebreakers to sleep on, and set up dormitories down on the dock. And they put up a high red board fence with strands of wire across the top so people couldn't get in. My brother Allan had the newspaper concession and he sold the men newspapers. He did well for himself — all those men with little to do. There was a tremendous amount of bitterness about these scabs. Most of them came from Pocatello, Idaho, which was a big railroad center. These new people changed the pattern of population considerably. In restrospect it seems like nothing, but it did make a lot of difference in the schools, a lot of kids came in, new kids from Pocatello. A lot of the local families left the area.

After the strike came the depression. We were never affected as a family by the depression because my father worked during it. But my brother Al, who got out of high school at that time, couldn't find a job at all. The ferries were going back and forth even though they weren't filling them. As for the town, it was very, very depressed. The men in the railroad shops were working only three days a week. I remember a man who came around selling broken cookies, and the hobos riding on the trains, coming in on the flatcars. The railroad was very tolerant.

Do you recall the Coaling Station on Paradise Drive?

My first recollection of the Coaling Station is just after World War I with the huge piles of coal and the gantry running. The big navy ships would come in. There again you had all those sailors coming down to Main Street! My sisters had some kind of romances with the sailors. I was too young. When the depression came they phased out the coaling station and all the men were sent to work on Mare Island.

Top: Carol's father was chief engineer on the Cazadero. *Below: Lyford's Tower, where Carol and Bob sold soda pop on Sundays.*

Left: Carol Creighton, Tamalpais High School, 1931. Right: Carol on a hiking trip, 1978.

But after the closing of the coaling station came another influx of young boys, which interested me more, the Maritime Academy! It was there for quite a few years. They had their lessons there and their boat, the *Golden Bear.* Of course there were more cars coming by this time, and the road got paved by the U.S. Government. World War II had started. So we had a beautiful paved road out to the Net Depot.

Do you remember the houseboats?

The houseboats were all down in Belvedere Cove. In the fall, October or November, they'd open the bridge and bring all the houseboats into the lagoon on a flood tide. And then in the spring they took them out. It was a big event. It was party time!

Belvedere in those days had a long row of arks — about forty — that made a crescent along the lagoon, all along San Rafael Avenue.

Italian gardeners lived in them?

Some of them were gardeners. The Colemans lived there, the Polacchis, de Tomasis, and Parianis. They all went to school with us, you see. There were railroad people living in Belvedere too.

What about the arks on the Tiburon Side?

They were the same arks. They were moved to the Belvedere side so that Belvedere would have enough children to open its own school. My husband, Jack Ericson, was born in 1912 and was four or five years old when he was living on one of those arks. There were ten or twelve arks on the Tiburon side then. His mother used to tell me that one day she looked out the window, and Jack and his brother had thrown all the silverware out the window. The tide was going out, and there was all the silverware sticking out of the mud! When their father wanted to go shopping, he rowed from the ark down to Main Street in Tiburon.

His father worked on the NWP as a steam engineer on the engines. He was sent all over the railroad empire. Jack lived in about every town that had a railroad depot, and Tiburon was one of them.

Do you recall the Nights in Venice?

Yes, very well. The Night in Venice was a big occasion for Belvedere society and the Corinthian Yacht Club. It was NOT a Tiburon event, not at all. It began on Saturday and went into Sunday and people barely got to work on Monday. And it was simply beautiful. All the houses in Belvedere were decorated very fancy. When we came down from Lyford's Cove it was inspiring, really, for a young child to see. There were barges in the cove, with musicians. The sailboats were dressed up.

When I was older, going on sixteen, Jack had a little sailboat that Hugo Keil gave him. I can remember sailing over with him to see the Night in Venice. It must have been the last one. It was really very daring of us to be there.

I didn't go to the dances. My sister went to them at the San Francisco Yacht Club, which used to be the Pacific Motor Boat Club. It had a beautiful dance floor.

Was there much communication between the two communities of Tiburon and Belvedere?

None at all. The people in Belvedere thought that only servants lived in Tiburon. They thought that anyone who went to old St. Hilary's Church was lowbrow, Irish or Italian!

Was it a racial or a social thing?

It was social snobbery! A friend of mine told me that no one in Belvedere went to Tiburon because Tiburon was just commercial. This distinction is gone now, though. It broke down in World War II when there was an influx of young men and women who were not interested in whether it was Belvedere or Tiburon. The view was really the same.

When the new young people came, Belvedere School was floundering for lack of students, and it had to merge with the Tiburon School. That was a big breakthrough. Tiburon voted against it, and Belvedere for it. Belvedere needed Tiburon. Isn't that interesting! So they joined schools and their kids were all in it together. When you get your kids together, everyone has to come together.

Olive Fetherstonhaugh, 1980.

Olive Fetherstonhaugh

1896–

Mrs. Fetherstonhaugh's long experience as an artist is evident in her actions and words. A small, handsome woman, she uses lively gestures and animated facial expressions. Her speech is full of vivid pictures, color, textures, shapes. At the time of this interview in 1975, her living room was crowded with mementoes of old friendships — books, paintings, shells, — representing a bond understood only by the giver and the receiver. In her studio, when she dons a smock and picks up a paintbrush, she becomes truly ageless.

Mrs. Featherstonhaugh, where did you come from, and when and why did you come to Belvedere?

We lived in Berkeley, on Canyon Road, overlooking the stadium. One day an artist friend of ours, Ray Boynton, asked us if we would like to drive over to visit Mr. Piazzoni and his family in Belvedere. It was the first time we had ever heard of Belvedere, to tell you the truth. So we drove to Richmond and came over on a big ferry to San Quentin and drove through this Oh! Beautiful countryside! I think this was about 1922 or 1923 — you know, I'm awfully poor on dates.

We arrived in Belvedere, and the lagoon was a beautiful big lake with a causeway to drive along. The Piazzonis lived opposite where the Belvedere Land Company is now, on Beach Road. They lived in one of those English period cottages. I believe they paid twenty dollars a month rent. Mr. Piazzoni was a very fine landscape artist. His wife was French and he was Swiss-Italian. We had a delightful little visit. We met his French wife and her mother and the two girls, Mireille and Romy. He seemed absolutely settled here in Belvedere at the time. Ralph Stackpole, a sculptor, lived not far away; they were friends. There was some other artist but I've forgotten his name entirely.

Next door to the Piazzoni cottage was the Belvedere Hotel, where the San Francisco Yacht Club is now. We were there in the autumn and the summer people had gone. And all the chairs were piled against the building. People used to sit there and watch the cove. It was a seasonal hotel, open for spring and summer.

On our drive back to Berkeley my husband said to me, "This is the place where I want to live."

We came back two years later looking for a place and the hotel was gone; the lake was gone, too — it was just bluish clay. Down in the cove there weren't so many little houseboats. We were stunned by the change. So much could happen in a couple of years! So then we looked around and found a place on Corinthian Island, Mr. Chamberlain's — quite a large place. He only came over on weekends to his part of the house. We had the loveliest garden, just beautiful. We thought we had arrived in Paradise. And then a few years later we discovered this house on Belvedere. Mrs. Ball owned it. She said she would rent it to us on one condition: we had to use the coal and wood stove and never replace it. That meant we'd have to heat the stove to heat the water in this great big heater. But we acceded to her request, luckily. She was a really nice old lady. And so we moved over to Belvedere.

How did you get to your art classes in San Francisco?

I commuted every day on the ferries. I went for three or four years. Mr. Piazzoni, whom I absolutely loved, was one of my teachers. He was living in the City then. I joined his landscape class. And I asked him, "Mr. Piazzoni, why did you move from Belvedere when we just moved there ourselves?"

"Because it is too beautiful," he said. "All I did was gaze out and say, 'Oh, look at the beautiful moon, look at the gorgeous sunrise!' I work better in the City, with no view, because I have to create beauty."

I used to see Mr. Stackpole on that Union Street car, too. He was a very nice man. He married a French woman. I loved going through the wholesale produce district on my way to school. You know after the war the GI's flooded the schools and universities; we had very good teachers then — I became a student again. Helen Rich and I both went back after our husbands died for a year of school with the GI's. It was the best period the art school ever had. People were really involved.

Were you giving art lessons at that that time?

No. I am now. I have taught off and on since I've been married. In Tiburon there was a little shop run by the Weinsteins, very wealthy people from Chicago. They wanted to have a hobby, so they had an art shop where you could buy people's paintings and also have some teaching. I had specialized in mosaics, so they asked me if I'd like to teach. Was I ever glad to! That was the beginning of my teaching. Very few people take mosaics now; it is sort of a specialty. I love it.

Did you study with Spencer Mackey?

No, he was from an earlier time. Mr. Mackey, Mrs. Mackey, Mrs. Albright and Mr. Randall were the teachers in the thirties. It was a much more academic school. The teachers had all studied in Rome, Paris, that kind of thing.

Oh, and Seldon Connor Gile was in Belvedere. He lived in one of the houses along Beach Road, not in the English cottages, but one with a broad balcony. He had his place filled with paintings. And he was out painting every day. He was either at the lagoon, or he walked along with his paintbox. He reminded me of the impressionists the way he worked in the out-of-doors. And he showed mostly at the Oakland Museum. And this friend of his, a very well-known artist, Louis Siegriest, used to come over and spend weekends with him.

Mr. Gile was a proud New Englander. And really what happened to him — the Depression came and his investments that he had retired on after years of work as an accountant were lost. He became frantic, and he sold everything he had, which he should not have done. He should have hung onto what he had because they were good investments. But they all went down in value and he sold them at the low price. So from that time on he was desperately poor. He sold his paintings, but you can't live on the sale of paintings unless you are an Andrew Wyeth. It's impossible, really. But he painted, nevertheless, he never stopped. I think he sold enough, just barely enough to keep himself and pay his rent.

Then he opened a library down there in back of the Belvedere Land Company building. It was very sparsely furnished, with very few books on the shelves because he was building it up. He said "Be sure to come in and see my library." He was terribly proud of it. And he had hung a beautiful painting there, the one Bunk Mersereau has, a long mural of Belvedere Cove. It is a beautiful painting. And he said to me, "What do you think of it?" I said it looked nice. "Nice!" he said. "You wouldn't find a nicer library anywhere!" He was so funny, such a character.

And finally he got his big commission from the Northwestern Railways, I think it was, to do murals for all their offices in Chicago and San Francisco. By that time he was a very sick man. He managed to get one done which hangs at the San Francisco City Office. He was never able to do any of the others because he died of cancer of the liver. That was very sad.

Could you show us some of your paintings?

I don't know where they are! I wish I had them but I don't. The only one I have from that time is this one of the lagoon before it was built up. The school was not there but the little barn was there, that is a very early one. Most of the time I'd go out by myself to paint. But I do remember sitting on one of those hills over there in Tiburon where the dairy was, with a friend. We were sitting on the ground with our paint boxes on our laps and suddenly a herd of cows came charging down the hill, going down to be milked, you see. I said to Laura, "I don't think there are any bulls, but if there are just keep still." And then charging after the cows came a bull, looking like a railway locomotive, a huge white bull. We sat there, and I had a paint brush; I held it just like this. We drew in our breath and we didn't even move, and he went charging past. I guess he thought we were stones or something. But if we had been foolish and tried to run we certainly would have been sorry.

You said you took the ferry into the City. What was your route?

The cutest little ferryboat came in to where Miss Huntington had her house on the east side of Belvedere. There was a little wharf there, and the ferry the *Marin,* really a little schooner, would tie up and people would go over the plank. It would go to Sausalito and you'd change to the big ferry going to the City. At Christmas the *Marin* always had a Christmas tree tied to the mast. And the big ferries had beautiful big trees that absolutely filled the air with scent. Inside we used to sit around sniffing the air. Oh, it was really a great time, a beautiful time.

Was there much traveling between Sausalito, San Rafael, Kentfield?

Well, you see, what we did then every week, in a landscape art class, was to meet at the ferry landing in Sausalito and then we'd get aboard the train, all of us — there would be about thirty of us, with our paint boxes and our lunch. And we'd get off any place every week. We'd go to Larkspur, Kentfield, and the Kent estate; we were always going there. The Kents gave us permission to be on the grounds. That was always the time when the grapes were hanging in clusters and the leaves were beautiful brilliant reds. We loved going there. Then we'd go to other places up the line. The little train would stop and we'd get off and paint. Then we'd get the train back to Sausalito, and I'd get on the ferry and ride back here to Belvedere. Oh, it was delightful!

And to see the trains on Sundays filled with people who had been out all day in the country, and they would have bouquets of wildflowers, which you are not allowed to pick now. And on the ferryboats there would be men strumming guitars or playing the banjo, or a game of cards. And all that was just another life! It is still alive in me. People were so leisurely, so carefree.

And no one locked their doors here, no one did. There was only one occurrance that made me lock my door. It wasn't the time of the Depression, it was after that. Margaret Prentiss, who lived above me, always took her dog for a walk every day, never locking her doors. When she came back one day she was frightened by a man who had entered her house and was hiding in her closet. He had taken some money from her dresser. The unlocked door must have tempted him. So after that I always locked my door.

Did you walk much around the island yourself?

Yes, in the morning it was gorgeous around on the west side, and oh, the fresh smell of eucalyptus! And no houses — only that big barn-like stable that Mr. Blanding had down there.

Did you know Mr. Blanding?

Yes, Mrs. Holmes asked if she could bring a young friend of hers to call on Mr. Blanding. So he said most certainly. We arrived there for tea on his porch. The same house Mrs. Booth lives in now, the big white house perched on the end of the island. Someone brought tea and we enjoyed it there on the porch. He was the nicest man, a very big man. Rather sardonic, you would say. He said things that would show you he was very much a man of the world. A little disillusioned, but interesting. I would say a very clever man, even brilliant. He gave us tea, and then he took us around the garden, a little tour of it. We then went to the Organ House, below, where he played the organ. He had two sisters who lived in a third house. That's my only memory of him, just that afternoon. I would say he was a sad man; I think he had a lot of sadness in his life. He seemed to know few people. I'm glad I had that experience because he was a man you wouldn't forget.

Do you remember the codfishery?

Oh, yes, on the west side of the Island. I went down there one day and sketched. A man was peeling potatoes inside the cookhouse. My goodness, two-thirds of the potato fell into the pail, he peeled so lavishly! And the smell at the codfishery was terrible. But a most picturesque place. The men all hung their working smocks on pegs in a long line when the dinner bell rang, you know the kind. We had a nice time drawing. We went twice. And the big black-masted ships were anchored in Richardson Bay, silhouetted against the Sausalito skyline.

There were not many houses in Sausalito then. But they were practically all English people living over there. Awfully nice English people. There was a joke — one of the writers on the paper said they were thinking of putting an American Consulate over in Sausalito.

What was happening to the lagoon at that time?

The lagoon began to grow little groves of willows and grass. You'd often see beautiful blue herons in little pools of water, and all this grey clay. It could be used to make pottery.

And there was a group of Italians who lived there along the lagoon in arks. They were mostly gardeners. That was quite a place. You know where you walk under the cork elms on San Rafael Avenue? Right along there — about nine or twelve arks with nice little gardens. They used to grow squashes on the roofs; they got more sun there and less salt in the soil. On Sunday you used to think there was a huge fight going on because they all shouted and talked to each other, they were so loud! They were very friendly, but it just sounded like a huge fight.

They were good gardeners, oh, marvelous gardeners. All from some place in Italy. They were characters, every one of them. Harry Pariani used to come and do special work for us; he was marvelous! He was up at 4:30 a.m., always walking the lane below us. He died long ago. Louie Soldavini still works on Belvedere, for the City now. His father, Vincent, was a very good gardener. Vincent went back to Italy and I understand he died there; he must have been in his nineties.

Marion and Lem Allen had a grocery store in Belvedere. We would go there and have ice cream. Marion and Lem were awfully cute. We used to have a monthly bill, and when I'd pay it, Lemuel Allen always would give me a chocolate bar.

What was the Depression like here?

During the Depression people used to come to the door begging for food. They used to ride in on the railroad train and they stayed in a sort of jungle. Nice men, every one of them. Boys that were so nice. They were principally from up north, Oregon, Washington. They were looking for work. They often came to this house because I'm on the road. All they wanted was something to eat. They never asked for money. Quite a number of people in Belvedere left a standing order with Lemuel and Marion Allen to give those men a dollar's worth of food. They always wanted coffee, bread, and a bit of meat or some apples. Lots of people did this. I used to cook a breakfast of bacon and eggs, toast and coffee. Oh, how they liked that!

But two lads arrived one day, nice young men about eighteen or nineteen. One of them just fainted on the back porch. He was so far gone. They had no blankets; it was October and cold at night. Their blankets had been stolen from them. They were sleeping on the hard ground, of course. So I was desperate about them. They didn't have the right clothes; they had nothing but shirts on, no sweaters. Terribly worn. I didn't have anything to give away because I had already given away my husband's things that I could spare. I had a dear friend who lived up the hill, so I called her up. Travelers never went to her house because they didn't want to climb all those steps. I asked her if she could give these boys anything because it was cold at night and they were going back to Washington. That's where they were making for; this was just when we had heard that the CCC camps were forming. Work farms.

She said she would be right down. Well, I've never seen such beautiful clothes. She had the most

Top: Gottardo and Beatrice Piazzoni with dog; Mireille and Romy Piazzoni with their grandmother, 1921. Below: The Farr Cottages, about 1930.

gorgeous white woollen sweaters and white flannel trousers and flannel shirts. And these boys couldn't get over it! She gave them each some money; blankets too. They were outfitted in the most elegant clothes you ever saw. So impractical, you know. It was so funny! But these were the things she had the most of.

Some people from this area had to move. There was one very nice man and his wife, I don't know what happened to them. They had been living here in Belvedere and they lost everything. They moved to the City and I think they were living in a room. He used to turn up here, trying to borrow a few dollars from any man he could find who had a job. He was white-haired, an older man; it was heart-breaking.

But Belvedere was hit principally by these men traveling through. They went into this commune or jungle here in Tiburon and waited for the trains. Nobody disturbed them; everybody felt for them, they really did. Not one of those men or boys was rough, or made any trouble. I think that was one of the distinguishing marks of the Depression, the lack of violence. We all pulled in our belts.

Do you remember some of the town characters? Miss Livsey? Smitty?

Oh, yes! Miss Livsey, a wonderful character. Her family came around the Horn in a sailing ship. She was English, a niece of Lotta Crabtree, a famous actress. She never married. She was like a character out of a book. Well, I'd say she was; it's hard for me to judge, for at the time I was very young and she seemed very old. I would say she was in her seventies.

Anyway, she inherited money from Lotta Crabtree when the estate was settled, so she had means to go and retire in Sausalito finally. She did lots of good work. There was a man who was very ill and he wasn't able to work. She knew they were very hard up, so she arrived one morning and put a check on the man's bed and said, "Don't you ever speak of that!" She did things like that, awfully nice things.

She had a cubbyhole of a post office next to the Allen's grocery store, in the present Belvedere Land Company building. She wore the most tailored clothes, sort of a suit with a stiff collar with a little tie and a tailored hat. And she had a parrot, often sitting on her shoulder. Sometimes at the post office window she would stand there looking at you with this bright, eager, rather lean face with very sharp, dark brown eyes, with her parrot on her shoulder; it's this vision that stays with me, it is how I'll always remember her.

She had an apartment upstairs and in nice weather the parrot would sit on the windowsill. There was a man, a commuter, who came down through that little park every day. And as he was walking he would hear a voice say, "Good morning!" And he'd take off his hat and say, "Good morning!" He didn't know it was the parrot upstairs. Finally he looked up one morning and saw the parrot gazing down on him. He told that story and thought it awfully funny. He felt like such a fool, taking his hat off morning after morning! (laughter) Oh, dear!

Miss Livsey was terribly funny about the mail. For instance she would give me a postcard and say, "I'm glad to hear that so-and-so is well." She knew everything. She was a very frank person, too. She'd tell people off, she'd tell them just what she thought.

She and I once went on a little binge together to see a show at the San Francisco Museum of Art. And we had an awfully good time. She had a very good feeling for art. And then she said we should go to the Palace Hotel, to the grill. So we did. She ordered a big plate of oysters, and as she was eating them she said, "You know, they are alive, but Oh! they're good!"

And Smitty, ah, Smitty. The man with the little tiny legs. What a figure he was. Very uncommunicative. I wonder if he ever talked to anyone?

Ah, there was a wonderful family, the Meenans —Johnny and his mother. They were the real kind of Irish that you'd read about in a book or see in a play. They lived in a tiny little house where the Ark Apartments are now. There were a lot of little cottages and old arks there. She lived in one that had a white picket fence around it, and she'd lean against it and look at you as you passed, and say, "And how are you today?" with her pompadour sliding down one side.

She would get quite a bit of work. I must say she liked drinking very much. When we were living on Corinthian those first two years, my mother was visiting us so we had people in for lunch. My mother insisted on my getting someone to wash the dishes and help. So I went down to the cottage and asked

Mrs. Meenan if she would come. "Yes, indeed I will!" After she arrived, Ted, my husband, was making martinis in the kitchen. He felt a burning eye fixed on his back. He turned around and asked Mrs. Meenan if she would like one of the drinks. "Indeed I would!" she answered, and took the drink and downed it. He didn't offer her any more.

She once said to my husband, "So they say you're Irish?"

"I am. I was born in Dublin."

"You were, were you! Well, your name isn't so Irish."

"No, I guess it goes way back to Anglo-Irish or Danish."

"Ah, there's been many a Swede buried in Ireland."

Her son, Johnny, also drank profusely. He had an old felt hat cocked on the side of his head and an old car he'd drive along. One day I was walking and he said, "Would you like a lift?"

"Thank you, Johnny, I'd like it very much."

"I never thought you'd accept."

"Did you mean it?" I asked.

"Of course I meant it." He was so pleased; I got in and we drove down to Tiburon.

He used to do odd jobs, and he'd work until he got drunk and then he'd be away for four or five days. Then he'd come back and finish the job. He had a dog that followed him everywhere. Once he had to go away and he came to ask us if we would take care of the dog for him for one night. "That's all I'm asking, just one night." So we said yes. That night the dog began howling when he was brought into the house. We didn't know what to do, so we fed him. We were very suspicious of his fleas. But we fixed up a place for him to lie down in our room. And I think that comforted him. In the morning I opened the door and he dashed out of that house like a bullet! He went as fast as he could go. And he would never come near me again, he was so afraid I was going to take him away from Johnny.

Then Johnny died, and they said it was just dreadful to hear that dog crying. And then a brother, whom I had never met or seen, turned up. He was a big, tall man with another battered old hat on and a long overcoat. He was quite pretentious — misquoting from Shakespeare. And he came to look after the dog, all to his credit; I think he took the dog away with him.

I was teaching art down on Main Street, at Mrs. B. Weinstein's. And she was horrified to see this tall, lank figure coming and asking for Mrs. Fetherstonhaugh. She wanted to know how I ever got to know a man like that.

"Well, I said, he is an old inhabitant of Belvedere. Everyone knows the Meenan brothers. Winifred Allen went to school with those two men."

Oh, then she did not object. But he was so funny, such a character. Now that was the Meenan family. I guess the brother went back where he came from.

Did you ever use the Belvedere Golf and Country Club?

Oh, yes. That was up at the north end of the island. During better times we enjoyed the Club. We used to have parties there, New Year's Eve parties, maybe five times. All the people were there. The Kirschmans — she was very young and pretty, and her husband, who is gone. Rather a younger, gayer set than the other people we knew. The Booles, the Holmeses, the Prentices. It was just a sporty little club and course, like the people who belonged to it. I didn't play golf, nor did my husband. We didn't belong to the club, but we were invited there. That's how it was. Our lives were too busy for anything like that.

The Holmeses had a famous Chinese cook. He lived with them for years. Great dignity — the king of the kitchen. I remember being there when a niece and nephew of Mrs. Holmes came over from Berkeley unexpectedly. We had been invited for Sunday supper. To my horror, Mrs. Holmes could not ask her own relatives to stay for supper because it would have upset her Chinese cook! And in her own home!

Did you ever have a Chinese cook?

No. But there was a Chinese vegetable man who used to go around. The most marvelous wagon with lovely fruits and vegetables and things hanging from the top. You'd go out and pick your fruits and vegetables at your front door. He came just certain days of the week; you could choose from what he had that day. He always gave us a Christmas present of tea or ginger. Of course we always gave him a little present. His name was Jason — Jason Wong, I think.

There were only about three hundred fifty people on the island then. They'd all meet on the ferry in the morning. The population was very much decreased in the winter; many families moved to San Francisco when October came. They came back in May.

Did they hire caretakers to look after their property?

No, I don't know of any that did. They would just cover all their belongings and move over to the City. They moved to a hotel or an apartment. They enjoyed the concerts and theater in the winter.

Did you have much contact with people from Tiburon, or were Belvedere and Tiburon quite separate?

Yes, I'm afraid it was like that. You know, I don't approve of it, but it was like that. Most of the people in Tiburon at that time were working on the railroads and ferries. I'm sure there were some artists living over there. I went to art school with Laura Ericson; Carol was very much younger. I knew that family, and a very nice family it was. They have all moved away.

Another nice family was the Andersons. Mr. Anderson owned the butcher shop on Main Street. The Beyries were next door, a grocery store; Chapman's was across the street.

During the war Tiburon became quite a tough place. All the sailors from the Net Depot. I remember going to Sam's one night for dinner, and we heard dreadful fighting outside in the street — smashing of windows! It was sort of an active evening.

My husband was an air raid warden on our street because, you know, we expected a Japanese invasion. I don't think there were any Japanese families on the island at that time.

Once in a while I was able to go to Angel Island. Helen Booth, who lives in that big white house on top of the island, needed someone to do the cooking. She found a Mrs. Rose, whose husband was in the service over on Angel Island. Right after the war there was a quarantine station on Angel Island. The Roses had a very comfortable house over there. He was in the service, and she wanted something to do. She was a very nice woman from the Midwest. And she became a friend to all of us who knew her. They had one of those very well-built houses in the harbor. She would invite us over and we would go on the government boat, and she would have homemade bread hot from the oven and coffee for us, and then we would explore the island. We'd walk to the top, before they had the radar on it. The most heavenly view, the most beautiful island, and all those empty houses. We felt privileged. And then we would come back to her cozy house and a warm welcome, and come home on the government boat. We did that many times. It has changed a lot; now we take that little car around the island. I love it just the same.

Did you ever sketch while you were visiting Angel Island?

I did when we went to see Mrs. Rose. We never saw deer on the island, but you knew they were there. People have seen them swimming across Racoon Straits. There is a lot of wildlife on the island — deer, raccoons, a great many birds. We used to watch flights of pelicans — perhaps fifty of them, drifting along low to the water. There are some now but not many. I've seen them, like little schooners on the water, floating around, just a sight. It was beautiful to see them. You know they are so ungainly looking out of the water, but in the water they are quite graceful.

Did I tell you of the Italian fishermen in Belvedere Cove? There was no yacht harbor then. The fishermen came in to fish the herring. They all came in blue and white boats with little lights burning at night. They stayed all night, calling to one another from boat to boat. They would have picnics on the shore and dance and strum music. A lot of people did not like the noise. The only thing I disliked — hated — was when they would shoot the poor seals and the seals would cry and cry. That was terrible.

In the early dawn it was a wonderful sight to see the boats all lined up in the cove with the sun rising. I went down and did many drawings. The gulls came first, before the herring, hundreds of gulls flying, and the blue and white boats, and the men in their tarpaulins. The nets going out from their boats, very colorful and beautiful! Very beautiful!

Oh, and the Nights in Venice were also beautiful, calm beautiful warm nights. I don't know why, but the weather always seemed different then. The first year we hung our balcony with Japanese lanterns. Everyone did. With candles inside — very dangerous. But I don't remember them causing any

Louis Siegrist and Seldon Gile on the porch of Gile's houseboat in 1920, sampling Gile's home brew. This was the meeting place of the Society of Six, a group of painters who ate, drank, talked and painted together each Sunday. The six are now recognized as among the leading impressionist painters of the bay area.

fires. I still have some of those lanterns tucked away in the cupboard.

It was such a small community, you see — only 350 people living on an island — far fewer houses, because each house held a family. All the houses were lit up, and everybody went calling on everybody else. We went walking and were invited to drop in here and there. There was a barge in the cove with a little orchestra playing; one piece was Moonlight Sonata. A divine night. Just a friendly, natural, glamorous time. You would go out walking and people would call and you would go in and see your neighbors and have punch and cookies. One year we invited people from the City, so we did not go walking. That year people came calling on us. It was the loveliest of memories. It was just one night in the summer, but you kept your decorations up for a while. It was always a full moon. Years later they tried to revive it but it was not successful. The community was no longer small.

And I never saw this, but I know that the women used to row their husbands over to the ferries, before we came. I always heard that the women did the rowing. And we used to swim in the cove. I used to walk down from here to swim. Once I caught a terrible infection. Probably the tide was going out or something. I was a year ill. So I never dared to swim again after that. I think too much sewage went into the water. But other people swam, and at times the water seemed nice and clean. A lot of young people met at the beach there under the palm trees. Too bad it had to be filled in as a parking lot, but far better what the yacht club did than what could have been done. But it would be lovely to have the Belvedere Hotel in the cove, with people sitting on the porch there in the chairs overlooking the cove.

Oh, I have one more thing to tell you about. Next door there wasn't any house, of course, just this grove of oaks. And in it nested those black-crested night herons. That go squawk at night time. And in that back bedroom window upstairs I would look out on them every morning and see them nesting there and hear them squawking. Squawk! You know. They'd go down and get fish and feed their young in their nests. And one morning I woke up and all the trees were white! It had snowed. It is something I have only seen once. Snow all over the oak trees and bushes, all over the birds. It all disappeared in three hours. Was that the big storm in 1924? Were we here then? I never know when it was we moved over here, 1924 or 25 or 26. My husband remembered every date; I never remembered one. It was about ten years after we moved here that the snow fell. It blanketed everything. It was beautiful.

Everything is beautiful here; I think it is all beautiful. Every day. This place is something!

An aerial photograph looking east shows Beach Road and the drawbridge (left), Corinthian Island (center), the entire railroad yard and ferry slips, and Racoon Strait, with the tip of Angel Island (far right). The Dobie ark (bottom right) was the last to leave Belvedere Cove. This picture is probably from the early 1920's.

The Bradley house on Esperanza, about 1910. (From left) sister Elizabeth Bradley, a cousin, Rosella (Hilary's wife), sister Agnes Bradley Kircher, brother Hilary Bradley, aunt Kate Murphy, Miriam and Graham Bradley in front of their father, and mother holding Mary Kircher.

Miriam Bradley Grbac

1899–

Brownie Grbac is a tall, stately, handsome woman, quick to smile. On the day of this interview in 1975 she wore white shoes and white sweater, a fresh, clean dress, her white hair adding to the impression of spotlessness. She is a good, honest, sincere woman whose first concerns in life are family, friends, and church. She lives in the house she came to as a bride; the house she was born in is just across the street, next to Tiburon School, where she taught for more than twenty years; Old St Hilary's is just up the hill. Although she has not traveled far, her life has been rich and full.

Mrs. Grbac, when and why did you come to Tiburon?

I came because I was born here! October, 1899, and I'm proud of it! My father was Tom Bradley, a railroad man, a car oiler. I don't know what year he came, but he was here when the railroad started, or shortly after. He came down from Sonoma County. My parents had a ranch in the Sonoma hills. My father was born in Pennsylvania, and my mother in New York. Her parents had the Sonoma ranch originally. My older brother, my younger brother, and I were all born here in Tiburon. The rest of the family — there were eight of us — were born in San Rafael and Sonoma County. I'm the only one left.

I was born down on a place in the railroad yards. It was two living quarters and a school for railroad children, between the railroad paint shops and Mar West. Many of the railroad workers were Irish and Italian, quite a number of Italians. The homes along Mar West were owned mainly by railroad people. Many of the railroad families of Old Town are gone or passed away. Harvey Anderson and I are about the only old-timers left.

There were few homes in Tiburon then. The Tiburon School building was two stories on the corner of Mar West and Esperanza. I was growing up in the house across the street, which my parents built in 1901. The schoolyard backed along our fence. There were no houses on the hill — it was all cow pasture. Cattle used to pass by our house, and St. Hilary's sat above us on the hill. And a few houses along Mar West, and of course the rest was railroad yards down below. The few houses next to the school, on the point, were built before ours. The contractor who built our house, Mr. Seally, had built the house next to the school. This part of town was known as "Irish Hill."

Did you attend the railroad school or Tiburon School?

I started school in Tiburon School. There were two classrooms, two teachers, and about forty children. First through fourth grade, and fifth through eighth. We had reading, writing, and arithmetic, what we should have now. I went on to Tamalpais High School. We went over on the little *Marin* ferry to Sausalito and then took the electric train from Sausalito to Tamalpais. This all took about an hour. We never missed the boat. I went to San Francisco State Normal School for two years and got my teaching credential, that was about 1920. I commuted from Tiburon and took the ferry from Sausalito.

I first was a teacher at Reed School. At the time Reed School was about where Jefferson Avenue is now, up on the hill in Belveron Gardens. There were about eight or nine children. All eight grades. They came from the dairies: Borges Dairy, which was at Reed Station (Bel Air). Some came from Strawberry, where the Lyford home was. And there was a Chinese family at El Campo. They ran a pig ranch there. About four came from there — no, five Chinese children came. When they sold out and moved to San Francisco there wouldn't have been enough children to keep the school open. I taught one year at Reed School and then they closed it. The children then went to Belvedere School.

When I taught at Reed School it was a one-room schoolhouse with a potbellied stove where we kept warm. We had to carry water in. The boys would go over in the morning and get a bucketful from the spring at the cow trough at what is now the intersection of Trestle Glen and Tiburon Boulevard. They'd catch the dribbles. That was all the water we had.

We all walked to school. I'd walk up the railroad tracks to the schoolhouse. There were no passenger trains by that time, only one in the morning and one at night. The children also walked. On rainy days we did not have school. It was too wet and too far to come. The children from the Borges Ranch would walk through the railroad tunnel. Well, I got halfway through and I got so frightened that a train would come through that I made them run out the other end and come back over the hill. It was a daily occurrence for them to walk through. Boy, did they tease me many times about that afternoon!

There was a Miss Reading before me and before her a Miss Hauss. Miss Hauss was quite elderly. She would walk through the tunnel with the kids. But my youngsters would tell me how she would nap in the middle of the day and how they would turn the clock ahead to go home early.

We taught reading, writing, and arithmetic. At that time you had to follow a county curriculum. We had a little booklet that we had to complete, so much for each grade. The children and I were just good pals — on our noon walks! When the school closed I taught at San Jose School in Ignacio, another one-room country schoolhouse. I had to board with the Pacheco family in Ignacio for awhile. My mother became very ill so I returned home and commuted every day by train. I was only there a year, and then came back to the new Tiburon School in about 1922. Tiburon still had two rooms, with four grades in each. I had the primaries, with about forty children, and Margaret Smith had the others. Now read this and weep! (Mrs. Grbac has pulled out an old county tax record). First installment, $15.99, second installment $15.89, total for the year, $31.79! I was writing a check for taxes the other day, 1975, —six hundred and some dollars for a second installment. And that house was built in nineteen and one, my parents' home. I'll show you something else, speaking of the butcher shop (we are shown a monthy statement from the butcher shop). Yes, of course we had no electricity or gas, we used wood and coal. A ton of coal for $2.65. As far back as I can remember, Myron Weeks' father had the coal in a little shed over in Belvedere. Here are some receipts mother paid in 1903 for the little place where we lived down there. Dr. Lyford owned all of this. Payment for one month's rent for a five-room house situated upon block two, section nine, Lyford's Hygeia,Tiburon Point, $10.00! (Dr. Lyford's and Hilarita Reed Lyford's signatures are noted on the receipts).

What were some of the changes in Tiburon?

Electricity came into Tiburon about 1913. The town had begun to build up. There were still railroad families in the 20's. It started to develop around Paradise Cove.

As a child I was not allowed to go into Tiburon, but all the other children did. That bothered me.

Top: The Bradleys enjoy a picnic at Ocean Beach in 1910. Miriam, already known as Brownie, wears a white bow in her hair (left front). Below: Mr. Bradley worked as an oiler on a crew like this one.

I wasn't allowed to play on Main Street. The rest of them, as soon as school was out, would go and swim down there off McDonough's Wharf, on Main Street. I was afraid. I had a terrible fear of drunken people. I would go down to do the shopping or pick up the mail, but if I saw a drunken man I'd cross the street. There were three or four of those characters.

Was Main Street a rough place?

No, not necessarily. I have been quite put out by articles talking about all the ruffians from the railroads. They weren't ruffians. It's like saying of the Wild West that everyone was a ruffian. I was teaching at that time and I had some very fine youngsters whose parents were with the railroad. The town was used mainly by local people; some would come in and out by horse and buggy. We did not have a horse and buggy. We liked to walk. If you came in horse and buggy, you would come by San Rafael Avenue, through Belvedere and along Corinthian Island. And even after horse-and-buggy-days they came in that way. There was no Tiburon Boulevard south of San Rafael Avenue — it was all water down there. And from Mar West to about Tiburon School there were arks and people living along there in the arks. They would row to Main Street to do their shopping.

The trains would pick up the milk from the dairies in big five-gallon milk cans and take it up to San Rafael. There was one stop at Hilarita and one at Reed Station (Bel Air). And then for our own milk there was a dairy at the other end of Belvedere, what is now Westshore. The dairyman would come around with his cart, then a horse and buggy, and deliver milk at the back door in a pitcher or by the quart. We got our milk from the dairyman and our meat from Anderson's and vegetables from the Italian vegetable man.

Where did you play as a little girl?

We'd take to the hills! We'd just go for a walk. Practically every Sunday my father would take to the hills and most of the time we went with him. So I know those hills — every bit of them! And then too on Sundays, you know how people now come on the ferry or by car. Well, then they would come over on the ferry and on all the beaches all along there were groups of picnickers. There were no houses then. We would walk in the hills, take in the scenery, and pick wildflowers.

Sometimes on a Sunday we'd take the ferry to San Francisco, out to Ocean Beach. We'd have a picnic out there or at Golden Gate Park. We'd walk down to the ferry and at the Ferry Building take a streetcar to the beach. Sometimes we would go walking over the hills to El Campo on a Sunday and think nothing of it — dance all afternoon and walk back. There was live music. The ferry *Ukiah* used to come in from San Francisco — it was the picnic boat — and land at El Campo bringing the picnickers.

Yes, we just walked over the hill, but the ones who came in by ferry may have paid something to get into El Campo, it was included in their fare from San Francisco. Oh yes, and you could buy refreshments (a smile to suggest that the "refreshments" meant liquor). At times yachts anchored there. And there were two motor launches out of Tiburon, August Oldag, or his father, had a big motor launch and also Sam McDonough. People would come over and rent rowboats and go fishing or to the beaches. They would string the rowboats out one after the other and drop them off. And on Sunday you could see these two launches going out with a string of boats behind them. And in the afternoon they'd go out and pick them up.

Do you recall the Italian fishermen coming into the coves?

Oh. Yes, they'd come into what we called Anderson's Beach for herring. It is called Lyford's Cove now. We'd go over there and watch them throw their nets. And we'd gather up a bucketful and have herring for dinner. And during Lent we would go over the hill to the codfishery and get enough dried fish to last us through Lent. No one from town worked at the codfishery.

Did you ever use the yacht clubs?

No, not as a youngster — we were railroad people! But during the summer and the Night in Venice they would be in the cove and decorated with paper lanterns; there were no electrics. The people in Tiburon did not decorate their homes — it was entirely a Belvedere affair. We would walk over to Corinthian Island and take it all in, then maybe go to a street dance in Tiburon. Well, those were some of the ways we amused ourselves!

Top: Tiburon School, 1925. Miriam Bradley, right, was teaching in the school she had attended as a child; the house at rear is her family home. Below: St. Hilary's, up the path from the Bradley house, was the center of the family's social and religious life.

Left: Miriam Bradley (center) at her college graduation, 1920. Right: Miriam (Brownie) Grbac in the 1970's.

So people really created their own fun?

Yes. We had no other amusements; as I say, we would go for a hike, sing at the top of our voices — not that it was musical. Then there were card parties, whist parties at the school building, and picnics, things like that. It was mostly visiting from one house to the other. This actually is how I met my husband. He was born in Austria and came here in 1921. His brother was already here; he had come in 1911. His brother Joe worked on the railroad, then did gardening in Belvedere until he passed away. My husband, Mate — pronounced Matt — first lived in the East Bay, then came here to join his brother. My parents and I were having a St. Patrick's night party — we always had a St. Pat's party, but this one was for a couple who were getting married in June. These young Austrian boys, my husband and his brother, who could not speak English, came to visit another Austrian and were brought over to the party at my house.

There were few social affairs. Once in a while St. Hilary's church gave a card party. And you know, the priest came down from San Rafael on the train; in fact years before that he drove down by horse and buggy. He came here one week and San Quentin the next. In 1920 or along in there we became part of Sausalito Parish, and the priests came over on the ferry. The church was also used by people from Belvedere; they would walk over for mass. They were, of course, the help, you know. At that time the people of Belvedere had live-in help.

Were people here affected greatly by the depression?

During the depression men only worked three days a week in the railroad shops. We all cut down. Many of the men would do gardening work in Belvedere, or pick up carpentry work around. People did not sell their homes or leave. Men did come to our door for food. There were always hobos coming through on the trains. And our house was marked. My mother always had something for them. And gypsies used to come. They would set up a camp and then come begging and ask to tell your fortune right at your door. I was frightened to death of them. They camped mostly out there where Mar West meets Tiburon Boulevard, around the railroad water tank. They would stay a short time and then be off again. The Gypsies only wanted money. While the hobos wanted breakfast, something to eat. Sometimes they would saw wood; they said they wanted a job, but if they could get away without working they would.

During the depression there were many vegetable gardens. All the Italians had good vegetable gardens. We had a garden, but not like the Italians'. They could make anything grow when no one else could.

In spite of the depression, I am getting a picture of great happiness and peace in your life here in Tiburon.

It was, it was! We made our own fun and gathered at each other's homes; we played cards, danced, sang and walked. We were never lonesome or bored. We did a lot of silly things.

Oh, we had the baseball team. One field, Judge Field, was where the Recreation Center is now (the Tiburon Peninsula Club), and one where the Reed School was. I remember my brothers talking about a ballpark where Hilarita Housing is, on the slope. Later, after the lagoon was filled in, there was one down on the flat. There was always a Tiburon team, and teams would come in from San Francisco and Oakland. Everyone went out to support the Tiburon team, and they would pass the hat to pay for the expenses. And they would all gather downtown after the game. The winning team would have to celebrate. Well, I don't think there ever was any real prohibition in Tiburon!

Sam was the bootlegger. The sheriff would come down and close Sam's place and take him up to the court house; while he was there his place would open up again. And of course the Italians had wine, and you could get it from them on the sly. They were allowed to make their own wine. They would get a permit and every year when the grapes were ripe and ready there would be winemaking. Each Italian had three or four big wine barrels that he would fill up for the year. That was kind of an event. They made it by stomping on it with their feet, all the kids and everyone else would go and help. They would buy the grapes by the wagon load, each family at a different time, so they could help each other. It was quite an event when the grapes would come. We would all get a bunch of grapes, and that was a great treat. That was the winemaking season. And that was life in Tiburon.

Dolly Payne Keaton in the 1920's.

Dolly Payne Keaton

1903–1982

Dolly Keaton was the daughter of Dr. Clyde Payne, Sr., one of the founders of the Corinthian Land Company and an early member of the Corinthian Yacht Club. Named for a famous ancestor, Dolly Madison, Mrs. Keaton and her mother lived in great style in their house on Beach Road. She golfed, skied, swam, and sailed at the grand resorts all over the world. At the time of this interview, in August, 1975, her gestures were elegant, her voice surprisingly strong and deep for a person with so small a frame.

Mrs. Keaton, when did you come to Belvedere? What brought your family here?

There was an old hotel right where the yacht club is now, called the Belvedere Hotel. And my mother and father and brother would come over from San Francisco and spend summers at the hotel. When our house was built in 1916 the Belvedere Hotel was still there. It was a huge thing.

Was it active at that time?

Oh, yes, it was. I remember the kitchen was right next to us; we could hear all the dishes and everything. And then later the hotel was closed and we would come over and take one of those little brown shingle cottages, the Farr Cottages. And we kept it year round until we built our house.

We have seen pictures of the hotel being torn down, but many people say it burned down.

It did NOT burn down. If there had been a fire our house would have gone too.

Could you tell us about the hotel when you came over with your family?

We stayed at the hotel, but I don't remember. I was one year old. I have a picture of me on the beach in front of the hotel then. We spent just the summers here, for we had a house in San Francisco.

Do you recall who ran the hotel, who owned it?

I don't remember. It was closed for a long time, and then it opened up again just for a short time.

Do you know when it was built?

Oh, god, I don't know. I think there was an old Hotel Belvedere where my house is, just a little shack sort of thing; I've seen pictures. I think the new hotel was built in the 1890's. I know it was just as popular as the old hotel in San Rafael. It was a nice place for people to go with their families.

What became of the tennis courts behind the hotel?

Oh, that became the Greyhound bus station. The tennis courts were across what is now Beach Road, where the apartments are, up against the hill. Then the buses stopped there when they first came to Belvedere. Don't ask me when that was — I don't have the slightest idea. And farther down on Beach Road was the old Pacific Motor Boat Club. And across the street was an old barn. Before our house was built I used to go down and feed all the cats, because no one ever fed them. I think there was a jail down near the drawbridge.

(Looking at old photos) Now here is a picture of the old hotel and the Farr Cottages and the drawbridge at the end of Corinthian Island, where all the boats and houseboats went through into the lagoon for protection. I can't see too well without my glasses. Now this was the Wosser house. They had twelve children. Yes, twelve! Then here is the Chinese laundry, and then I guess the jail was in here.

Your father built your house in 1915 and you moved into it in 1916? From whom did he acquire the land?

It was leased from the Belvedere Land Company, and then when Harry Allen took over the Company my mother bought the lot from him.

Dolly, someone told us that when your father built your house he used some pieces of the Pan-Pacific Exposition, is that right?

Yes. There were several romantic stories that the house was barged over here, that it was the post office of the 1915 Panama Pacific Exposition, but that is not true. The house was designed by my brother, Clyde, who is an architect. The tile in front is from the Italian Building. And all the lumber in the house was second-hand lumber. Up in the attic you could still see the old plaster, the old mortar on it. But I don't think that the railing or the arches or anything like that were from a building at the fair. My brother designed those. Just the tile and the lumber. My brother was building apartment houses in San Francisco at that time and his workmen came over on their days off and worked on our house for nothing because they liked him so much. My brother lived at home with us. He was at the University of Pennsylvania in architecture, and then he'd come home. Then World War I came so he went in. They had just started naval aviation at that time. Clyde built and flew his own airplane when he was fifteen.

Can you tell us about the lagoon?

Well, in the cove people had arks that they lived on in summer, and also boats there. You know where Beach Road goes down and then meets Main Street, well, there was a drawbridge there, and in winter all the houseboats and the yachts were taken into the lagoon before the storms for safekeeping. The lagoon was very calm; it was all water then.

Did you know any of the people who lived on the arks?

No, I didn't. But I know one of them belonged to Clarence Dobie. He wrote a history of California. He had one houseboat. Then they were moved down by the water below the firehouse, all along there where all the Italian gardeners lived. The lagoon was all water then. And I don't know what damn fool — excuse the expression — filled it all in.

We understand the railroad company did some of the filling.

Maybe. But then Harry Allen dredged it out and made it a lagoon again.

Is it right that only one dirt road led into Belvedere?

All the roads in Belvedere were dirt. Naturally you came over here by ferryboat. The driver would meet the ferry and drive you home in a horse and wagon. That was in the early days.

Did a Chinese vegetable man stop by our house?

Yes, Jason was his name. Oh yes, he came around with beautiful vegetables. Too bad someone doesn't do that now. We couldn't wait for him to come. Mother would go out and look at the peaches and whatever he had. And of course you know the Allens, Lemuel and Marion, had the grocery store on Beach Road.

The Payne house was built in 1916 on Belvedere Cove, next to the Belvedere Hotel and the Farr Cottages. The Payne house is now a part of the San Francisco Yacht Club; the beach in front is a parking lot.

Did you go down to Main Street often?

Oh, yes. There was Beyries' Grocery Store. Are there any of the Beyries left around here? I guess not. And Kelley's.

Were the Nights in Venice still going on?

Not as regularly as they were in the beginning. But then later on we had two of them. I was around eighteen when they had one, and they had another after that.

Did you know Miss Livsey?

Oh, good heavens! Miss Livsey! We'd have Miss Livsey over every Thanksgiving and every Christmas. She was a character; she really was. And boy, if she didn't like somebody she didn't like them. She didn't have any family. She had a world back East. Lotta Crabtree, who was a singer in the mining days, was a relative of hers and left her some money. She was a second cousin or something. How much Miss Livsey got I don't know. She went east to get the money and was entertained royally when she got there, while she was waiting to get the money. She was invited there.

She had a parrot that was always with her. Did she bring it to dinner?

No! She lived above the grocery store, and the post office was right downstairs. In that building were the Belvedere Land Company, the Allen's grocery store, the post office and the telephone company. And Miss Livsey was the first one I knew of who had a radio set. It was one of those things with earphones and a crystal, and you had to get this whatever-it-was exactly on the right spot to get anything. It was called a crystal set. We would go over there to hear the radio.

I take it she liked you?

Yes, she did.

Did Miss Livsey ever marry?

No.

What did she look like, what was her dress?

Well, she wore those things that had bones in them and you had to tie them. And she had a stiff, stiff collar, and she was very, very thin. She was tiny; I don't think she weighed more than ninety pounds. She wasn't very attractive, but she was awfully nice.

And the telephone company. Did anybody tell you about Debbie Wosser and Julia Wosser, the telephone operators? Oh, they were wonderful! If I was going up to Kadah Becker's, I'd call up and say, "Julia, I'm going up to Kadah's place; if I get any calls ring me up there." It was very, very informal. And they knew everything that was going on! Debbie was Jake Wosser's mother. And then Lizzy O'Connell was an operator too. These women were all married then.

Did you ever go to the codfishery?

Oh, god, it smelled to heaven over there! I think it burned down. We used to go over there after the codfishery was gone, but it still smelled!

Did you know the Italian gardeners?

Oh, yes! We always had one working for us. Harry Pariani. He had a fit when I wanted to put in a vegetable garden once. He raised hell with my mother. It wasn't our garden — it was his garden. And he planted what he wanted, not what you wanted.

The Belvedere gardens were just beautiful. Oh, the Lathrop's garden was exquisite. The ones in the old Rey house, and the old Stephens house too.

You were quite a golfer, weren't you?

Oh, I just loved that old golf course! I don't golf anymore. I used to love to play. The golf course was nine holes. The old club house is still there, and the tennis court. It was a private club. A few people from Sausalito belonged besides the people on Belvedere. When they couldn't afford to keep the golf course up anymore they closed it down and just had a caretaker, a man and his wife and their little boy. And then the members would have dinner parties there and we'd do the dinner ourselves and put on skits or have poker games in the clubhouse.

We've heard the Belvedere course was tricky.

It was. I liked the first hole. Because you were way up there above San Rafael Avenue, and if you got your ball over just one ditch it would roll all the way down to San Rafael Avenue! It was quite a hike back up. And then one hole they called the Matterhorn, way out on the end of the island, but the

Dolly with her father, Dr. Clyde Payne, and brother Clyde, on the beach in front of the Belvedere Hotel in 1905. Corinthian Island is a bare hill except for the old Yacht Club. Angel Island is in the distance.

The north end of the Belvedere Golf and Country Club, with Mt. Tamalpais in the background, in the 1930's, when Dolly Keaton was an avid golfer.

tee was down here and you had to shoot way, way uphill. Well, you needed to be a goat to climb the golf course. But it was fun, it really was.

Dolly, after your father built your house in Belvedere, did you come to live here permanently?

No, we still had our house in San Francisco — we came just for the summer.

When did your family begin living in Belvedere year-round?

My father bought an orange grove down south. He and my mother separated — I suppose you'd call it that. My mother and I would spend the winters at the Fairmont Hotel and the summers here in Belvedere. And after I got married mother moved over here permanently. I think it was 1929 when I got married, during the Depression. I lived in Los Angeles.

You know it was so nice here at my house when we had a beach; now we don't even have a view because all the boats are so high on the dock I can't even see San Francisco. And the parking lot, oh! We used to have a dock and a float in front of our house.

When did you move back to Belvedere?

When I got divorced.

Did your family use the San Francisco Yacht Club much?

Yes, my father, Dr. Clyde Payne, Sr., at one time was commodore of the club. And he had a stinkpot. Here is a picture of Cliff Smith when they were tearing down the old Belvedere Hotel and getting ready to put up the new San Francisco Yacht Club. I can't remember when they started to build the yacht club.

I can't think of anything else to tell you. I feel a little disconnected, out of touch with things, because you know looking back over seventy years is a little hard! You can get some other pieces from other people, and before you know it you will have the whole story!

Robert Keefe in 1978.

Robert Keefe

1932–

Our interview with Bob Keefe was at the St. Francis Yacht Club in July, 1975. He was Commodore of the club at the time; Bob and his children are the third and fourth generation of Keefes who have sailed on San Francisco Bay. He has an impressive collection of yachting memorabilia which has been handed down from his grandfather, "Boss" Keefe, who was long a mainstay of the Corinthian Yacht Club. Bob is a healthy, tanned yachtsman with a strong, booming voice and a gracious manner.

Bob, how and when did your family come to Belvedere?

Well, I'm glad you asked. It's a quarter to three; with luck you might get home for breakfast. Actually I only know fragments of the story, because my father is dead and my mother is alive but not rational. My grandfather, the scion of the family, died in 1915. I wasn't even born until 1932, so a lot of this has to be family hearsay. But I do have my grandfather's diary. He wrote in it every day of his life, from the 1860's until he died. Most of it is about business; he was an interior painter and decorator. Very little has to do with Belvedere or Tiburon. He'd write, "I spent ten cents too much on cigars." He never gave a dime to anybody.

He came to San Francisco from Boston when the original Palace Hotel was being constructed, in 1875. He was recruited, if you will, to do the decoration in the Palm Court. Whatever money he made, whatever success he had, he had it here. When he came out from Boston he was just somebody on the train. We can find no record of any formal education he might have had. He was born in Ireland, although one document says he was born in Boston.

Sometime in the late 1800's my grandfather made a lot of money. So during the last twenty years of his life he did not have to work any more. He traveled all over the world and bought things. He bought things in Rome, in Hong Kong, in Cairo. Then he brought them home and sold them in San Francisco. The big Flood mansion, where the Pacific Union Club is today, the Roth house — he would buy all over the world for such clients.

During this period he developed a very serious love for the Corinthian Yacht Club. From about 1895 until 1910 or so he did whatever the CYC needed,

At the Corinthian Yacht Club on Ladies' Day, 1915, the ladies wore bathing caps, knitted wool bathing suits, and goggles; the gentlemen appear to be chilly. Main Street is still open on the water side; the McNeil building (dark roof) survives today, as do the houses on Mar West (right rear) above the railroad yard.

including financing. It never was a successful club from a financial standpoint. If they ever needed a couple of hundred bucks, one way or the other he got it. So they made him honorary port captain in 1899, and he was port captain until the day he died.

Here is a program on Corinthian stationery, dated Saturday, April 28, 1906, ten days after the 1906 earthquake. It lists J.F. Keefe, Frank Stone, and other members of the yachting fraternity. The CYC was the yachting center on the Bay, and was tremendously powerful. It was the Bohemian Club on the water.

There was nothing very democratic about my grandfather. He was an autocratic individual, with a big mustache and a cigar tucked in his mouth most of the time. They called him "Boss Keefe"! He also did a very strange thing: when my grandmother died he married her sister immediately. I have a clipping saying that they had been generally regarded as brother and sister for years! He had to get a special dispensation from the Catholic Church. They went on their honeymoon in an automobile, which was pretty unusual in that day.

Most of the Corinthian Yacht Club members were Catholics. If you were a Catholic you were somewhat welcome, but if you weren't you had to have some pretty good reason to be there. Like the Stones — Lester always used to be kidded about being a shirt-tail Catholic. And since Catholics had to go to church, they all went to St. Hilary's.

Do you know anything about the building of the church?

No, I don't, but in the Keefe company records there are notations about St. Hilary's. One thing my grandfather did very early in San Francisco was to corner the painting business in the archdiocese. Nobody turned a paintbrush in the church in the San Francisco archdiocese without the Keefe Foundation. Period. Nobody bid on the work. He just did it. What he had to cough up for the archbishop Lord only knows, but that was the deal.

Were women allowed in the CYC then?

There were no ladies; ladies were not welcome, they were not invited except for once a year on opening day. My grandfather would leave the City for the CYC on Friday afternoon and he wouldn't get home until late Sunday night. After ten years my grandmother had had enough of this. So my grandparents agreed to establish a weekend residence in Belvedere. My grandfather looked around for property, but there wasn't anything he wanted to buy. All it was supposed to be was a summer place for my grandmother and the kids to hang their hats while he was with the boys over at the CYC.

Finally he bought a waterfront lot on Beach Road, right down from where the drawbridge used to be. He was going to build on the lot, but then he got wind of a ship being junked down on the waterfront. It was a four- or five-hundred foot steamship which my grandparents had travelled on back and forth to the Orient. The *China*.

He bought from the wreckers the whole first class salon — the big sitting salon, dining salon, lounge from the ship. He picked it up on a barge and brought it over to Beach Road and put it up on pilings and it's there to this day. My grandfather named it the *Ruddigore;* I don't know why. The ship had been part of the Pacific Mail Steamship fleet.

When my grandfather bought it, everything came with it: bedding, dishes, silverware, the silver service, pillows, everything you could think of. I remember as a little boy seeing the dishes, with a picture of the ship baked into the glaze.

So he put this thing together. It must have been well before the turn of the century.

The only way you got to Belvedere then was by ferryboat. You got the ferry from San Francisco to Tiburon. The last ferry left Tiburon at 7:00 p.m. So every Sunday about 6:30 they started closing down and guys ran down Main Street. If you didn't get the ferry you were there until the next day. So my grandfather would get out of the CYC and my grandmother would bring her boys from the place they put together in Belvedere and they'd take the boat home to San Francisco. It was a way of life.

Then on April 18,1906, the family home in San Francisco was destroyed, and my grandfather moved the whole family lock, stock, and barrel, to Belvedere as fast as he could get there. It was apparently quite a struggle, with my grandfather, grandmother, two boys, a Chinese servant, Ah Sing, and an uncle and an aunt. The house on Castro and 21st Streets had been maybe five stories high; he had a tremendous family. And they had to move into this little ark. Not all of them lived there permanently of course; they shot my father off to boarding school somewhere. I can remember my father saying that

Top: Members of the Corinthian Yacht Club, 1890's. John Pew is at far left; "Boss" Keefe holds his son at top; Frank Stone is a blur at right. Below: The first Corinthian Yacht Club, built 1886, on the tip of what was then Valentine Island.

people were pouring out of San Francisco and they were scared to death that somebody would just take over the ark. There was a lot of that going on. People were driven out by the earthquake and the fire, and if you had a home in Marin County you might suddenly find a bunch of guys sitting in it who weren't about to leave!

Well, they got over there and lived in this ark for about three years. My grandfather died in September, 1915; the ark was part of the estate. His wife had no more interest in it after that. I think it was torture for her to go over there. She sold the ark then to Lord knows who, and who knows how many owners it has had since that day. The only thing I have left besides the painting is a small boat, a thirteen-foot wooden pulling boat. "Pulling boat" is a ship's term for rowboat. I have it in my locker at the St. Francis Yacht Club. One way or another it has been preserved; why it of all things should still be with us I don't know. It is a beautifully built small boat that they used to row around in the lagoon. At the turn of the century ladies' rowing was a very big thing in Belvedere. Ladies wore hats four feet wide and the funniest looking costumes you can imagine.

How was it that your family happened to bring Ah Sing with them from Hong Kong?

Well, they had been on one of their trips and they had hired him for something over there. And they liked him, so they brought him back. He was with the family until he died. I have found the bill for Ah Sing's funeral.

We would like to know more about the Chinese servants that so many Belvedere homes had. How did people go about getting houseboys? It seems that once you had one he was with you for life.

Oh, I think so. If you had a good one you hung onto him, and they probably paid them nothing. And I know where Ah Sing lived over at the apartment house. He was for all practical purposes a slave. Only he didn't know that, I suppose.

(Robert Keefe is looking through his collection of photographs and mementos).

Here is a note on the history of the CYC. It says, "any gambling had to be done with a 10-cent limit; this was based on the firm view of the beloved John F. Keefe, Port Captain from 1905 to 1917." But he died in 1915. "Thereby the wealthy executive and the worker from the iron foundry could be at ease at the same table." That doesn't sound like my grandfather! He'd take the money right out of the pockets of the iron worker!

Was the CYC pretty exclusive at the turn of the century, or could you just put your money down and join?

Oh, no! It was very, very exclusive. It was hooked up with the Elks. If you were a member of the CYC you were a member of the Elks downtown. They had big Elk's Teeth with the CYC badge painted on them. There were only three Jewish members of the CYC ever. And everyone had to participate — no one could belong for the sake of belonging, you had to be over there on the weekends. It was a real part of your life!

You said the club fleet was anchored in front of the club. Did they sail over for the weekend or were they there year-round?

They hung there on their moorings, for the most part. There wasn't anywhere to come from really.

People came over on the ferries and the boats were moored in Belvedere Cove. We still have Opening Day, but what we lost in the sailing fraternity in San Francisco Bay is Closing Day. On Closing Day, they towed the fleet into Belvedere Cove, through the drawbridge, and into the lagoon, where the boats were put away for the winter. They came out on Opening Day in April.

Did many of the men living on Belvedere belong to the CYC?

Yes, I think so, those who were yachtsmen did. Gordon Blanding was very active in the CYC. He had his boathouse on the point of Belvedere. But not a lot of people lived on Belvedere at this time; it was still a summer resort.

On the weekends did people spend the night in the CYC or did they stay on their boats?

A little of both, probably. Certainly they lived on the boats, but underneath the main deck at the CYC they had something called 'Pneumonia Alley,' a batch of rooms where their lockers were. And the rooms were like clubs within the club. There were five or

Top: Ah Sing with Mrs. Keefe (left), her sister (right) and Harold Keefe (rear). Below: Corinthian Yacht Club members march from the ferry down Main Street to a clambake, 1900.

six guys in a room and you were invited to join this or that little group. It would be like belonging to the Bohemian Club and then in turn belonging to a camp at Bohemian Grove. Some of the rooms were quite ornate.

They once had a tremendous howl over the subject of the ladies out rowing. Some of the members said that those women did not belong to this club and they could not fly the CYC burgee. So they had a great internal upheaval about can the ladies or can't the ladies, all the same pettiness that goes on today went on then. But you have to remember at that time ladies were not welcome in any men's club — there wasn't any such thing as a co-educational club. The Pacific Union Club, the Bohemians, the Elks — there were no ladies. The Jewish gentlemen organized the Concordia Club in the city to meet their club needs.

Did your family ever talk about the arks in Belvedere Cove?

I know there were a lot of men in the CYC who were forced to do the same thing my grandfather did, to keep peace in the family. So that the women would not be left in San Francisco every weekend. I remember my father saying that one of the reasons my grandfather wanted to go there was because my father was very young and he figured that the kid would never fall off the porch and drown himself because the cove then was very shallow. They have never been able to keep it dredged out successfully.

Did you hear mention of Tiburon's Main Street by the CYC members?

Well, it wasn't all bars then. Those guys who worked in the yards, on the trains, and on the ferryboats supported the town. It was just a little country town, with a post office and bar. I can remember my father saying that when they went on the boat they had to take everything! The groceries, everything, and the Chinaboy had to take all the cooking stuff.

What kind of sailboat races did the CYC have?

They had a lot of races. They also did a lot of cruising. They cruised as a fleet to the Napa River or Vallejo or Steamboat Slough. Or they'd go around the corner and anchor at Paradise Cove. There was more comradeship than we see today in club life. Of course yachting was not as big as it is today; there weren't that many clubs, or that many yachts. That picture of the boats in front of the CYC shows most of the yachts on San Francisco Bay.

The CYC split out of the San Francisco Yacht Club. It is well known that the St. Francis split out of the San Francisco Yacht Club, but not many know that much earlier the CYC was a splinter group out of the San Francisco Yacht Club. In this newspaper article it says, "A group of zealous young yachtsmen met in San Francisco on the night of March 16, 1886. They had disassociated themselves from an existing yacht club because of its members' inclination to sail large and expensive vessels." The existing yacht club was of course the San Francisco Yacht Club. The CYC bought the land from James B. Valentine — the tip of Valentine Island. When the first clubhouse was perched on the tip of the island in 1886, it became Corinthian Island.

That first little clubhouse was destroyed in a fire. And then they built that great white mausoleum which my grandfather designed. He had been all over the world and he just had to have those big Corinthian columns. He put together this idea of how it should be, a totally inefficient building, so big they could never heat the place. A big ornate thing is what he said they should build! Why it hasn't burnt down by now, Lord only knows!

Robert Lamoree in the 1970's.

Robert Lamoree

1898–1983

Robert Lamoree married Maude Masterson, daughter of Harry Masterson, one of the founders of the Corinthian Land Company when that island was developed in 1907. Mr. Lamoree was a big man — well over six feet tall — whose large frame and booming laughter filled the room as we talked with him. At 77, he was healthy, active, full of vitality, with snow-white hair and thick glasses. His voice was affectionately teasing, full of humor and warmth. The interview took place in May, 1975.

Mr. Lamoree, when did you come to Belvedere?

I came in 1936. My wife Maude — her family built a home on Corinthian Island in 1907, after the San Francisco fire and earthquake. My wife's roots were here in Belvedere.

What was your wife's maiden name?

Maude Masterson. Her father was Harry Masterson. She and her sister, Eleanor, graduated from the old Belvedere grammar school in about 1914. Then they both graduated from Tamalpais High School.

What was Harry Masterson's business in 1907?

He was president of the San Francisco Lumber Company — pretty important in San Francisco in that day.

Did your wife's family at one time own the Belvedere Hotel?

No. The Belvedere Hotel went kaput! Harry Masterson and some other jokers bought what was left of the hotel. The cottages that are there now used to be part of it. People rented them and took their meals at the hotel.

Did people live in the cottages the year round?

Some did in the cottages, but in the hotel only in the summertime. There used to be a lovely tennis court where the apartments are now, across from the San Francisco Yacht Club. The nicest thing I possess from the Belvedere Hotel is this spittoon from the bar. A great brass gaboon, with heavy lead weights in the bottom of it. In those days the boys used to chew a lot of tobacco.

When did the family become involved with the hotel? In the early 1920's?

Long before that. See, the Mastersons came over and bought a lot on Corinthian Island in 1907, from the Corinthian Island Land Company. They were burned out in the San Francisco fire. They lived in a hotel in the city until their house was ready in about 1907 or 1908. It is the big house on the north end of the island, with the red roof. That's where I used to court my first wife, Maude. And the Dave Plant family built on the other end of the island; that house was always white. Here's a list of the old-timers on Corinthian Island: J.H. Masterson, the Plants, a fellow named Esterbrook, who was the town clerk, Howard Belcher, the Kelleys, the Donzells, the Yates, the Preussers, the Taylors, and a lot of newcomers after that. The Masterson lot was $750. The Plant lot was the most costly of the bunch, $2,500. It was the choice spot.

The Corinthian Land Company was founded by W. H. L. Cockron, Sidney L. Plant, Fred Kelley and J.K. Kelley. It was founded in 1907 for a capital stock of $100,000 and 100,000 shares, a dollar a share. And this document shows that on July 22, 1907, J.H. Masterson bought 750 shares of the Corinthian Island Company and the lot #11. The document is signed by old Kelley as the Secretary and Cockron as the President; it has the corporate seal. This is real history.

Let's go back to the hotel.

Well, it was abandoned, and then Masterson and Dr. Payne and some of his old pals bought it for the hay that was in it. For years after it was torn down you could see the old concrete foundation, before the San Francisco Yacht Club took over the property.

Were people then still renting the cottages?

They were renting from the Belvedere Land Company.

And what do we have here? This is the Belvedere Land Company, 114 Post Street, San Francisco, it's their souvenir of Belvedere. A friend gave this brochure to me in 1940. He found it in Piedmont and knew I'd be interested in it. It gives many names of people who lived in Belvedere at the turn of the century or just before — Henry Cockron, Henry Crocker, George Page, and William S. Keith — half the big shots in San Francisco had summer homes over here. And here is Fred W. Boole, Freddy Boole's father, and old Hugo Keil, the uncle of Russell Keil; Arthur Page, and Bing Rey's daddy, V.J.A. Rey. Rey had that big house up on the end of Golden Gate Avenue; that house was built in 1893, about four years before Bing was born. Bing was born in the city and brought to Belvedere and raised there on top of the island. They had a hayfield, a family orchard, and chicken coops, all up on the island between Blanding and the Becks.

Was the Masterson house one of the first on Corinthian island?

Well, the Plant house was the first, Fred Kelley was the second and the Masterson was the third.

In 1936 were most of the residents living here year round?

Almost all were year-round people. Maybe Miss Huntington who had that big place on the water was just here summers. But all were here by that time year round. Now here is an old map of Belvedere during the war. It says World War II district 1, firemen C.M. Kretchmer, Bob Lamoree, Alexis Becker, Henry Kirschman. You know those names don't you? We were fortunate to be firemen; the firemen only had to go out when the alarm went off when there was a fire, but the air-raid wardens had to go out on every alert! Maude Lamoree was an air-raid warden. June Kirschman, Audrey Rey, and little Lucille Boole were air-raid wardens, and they'd all have to get up out of bed and put their hardhats on and walk up and down the streets, and the firemen would stay in bed and laugh.

Where did you and Maude live?

We first lived at 420 Golden Gate Avenue. Then in 1953 we sold that place and moved across the street, into Mary Monahan's old place, 427 Golden Gate. We bought our first house from Britton Rey's aunt, Mrs.Lavery.

You bought your house about the time of the Depression?

Yes. Oh, a dollar was a dollar in the thirties, and money was tight. You know the Wilson lot, it was a big piece of property, that pie-shaped piece going all the way down Golden Gate to Madrone. Wilson's lot was for sale at one time for $10,000 and

Top: Corinthian Island, 1926; Masterson house on left end, Plant house second from right above CYC. Main Street is still backed by the lagoon; the railroad yard and Donahue Building, upper right, the ferry Marin *at the dock. Below: David Plant, Harry Masterson, Dr. Clyde Payne, (unidentified).*

Top: Mrs. Masterson with Eleanor and Maude. Below: Maude wading, Belvedere Cove.

they couldn't find any buyers. We used to have big parties up on the Wilson lot. Big picnics, and we had a fair with games, and throwing balls at the girls behind the screens. A regular fair, more fun than a barrel of monkeys. Everybody went — the Keils came over from Tiburon — everybody went!

Did you know Miss Livsey at the post office?
Yes, I knew her very well. She ran the post office just as if she owned it! At Christmas time, if you were expecting a package and you'd ask if it had arrived, she'd say, "I don't know. They're all there in a pile in the corner. You can look through them yourself." She was an independent little thing. She had a parrot that was her great pal.

Did you use the Allen grocery store?
Lem and Marion Allen had the finest grocery store in Marin County, the equivalent, on a smaller scale, of the Goldberg-Bowen store in San Francisco. It was classy! The finest of everything could be obtained there. Everything was hand-picked — caviar, everything. And they were just the cutest couple you'd ever seen. Lem was a typical New Englander and Marion just busy as a bee around there, just as she is today, full of life! She's a kick! Between the Allen Grocery Store and the Chinese greengrocer, Jason, you had everything. Jason used to come around all through the top of Belvedere Island. And if you were home you went out to look over what he had on his little truck. But if you were away you just left a list on your door of the things that you wanted. He'd take the list, fill the order and write it in his black book. Every customer had a book and he'd write down what he had delivered and the amount after it and you'd settle up at the end of the month.

Do you girls know about Bill Barr? He ran the garage. Bill Barr was one of the characters of Main Street. He just ran the little barn and pumped a little gas and drove the taxi. The taxi would meet the bus in those days and you would buy ten tickets for $1, and he'd take you up to your home. That was old Bill Barr.

But before that, in the old days, when Crocker and Masterson and Doc Payne and a lot of the old-time bigshots got together for their poker game on a Saturday night, he would be called up to bring the gang home. Bill Barr told me once, "They were a funny old bunch, they'd call me and I'd come but they wouldn't be ready to go. So they'd give me ten bucks to sit down and join in the game. Then they'd play more poker, have a little grog with it. And I'd play until they were ready to go home." Bill had a contract with the Belvedere school to pick up one or two children way over on Paradise Drive. The Tiburon school district was nice and uniform. But every school district that disbanded they'd attach onto Belvedere district, way over to Strawberry and Paradise Drive and Corte Madera. We had the biggest district with the one little school up there.

Can you tell us more about Main Street?
Yes, there was Harvey Anderson's Meat Market; Harvey was a hell of a good butcher! He also tended bar at a few places in town. He can give you the dope on Main Street.

One character you should have in your record is Old Johnny, an Irishman who was the handyman for all the widows and the old people on Corinthian Island. Corinthian Island at that time was called Vinegar Hill. Johnny liked his booze, but when he was in good shape he could do anything, old Johnny Meenan! He had a little room that he lived in for years underneath the cottage where the Salvage Shop was. He had a dog that followed him everywhere — that dog just loved Johnny. He was a tough-looking old Irishman. He just liked to get drunk too much.

And another great couple on the other end of Main Street, a wonderful couple, were the Oldags. August was a Norwegian. If you wanted anything fixed you took it down to August. They owned the hardware store before Randolphs. August also had ten or twelve little skiffs, rowboats you could rent and take out fishing in Raccoon Straits.

Any memories of the Belvedere Country Club?
Sure, I remember the Belvedere Country Club. As a matter of fact I went to dances there before I got married; I took Maude. I can remember it just as if it were yesterday that we were dancing around! Oh, we used to have fun there. I met Maude at U.C. — we were classmates.

Did you enjoy the Nights in Venice?
The Nights in Venice were still going, and they went way back, before the turn of the century. I still

have the set of lights that went around the deck of the Masterson house on Corinthian. It was a big affair; everything was lit up. People really planned for it, and spent money on it — they really decorated and entertained. Most of the arks had moved out by then. There were only two left when we arrived. We didn't like it very much even with those two. It wasn't much fun swimming in the cove when people were living on the arks.

I'll tell you another interesting thing. Years ago in the twenties before the San Francisco Yacht Club moved over from Sausalito, the cove was pretty well silted up. And at a very low tide I have walked from Corinthian Island across the cove over to Belvedere. It was that shallow. They spent a lot of money dredging out the cove to get the yachts in there. There used to be a sandy little beach there called Johnson's Beach, where the palm trees are now on Beach Road. People used to take a picnic lunch and the kids and swim there. It was a lovely sandy beach, Johnson's Beach.

The Belvedere Land Company, through Winnie and Harry Allen, made available to the citizens of Belvedere a piece of property on San Rafael Avenue, about 100 feet, two big lots. We bought a couple carloads of beautiful white Del Monte sand and had it delivered to the Hilarita Station. Then we borrowed the city truck and hauled the sand over to the edge of the lagoon. We also put in a diving board. The codfisheries were being dismantled, and Allens gave the male citizens permission to go over and take some of the big brine tanks apart — they were doweled together, 3 by 12 pieces of redwood, maybe twenty feet long. We got them back to the dock and had August Oldag put them on his little launch, and he brought them around the cove into the lagoon and we made a dock with them. We had a fine swimming place there, so fine that people from all over Marin were coming over to use it. And they bumped into a tough policeman — the only one we had — Doc Oldfield. He was the tax collector, the dog catcher, the chief of police and street sweeper! He and George Stevens, his partner, used to sweep the streets of Belvedere with palm fronds from Johnson's Beach.

The town was so lovely to live in and so small that if your saw needed sharpening you'd take it down on a Sunday morning to Doc and he would sharpen it.

We didn't have a city manager. We had one clerk, old Esterbrook, who kept track of the bills and the payrolls and all that. The city council took care of everything, and one member was elected as mayor and that is how the town was run. It was a lovely town to live in.

Belvedere children dressed for a birthday party in the ballroom of the Corinthian Yacht Club about 1910. Maude Masterson is fifth from left; her sister Eleanor is seated at the head of the table on the left. The party, with a circus theme, featured a toy three-ring circus as centerpiece, an adult clown (at rear), and a poster from the White House toy department in San Francisco.

Mary McLean at the Panama Pacific Exhibition in San Francisco, 1915.

Mary Copeland McLean

1894–1981

Mary McLean was married to Sandy, son of one of the two McLean brothers who built many of the earliest houses on Belvedere around the turn of the century. She raised her six children in the Neil McLean house, across McLean Lane from her parents-in-law. Mary was a small, delicate woman, no more than five feet tall; she wore her hair in a tight bun. Her manner was modest and unassuming. During the interview in 1975, her voice was full of joy and laughter as she recalled her children's antics and the scenes of an intense family life.

Could you tell us when your family first came to Belvedere?

Oh, yes, you must mean Sandy's folks. They came to Belvedere in 1892, and they lived in the old *Tropic Bird.* Do you know the *Tropic Bird,* the ship that was on the beach in Belvedere? They lived on that until they built two houses up on the hill in Belvedere.

Was Sandy's father Dan or Neil McLean?

Dan was his father; Neil was the brother who built the house that we lived in for many years. The *Tropic Bird* was what was left of an old ship; it had been made into two apartments. Neil lived in the upper one, and Dan in the lower one.

Where did they build their houses?

On McLean Lane. It was Myrtle Lane, but when they moved in they changed it to McLean Lane. They bought two lots, one on each side of the lane, and drew straws to decide who would have which. They broke ground on July 4, 1894. Dan moved in first, but the house was not quite finished. Uncle Neil waited until his was finished.

Were the McLean homes among the first on the island?

Yes, I think so, there were others but not many. I think the Pew house was there. Mr. Pew owned the fishery. That's how the Lemuel Allens happened to come out to California. Charles Allen, Lemuel's brother, came out first; he was a manager at the fishery. And then Lem and Marion came out afterwards. You know the apartments down there before you'd come to the old drawbridge, on the left, well, Neil McLean built those, and he built a lot of the

Top: Dan McLean in front of his coal and ice company on Beach Road. The two houses at center belonged to Neil and Dan McLean. John Pew's Pagoda House is at far left, Presbyterian church far right. Below: The Dan McLean family on their porch in 1894. The baby, first child born in Belvedere after incorporation, was named William Belvedere McLean. Photo was taken from Neil McLeans' porch.

barracks at the Presidio. I think he owned the apartments he built on Beach Road. Dan bought them from him and then eventually Dan sold them to Mr. Benson.

Were the two brothers from San Francisco?

No. Dan had been living in Los Angeles, and Neil asked him to come up and go into partnership with him.

And what was the business?

Well, first they were in the coal business. It was right down at the foot of the hill where all those apartments are, where the dentist's office is, I believe that is where they were.

Did they sell out to Myron Weeks?

No, it was someone else; Mr. Weeks owned it later. The coalyard was moved down onto Beach Road. Do you know where the Japanese laundry was, down in that group of buildings by the drawbridge? Well, it was in there at one time. They delivered all over Belvedere Island. I don't remember how long they were in that business before they went into the contracting business.

Were the McLean houses the first ones they built here?

Yes, I think so. But they did build quite a few of the homes on Belvedere.

Mrs. McLean, did you grow up in the area?

No, I'm from San Diego. I was living in San Francisco when I met Sandy. Sandy was about one and a half years old when he came to Belvedere, so he grew up here and he lived his whole life on McLean Lane. He lived in one house or the other, because when we were married we moved into Uncle Neal's house. He went to the Belvedere School.

Was Miss Boynton his teacher?

Yes, indeed, I remember his mother talking about her.

Were the McLean families full-time residents of the island?

Yes. Most of the families up on the hill were seasonal, but the McLeans were here all the time. And the Italian gardeners were full-time residents. They lived along the lagoon, across from the firehouse; some of them lived in houses, but most were in arks. We knew some of them, and we also knew the Coleman family, who lived in a house down there.

When were you married?

In 1914.

Did you move to Belvedere then?

No, we lived in Sausalito first and then in Tiburon, up by Hilarita Station. Then we moved over to Belvedere in 1918. We rented Uncle Neal's house until he died; then Sandy's aunt sold it to us, at a very reasonable price. Oh, when I think of what they get for a house nowadays! We moved into that house on McLean Lane just twelve days before Scottie was born.

Most of the people who worked on the railroad lived in Tiburon, and you lived in Belvedere. Did you socialize much with those who lived in Tiburon?

No, not much. You know the people of Belvedere — well not that we did, but the people in Belvedere just thought they were above the people in Tiburon and they never got together in anything. Of course, I had a few friends in Tiburon, but I didn't go out much. I had no chance to. With no car I had to walk everywhere. But my six children walked all over. I had four and then when my youngest daughter was nine I started all over again and had Bob and Bill. It was just like having two families.

Was your husband, Sandy, a carpenter too?

Yes, he was when we were married, and then later, about 1918, he went to work for the railroad. He worked there for forty years, in the mill, until he retired.

What did your husband do for the railroad?

Sandy worked in the mill, where they prepared all the lumber for repairs on the cars and the different stations. Boxcars always had to have sides put in, that sort of thing.The trainyard here had everything — a mill, a paint shop, toolmaking, and the roundhouse where they took care of the engines. It was a complete maintenance center for the whole railroad.

Did your husband have a fishing boat?

Yes, but he didn't do any commercial fishing. But, oh, he loved to fish! He kept his boat anchored in the cove. And later he kept it at Manny Olsen's in Richardson Bay, for many years, anchored offshore.

Do you recall the fishermen who would come into the cove for herring?

Oh, yes. My husband was very fond of herring. He used to bring it home by the bucketful! The herring were so thick you could go down there and dip your bucket in and bring it up full. The seagulls would come in first and then the fishing boats would come in and spread their nets and stay for hours.

Did you at one time work in the post office?

Yes, I did, at Belvedere and Tiburon. I started at Belvedere in 1941 and worked for five or six years, and then I left it for two or three years and then went back to work at the Tiburon-Belvedere post office.

Do you remember Miss Livsey, who worked at the Belvedere Post Office?

I certainly do.

What is your impression of her?

Well, if she liked you she was so sweet and dear, and if she didn't like you just look out! She was a typical old maid. And all the children used to torment her, tease her and run in and out of the post office. She had a parrot that was given to her by a woman who lived in one of the arks... I don't know where it learned its language, but it did have a great vocabulary!

I assume it was not the vocabulary typical of an old maid.

No, it wasn't! When she wasn't busy she used to come out of the post office and walk up and down the sidewalk with the parrot on her shoulder. You know, women did not smoke in those days; it was considered terrible. Well, she lived in that house on Acacia that Jim Rey lives in now, and her bedroom was at the back of the house, above a sloping roof to the shed. And that roof was just covered with cigarette butts. She would evidently lie in bed and throw her cigarette butts out the window. It was a wonder she did not burn the place down.

Did you go over to El Campo with your children?

No, not often, only when the school went on a picnic over there. But the older children used to walk over there, over the hill. The hills were full of cows and wildflowers. It was beautiful in the spring — the lupine and poppies and wild violets — just beautiful. We hated to see houses built there.

Did a Chinese vegetable man come to your door?

Yes, he came over on the ferry two or three times a week. He had a horse and wagon when I started buying from him. I'd go up to the wagon and pick out fruits and vegetables.

Did you go into Tiburon very often?

No, not very often. You see, you telephoned the grocery, and they'd deliver your order. So I did not get out often when the children were young, except when I went to the city on the ferry. I called Beyries. The first grocery store was Carpenter and Chapman in Tiburon. Mr. Beyries worked for them for years, and then he started his own store. Carpenter and Chapman were on the water side of the street and Mr. Beyries was on the other side, in the middle of the block. We used Beyries and then finally we traded mostly with the Allens.

When did the Manteganis open their grocery store in Tiburon?

Mr. Mantegani was first a gardener for people who lived on Paradise Drive. Then he went to work for the railroad as a section hand. I don't know when he started his grocery store. But it was not until his two sons, George and Fred, were old enough to help him.

Did you get your meat from Anderson's Meat Market?

I'd telephone an order, and Beyries would deliver the meat along with the groceries. There was a door connecting their two stores. He'd also deliver the mail.

Main Street had a reputation for being rough. Was it?

It was at times because of the saloons. Men used to come from the fishyards and the coaling station. It used to get quite rough at times. There were lots of bootleggers around. Sam Vella supposedly got rich during prohibition. The Italians who lived down in the arks always made their own wine.

Who lived in the arks across the lagoon on the Tiburon side?

Mostly the railroad workers. When they came down to Main Street they walked either on the railroad tracks or on dirt paths; that's all there was. They owned their arks and they didn't pay berth rent. It wasn't thought of then.

Did you belong to the yacht club?

Sandy belonged to the Corinthian for years, and to the San Francisco.

Were women allowed in the Corinthian Yacht Club then?

No. Women were not allowed to vote then. I can remember when I first registered to vote. Dan McLean said everyone should register, everyone should vote. He took it upon himself to see that everyone in the family voted. It was just terrible if we didn't. And I served on the election board for many years.

Were the people in Belvedere affected by the Depression?

Well, we were, I know. I don't know about the people further up on the hill, I suppose they were, more or less. But it was pretty hard on us. The railroad men only worked two or three days a week. I think most people found extra work — my husband did. At the time George Hall was the boat assessor and he gave Sandy a job assessing boats all around the bay. We didn't have too hard a time. I don't think people were as hard up as they are now, because we didn't need so much. We didn't need radios, TVs, automobiles, that sort of thing.

Did you have electricity?

Yes, but we didn't get gas until 1929.

What about your telephone service?

We had the kind you'd crank the handle on to get the operator and you'd tell her what number you wanted.

Were your in-laws affected by the 1906 earthquake?

It scared them to death. They moved all the mattresses downstairs onto the kitchen floor and slept there for weeks.

Where did your children go to school?

The old schoolhouse is still there. They were the nearest ones to the school and the last ones to get to school in the morning. There were no houses between our house and the school then and they just ran along the path and up the hill.

Were all the pupils year-round residents then?

I don't think so. Winifred Allen went to school with my husband and her family were summer residents. But when my children went to school I think everyone was here year round.

Do you remember the big schooners on the west side of the island?

Big fishing boats came in on the west side of Belvedere where the old fishyards were. They would go up to Alaska to fish. The men lived on the boats, but there were also living quarters above the fishyards. The men would spread the fish on the racks to dry and salt them, and then turn them, and pack them for the market.

Sometimes Sandy used to walk over to the fishery and buy three or four salted codfish and bring them home and we'd hang them up at the back entry on a nail and when I wanted some codfish I'd take a sharp knife and whack off a piece and freshen it. We had lots of codfish.

Did you ever see the fishermen on their way to town?

Oh, yes, on their way to drink. The path went up the hill from the foot of McLean Lane, right by the schoolhouse. I used to watch them sometimes. I never thought they'd make it on their way back. On the other side of the hill it was steep, with wooden steps most of the way. I don't know how those poor old guys ever made it. They were just old seafaring men, some of them pretty disreputable.

How did the Belvedere residents feel about these men?

They didn't think anything about them because they were was just there. The men didn't bother anyone. They just went down to Tiburon to have their fun and went back to the fishery.

Sandy McLean repairs his boat at Manny Olsen's boatyard at Hilarita, 1922. Below: Mary McLean in 1919, with Edith and Donald (Scotty).

Did many of the families have Chinese cooks?

Yes, several families on the hill did. But I can't give you any names. Mrs. Meenan came in to do the washing for Mother McLean when her children were small. Mrs. Meenan had a son Johnny who was one of the town characters. They lived at one time on an ark on Corinthian near the bridge. And Johnny was a handyman of sorts.

Do you remember the raising of the drawbridge?

Oh, yes! We used to go down every year and watch the arks being towed into the lagoon in the fall and out again in the spring. It was really something to see, all the people lined up on both sides of the bridge. If anyone on that day wanted to get to Tiburon or Belvedere they would row across to the beach on the other side, for the bridge was up all day. It was a festive time, like the opening of sailing season. At the end of the summer the houseboats and the large boats and yachts would be brought into the lagoon to anchor there for the winter. The lagoon was deep then and there was quite a current going under the bridge. That is where my son Scotty learned to swim; someone just pushed him off the bridge and it was sink or swim! We used to go down to the beach. There were no buildings there then. Oh, if I had known what those boys were doing down there I guess I would have had heart failure. When Bill was about three years old his big brother, Scotty, would ride him on his back in the water, swimming from the beach over to the Yates' on Corinthian Island. Scotty was always good to his little brothers!

It was a lively place to raise your children?

It was a marvelous place for children. I had six: Edith, Donald, Madeline, Shirley, William, and Robert. There was so much freedom. You never worried about them; they wandered all over the island. We had a pointer that followed Bill everyplace, and if I didn't know where Bill was all I had to do was go out on the front porch and look for the dog. We didn't worry much about them for there were not many outsiders here then.

Did your family play on the baseball teams?

No, my family wasn't interested in any sport but sailing. They sailed from the time they could walk. Sandy always had a boat and he built Scotty his first boat. They lived in and on the water, the lot of them!

How did the people of Belvedere socialize?

Well, the two McLean houses were side by side down here at this end of the island all by themselves, and the only other person I really saw was Mother McLean. We were back and forth all the time. And then I joined the Mothers Club at the school and we had card parties once in a while. Before that I didn't do much.

Didn't do much! With six children?

Oh, yes, I didn't have time to do much else. I'm glad my son Scotty is living in the old house now; it is nice to go back and visit there.

You said there were only the McLean houses at this end of the island. Were there no other houses at all there?

Well, the arks and some houses were down on the water. And way down at the end of Belvedere at the end of San Rafael Avenue, just before the spit and where Westshore is now, there was a little house. Joe Rose lived there; he worked at the dairy that used to deliver milk to us. Of course a lot of arks were torn down. Did you know that Sandy's father, Dan McLean, was the originator of the Belvedere Volunteer Fire Department? Dan was the first fire chief. Then Sandy joined the department, and all my boys did as soon as they got old enough, and now my grandson Jock is, he is the fourth generation to be in the Belvedere Fire Department.

Mrs. McLean, you have good memories of your family life here in Belvedere, don't you?

Belvedere was a quiet place, and very beautiful in those days. The children loved it here and so did we.

The Belvedere Fire Department, 1936, when the station was on Beach Road near Cove Road. Firemen showing off the new GMC trucks are (from left) Elmer Benson, Oscar Hurst, Paul Hilton (on running board), Charles Polacchi (in driver's seat), William Beyries, Dr. R.J. Milzner, Laurence Mersereau, O.J. Oldfield (seated on bumper), R.C. Weeks Sr., A. Bernard, William Barr, W.A. McLean (seated on bumper), George Hutchins, Ray Weeks Jr. (in driver's seat), Paul Stevens, Dan McLean.

Laurence Mersereau

1907–

We interviewed Bunk Mersereau in June, 1975, on his home ground: the Belvedere Fire House, where he was Chief for many years. As we spoke other firemen milled around, monitoring police calls and other fire stations; Bunk kept one ear tuned to the commotion, speaking to us softly and slowly. Short, direct answers are his style. He speaks his mind freely, in language that is vivid, terse, colorful. He is a very handsome man. Some of his stories made him double over with laughter; his great affection for his old friends and acquaintances is clear in every tale he tells.

Bunk, when did you come to Belvedere?

I came with my parents, my sister, and my brother from New Jersey. My dad invented vacuum canning; he sold everything in the east and came out here to set up a new business. We arrived in San Francisco in 1918. Two years after that, we came to Belvedere. I was about 12 years old.

Just at that great age to get into trouble around town.

I think we found it all, with some help.

Did you and your brother and sister go to school here in Belvedere?

No, not in Belvedere. We went to San Francisco. My sister went to Miss Burke's and my brother and I went to Potter High, which is no more.

How did you get to school?

By ferryboat, of course. Only way to go!

Were your friends children here in Belvedere, or did you have friends coming from San Francisco?

My friends were here in Belvedere — Bernon Mitchell, Bob Tuckey, people like that.

Did your family belong to one of the yacht clubs?

My father was in the Corinthian Yacht Club. The San Francisco Yacht Club wasn't over here yet. It didn't get here until 1926. But we had motorboats here, the Pacific Motor Boat Club. It was a private club, built in 1912. Bernon Mitchell had the old *Fighting Bob V.* I had my boat, *The Shrimp.* It was all power boats then.

We understand the San Francisco Yacht Club used the same building for awhile as its clubhouse.

Yeah, they did. That is an interesting story. Cliff Smith was Commodore of the San Francisco Yacht Club at that time. The members wanted to move the club out of Sausalito to a quieter mooring ground, away from the wake of the ferryboats. They picked Belvedere Cove. One group in the club didn't want to move here — these were the big money men. So they decided to break off from the club and go over to San Francisco. That's how the St. Francis Yacht Club was formed, as a break-off from the original San Francisco Yacht Club. That's why feelings have never been good between old timers of the two clubs.

The San Francisco Club didn't have much money when they came here, so they leased the old Motor Boat Club house. I guess the Belvedere Land Company owned it then and they arranged a lease. We were all supposed to be taken in as junior members. Then the word came out that they weren't going to take us in, we were too rough for their group. Mitch's brother, Emery, worked for the State Attorney General, and we found out that, oh hell, we juniors owned all the furniture, so they were sort of compelled to take us in.

Then the Motor Boat Club merged with the San Francisco Yacht Club?

Yeah, they purchased the property, their present location, from Belvedere. The Belvedere Hotel was still up then. Why they didn't move into that I don't know. It was a good building, with bedrooms and everything else in it, and a good porch. But they didn't. They built the present building instead. A group of us helped build the foundation for the deck and clubroom, and it has been gradually extended.

What happened to the old Belvedere Hotel?

They tore it down.

Was there a fire?

No, not during my time. Some people say it burned down, but it never did.

Did the hotel still have paying guests when you came to Belvedere?

No, it was just about at the end of its rope. There was a mild depression on about that time, 1921. It wasn't operating. The hotel had been used in summer months. People would come over from San Francisco and stay. And people in Belvedere had guests stay there. It was a nice place.

Do you recall the Night in Venice?

Well, it sort of fell apart after a few years. About twelve or fourteen of us young fellows, members of the Pacific Motor Boat Club, we started it going again. We got gondolas from over there in the Palace of Fine Arts, to come over and paddle around; a guy played the banjo. Everybody lit up their houses with lanterns. It was a beautiful evening. Boats came from all over the bay. I don't think anyone in boating today knows what the Night in Venice was like.

Where was the Pacific Motor Boat Club located?

Well, from the San Francisco Yacht Club going straight down toward Tiburon, it was the first apartment house with the peaks in them, just before the drawbridge.

Did the Club have lots of social functions, parties?

Lots of booze! (laughter)

That was getting close to Prohibition, wasn't it?

That was right in it.

Should I ask who supplied the liquor?

Well, you had all kinds of suppliers. Sam Vella of the Old Anchor Cafe. He started out in an old army tent, right down there in Tiburon. Just off Main Street.

What was his business?

Bootlegging!

Bootlegging in a tent! What was his legitimate business?

Bootlegging! (laughter) Sam and Mike, I forget Mike's last name.

So Sam and Mike arrived in town and put up a tent...

That's about it.

Where did they get their liquor?

For some time, they distilled it in that cemetery north of San Rafael. Sam and Mike did most of the work. Then other bootleggers decided to work together. McHarvey, he was in the old McNeil Building and another guy was there where Art is. And one of the last buildings in Tiburon, where the parking lot is now, that place was built for a bootlegger. There was a bootlegger there by the name of Andy White.

Did he have a legitimate business?
Bootlegging!

Nobody made any attempt to cover it up?
Not around here. Everybody drank!

What happened when the sheriff came down for a raid?
Mitch's father was the first prohibition officer in the state of California, and no raid ever came into Tiburon unbeknownst to Mr. Mitchell. You knew there was going to be a raid because a Coast Guard cutter would be lying off Corinthian Yacht Club. That was one of the signals. Everybody would watch and phone in when they saw a strange car coming over Tiburon Boulevard. There weren't so many cars then that you couldn't keep track.

Bootleggers didn't carry much liquor right in their places. They had other places where they kept it, then they'd go and bring in what was necessary. They had a hatch and would dump it down in the bay so there was no evidence when the agents arrived.

All the bars here were going full force during Prohibition. That Coast Guard cutter would pull in and — I don't want to mention the skipper's name, he might still be alive. I think he got heaved out of the Coast Guard because he got caught. He had a great tenor voice. He'd come and sing songs.

The yacht clubs had bars too?
You had your own liquor in your locker. You came out and poured it at the table. All the Italian gardeners made their own wine. They had a license to make 200 gallons a year. Then off that they'd run brandy, and they'd sell it. And you'd get a gallon of white wine for 35 cents and a gallon of red for 25 cents. They'd buy the grapes on the open market — it was legal. They each would get a ton of grapes, delivered by train primarily.

Did you ever help make their wine?
I always jumped on the grapes, yeah! And I drank it after I got old enough.

Where did they make the wine?
They made it right in their yards. They had a big barrel where they'd crush the grapes and get the runoff. They'd age it, then bottle it and then drink it! The families helped one another.

And Bunk Mersereau!
Yeah, I wanted to see where they ditched it! (laughter)

Did you have any contact with the codfishery workers?
Not much, but I did work over there a couple of summers.

What kind of life was that?
Oh, it was a job. First we would unload those boats, then we'd put the fish out on drying pans.

Did they hire many local kids?
I think Mitch and I were the only ones.

What were you paid?
About 15 or 20 cents an hour, if that. I don't remember. We just worked to get some money.

You never ate with the workers?
No, I got better food down in Tiburon.

How many people were living at the fishery?
It varied. Sometimes they'd have sixty people out there, when the boats were in. And on this hill up here, Oak Avenue, there was a big fig tree. The crew from the fishery would go down to Tiburon and get half loaded. They'd get as far as the fig tree and go to sleep. Then Belvedere passed an ordinance about walking around drunk, but they never arrested any of them.

Was there a jail in Belvedere?
Yeah, right down where the old icehouse was, between Cove Road and the drawbridge, on the north side.

Top: Beach Road in the 1920's; Pacific Motor Boat Club, which merged with the San Francisco Yacht Club, is at right. Across the street is the old barn, used as a garage. Below: Bunk Mersereau on the deck of the Pacific Motor Boat Club, early 1920's.

Who was put in jail?

Whoever was out of order.

Did you ever find yourself there?

No, I never made that one! No, very few people were ever locked up in there. Doc Oldfield was the sheriff, and before him a relative of the McLeans. A Wosser — I can't think of his name — he was the judge.

What else was near the jail? Was there a cluster of buildings?

Yes, there was an icehouse, a woodyard, the jail, and what have you.

Who ran the icehouse and woodyard?

Ray Weeks, Myron Weeks' father. They delivered by horse and wagon all round Belvedere. The people in Tiburon did not have enough money to buy ice.

Did you ever spend much time with the people of Tiburon?

Yeah, I lived down there, in Beyries' grocery store, upstairs. They had twelve rooms, and I had one of those for a number of years. They were boarding rooms, operated by the H and H Cafe. Two colored people owned it, Henry and Hazel Hunt. That was the best food in the whole country.

Who else lived in the boarding house?

Primarily railroad people. The cafe was right opposite Sam Vella's, across the street. We used to pay by meal ticket; it cost $20 for a meal ticket for a month, and six dollars or ten dollars for our rooms.

What time period are we talking about now?

Around 1924, 25, 26 when I was there. The Hunts were still in the business in the '30's, I know that. Old man Hunt died in the '30's. Hazel Hunt used to keep the rooms up. She had three stepchildren, Hayward, June, and I can't think of the other guy's name. A very interesting thing — in the spring of the year the loggers would start going back up the logging country, by train from here to Eureka. They'd hitch a ride on the railroad. They came in here broke after being drunk in San Francisco all winter, no money, they'd stop in Tiburon. Hazel would always give them something to eat. She always sent them out with a lunch.

The Hunts weren't making any money. We used to help her wash the dishes at night. Amos and Andy were on; they loved that. Well, I once said to Hazel, "You're not making anything yourself, why give them a lunch too?" She said, "Well, one of my children may need a lunch one time!" They were quite a family.

What other businesses were there on Main Street?

An old hardware store right next to 39 Main — I can't think of his name, the fellow who had that store. It was all boardwalk in those days, and dirt road, of course. In the early years there were only a couple of buildings over on the water side, including the McNeil Building. You then had the Oldag's Boat Works, Sam McDonough was off the McNeil Building. They leased boats to people going bass fishing. They'd tow them, a string of them behind a launch and drop them off and pick them up at the end of the day, or they could row home.

People used to row to Tiburon to do their shopping. Of course the lagoon went all around into Tiburon. The water used to come up to the firehouse during high tide. The little country road in front of here was covered most of the time with water. We rowed into town quite often.

And there was Anderson's meat market, and Kelley's and Chapman's groceries. Sam Chapman's father.

In 1921 a fire took out quite a bit of Main Street. A guy came in a tugboat and pumped what water he could. It was to no avail; there was a wind blowing and she took off. That pretty well leveled Main Street. Everybody just stayed and rebuilt. The Hunts came in about that time. Old man Hunt was a chef on the Southern Pacific, on the "Lark," going back and forth between San Francisco and Los Angeles. He came over here and opened this place, his cafe. Of course they had the railroad shops here then too. He knew how to cook! He could show up all the chefs in this part of the county, old man Hunt!

Can you tell us about the arks that were here? No one seems to know just where they came from. Were the arks built here, or somewhere else and then brought in?

I can't tell you where they came from, but we had an old fellow by the name of Stinky Wilson, who lived on Corinthian Island, used to haul them out once a year and tar them. He could have built a few. Stinky was an expert. He would just pull the ark up on the beach anywhere, jack it up, and start firing his tar. He used the big mops. He'd scrape all the barnacles off and mop on the hot tar. I remember seeing all the arks, just took them for granted. Now they are all gone.

I remember a couple of them moved up Acacia Avenue, and right up what we call Fig Tree Hill, Laurel Avenue. There are about four or five up there today on land. Then you have a couple of them moved up on Corinthian Island. They just raised them up off the beach and jacked them up.

Were the arks owned or rented?

Most of the arks I remember were leased, somebody renting to somebody else. San Francisco people owned the arks, mostly.

Had any of these arks indoor plumbing?

Just a box over the water. A one holer. You had a tide circulation so it didn't bother anybody.

Where did the arks go, did they just rot away?

Mostly they were hauled out of here, some around by Paradise. And to where Cappy Robinson had his club. And somebody took one over to Oakland. No one kept a record of them. Old Lady Tuckey, she knew all about the arks, but she's not here anymore. Old Lady Livsey is gone, too. The Belvedere postmistress. She knew everything that was going on.

Do you recall the railroad strike of 1924?

Oh, I remember it all right. Doug Wosser, friends of mine were on strike. They had pretty rough times. The railroad brought people in from Idaho to break the strike. Dr. Milzner treated all the strikers' families. He never charged them a nickel when they didn't have any money. He saved the lives of Bert Hooper's two daughters. He had to pick up one girl at two-thirty in the morning and take her on the ferryboat to the hospital where he worked. He operated on her and saved her life. She is still alive today. And then the second one got sick, and he did one and the same thing. People worked together then.

Wasn't there a lot of animosity between the townspeople and the strike breakers?

Oh, yeah. There was never any love lost! A bunch of strikebreakers hung on for years and even retired in the railroad, but they were always remembered by those who went out on strike.

A lot of the strikebreakers actually settled here then?

Oh, yeah. Most of them.

Were a lot of the strikers forced out?

Some went back to work for the railroad again. The railroad accepted them. Some chose not to go back. Like Doug Wosser, Jake's father, went to work as a mechanic over in Oakland. He never went back. A lot didn't.

What caused the demise of the railroads? The strike? The Depression?

Trucks! You can get a truck up to Eureka a lot faster than you can get a railroad train.

Did many of the railroad people have to leave?

Oh, the railroad was eventually just phased out. Then the ferryboats went. There was just less and less work in the shops. Some people left.

Did the codfishery close about the same time?

Yeah, there were a lot of big changes from the 20's to the late 30's.

Was the area hit hard by the depression?

You bet it was hit! Yeah. The railroad cut down to a two- to three-day work week. I was not working for the railroad then; I was with the U.S. Rubber Company.

Did some of the Italians turn to gardening at that time?

Some of them did, yes.

Did you know any of the gardeners?

I worked for Pete de Tomasi in the gardens. And then Harry Pariani, he was all talk. He wasn't half the gardener Pete was. No, he was not a railroad man. There were fellows who worked for them in later years who had worked for the railroad. Pete paid a little more than Pariani too. They both had good businesses, with many gardeners working for them.

Pete did a lot of stone work on Belvedere. I worked on the old Sloan place, 345 Golden Gate Avenue, the place with the big high wall around it. Both Pete and Harry did work on that wall. It took us darn near a year to build.

Where did you get the rock?

Out of Sonoma. It came down by train. Most of the rock for the other walls came out of the Tiburon hills; there's good rock over there. We loaded it on wagons — brought it over by horse and wagon. We got thirty-five cents an hour. But Pete paid fifty.

They both came over from Italy intending to become gardeners?

Yes, de Tomasi brought Harry Pariani over. There was rivalry between them in later years.

Did they bring their families with them?

No, they brought their wives over later.

Are there any of their sons still working as gardeners in Belvedere?

Pariani had all girls. Pete had all girls, too, I think. The girls were very bright and were very good students at Tamalpais High School. I think most of the gardeners came from Paloma, Italy. I remember Rosie de Tomasi. She was a good girl. I know sometimes on a Saturday night I'd want to go out and I didn't have any money, and I'd go to Pete and say I wanted to borrow five bucks. I'd always get there at dinner time, you know. They'd invite me to sit with them. Pretty soon the old wine would come out and I'd stay to dinner. And as I was about to leave, Pete would call out, "How much you want?" He'd say, "Rosie, write out a check for ten dollars!" Christ! You could go to San Francisco for two nights in a row and hit every place in town for ten dollars!

Let's go back to Main Street. During Prohibition, all the bars were in full swing, serving the railroad men, the yachtsmen on the weekend, the codfishery men coming in from the sea. Where were the women? Were there prostitutes on Main Street?

Yeah! McHarvey had a bootlegging place in the McNeil building on the ground floor. Upstairs were rooms, and he used to have prostitutes up there. Until the old gals in the Tiburon Hills would make a fuss, and they'd run them out for a couple of days and they'd be back again. It was a rough town!

Prostitution was an accepted fact of life in Tiburon?

I don't know if I'd put it that way, because they'd run them out every so often, but they would come back. They were from San Francisco. There was also an ark up in Greenwood Beach, when they were putting the highway through here. You had all those laborers on the highway, you know, and you didn't build highways as fast as you do now. It was all dirt and sod. They had bootlegging out there, and a little prostitution on the side, that lasted for about three years.

Tiburon didn't have a law enforcement officer at that time?

No, we had the sheriff's office in San Rafael. You didn't need cops in those days. You had fights now and then, but nobody got killed. There were no guns, no knives, no dope. There weren't all that many loose women, either. That shouldn't be exaggerated; they did have them though, they were available at times.

Were there any restaurants besides the Hunts'?

No, there was only the one. And Sam Vella didn't get into the restaurant business until Mrs. Hunt was having bad times and wanted to leave. Harry Hunt was killed in an an auto accident, and she was having a tough time. She made up her mind she was going to get out of it, and only then did Sam start up a restaurant.

Where was his business located then? Was he still in the tent?

No, that was long gone. He had the place where Sam Vella's is now. He was in the tent a couple of months until he had a shack built, about twice the size of this room, right on Main Street.

He was just bootlegging, no restaurant!

Yeah, just booze then. He would cash guys' checks; the 10th and the 25th were paydays, so he had money there to cash the checks.

Bunk Mersereau worked at the Union Codfishery as a teenager, earning fifteen to twenty cents an hour. This picture, from an earlier period, shows men cutting dried fish for packing.

Who were you working for when you lived on Main Street?

It's hard to say. I went to work very young, about fifteen, after my father died. My family moved to San Francisco, but I stayed here and went to work. So then I was on my own. I don't know if the railroad shops were the first place I worked. I worked for the gardeners, of course.

The railroads were unionized?

Yes, but you could go in and get a job as a laborer. They didn't compel you to join the union. I worked in the Brown Hoist Crane — that was a good job. There was a big lumber yard up there — the old mill Sandy McLean was in. They were rebuilding box and flat cars. You had to go up to the yard and pick up the lumber and bring it down to the shop, put the boilers in the steam engines, lift up the boilers. All kinds of work — loading up flat cars, getting folks all the tools they needed.

Were there lots of young boys your age working?

Quite a few in the summertime. Bob Tuckey worked there. I started in the summer, but I kept on working. It was a rugged job. A lot of kids didn't like to work hard. Once there was a wreck up north, a car had rolled down the bank, and they sent out a wrecker, a big Erie, a powerful unit, steam. A train would tow it up on a flat car with the various tools we needed to pull this rig up out of the river. It was springtime, and we lived aboard the caboose. These drunken loggers would come into the town and mooch rides up the line. Usually they rode the brakes, but if they were pretty good guys we'd bring them in the caboose and listen to their yarns.

The fellow I used to room with down at Hunts', Scotty Ross, was quite a character. He was a Scotsman who came to New York after World War I and went into bootlegging and running prostitutes. Then he came to San Francisco and got mixed up with a guy named Bishop. Old Man Bishop worked in the railroad shop. Somehow he and Scotty became partners in a bootlegging business over in San Francisco, down on the Embarcadero. We used to go there after the prize fight and have a couple of shots. The joint was raided and they were both put in jail. Bishop went to San Quentin, but Scotty didn't stay in jail because everybody liked him. Everybody liked Scotty but we didn't much care for Bishop.

Meantime, before the San Francisco venture, Scotty was a boatbuilder, and a good one. He built a boat about fourteen feet called the *Bonnie Doone.* Bishop bought an outboard motor, so they joined up.

So the boat was always lying on the mudflats just inside the drawbridge, and the kids were all using it at high tide. They'd come scooting through there using it like a surfboard. Bishop didn't like that and put a stop to it. Scotty said it was okay. This went on for several weeks. Scotty and I were living together down in Room 12. One Saturday morning he said, "Come with me, Bunk." He got his saw and all his measuring devices. So we get down to the *Bonnie Doone* and he scientifically measures it and draws a line right across the middle. I got on one side of the saw and we cut the boat in half (laughter).

So Bishop takes Scotty to court. Everybody in the country went over to the court in Sausalito to see the boat that had been cut in half. The judge fined Scotty five bucks. Scotty asked Bishop if he wanted the point or the blunt end.

Christ! I'm laughing so hard I'm crying!

Then Scotty got mixed up with the bootlegging with McHarvey and they did get knocked over all right. So they went north someplace and I lost track of Scotty.

Did you know Mr. Blanding?

Oh, yeah. Blanding didn't die until the early 40's. I knew him quite well. He was a very fine man. He put in all the roads in Belvedere. Anybody who was raising any money would go to Blanding and always get a $100 check. That was a lot of money in those days. He stayed at the Fairmont Hotel in the wintertime.

His sister married a man named Titus, who was going to build up the north end of Belvedere while Blanding built up the south end. Blanding's main house was on top of the island, his boat house on the east side of the point and a stable house on the west side. But the plan never materialized fully.

I knew Mr. Titus very well. I used to exercise his polo ponies in Burlingame in 1918–1920.

What haven't you done, Bunk?

Made a million!

Top: Main Street, 1920's, with the H & H Cafe at right. Bunk ate at the cafe, owned-by the Hunts, and lived upstairs in the building next door. Below: Main Street, water side, 1930's.

Bunk, how did you get this job as firechief of Belvedere?

I'd been around a lot, fighting fires here since 1921, except when I was away for seven and half years in Los Angeles. I came back in 1944. Of course, I was right back in the fire department, and in 1946 I was made fire chief. The first fire I fought was in 1921.

Where did you get water to fight the fires?

From a tank on top of the hill. There wasn't much water. The pressure wasn't worth a damn. So what usually happened was your house burnt to the ground! But they were slower burners than the ones they have today. You were always able to get all the furniture out of the house and people were always watching it, arranging where the people were going to stay. Most of them left town after their houses burnt down. In the 20's Belvedere had about 250 to 300 people. Everybody knew one another well.

Were the dairy ranches still in operation?

Oh, Yeah, there was one over where Reed School is now. It caught on fire. And the Belvedere fire department used to take care of the whole peninsula up to 1941. Well, that ranch caught on fire once. We used to carry a small tank of water right on our truck. We ran out of water and the place was still burning. The rancher had 25-gallon cans of milk sitting out there, so we poured that milk into the tank and got the fire out. He was one mad Portagee because we were burning up his milk! We saved the barn, though.

Did the dairymen and their families use Main Street with the rest of you?

Oh, yeah! We were all one family, this whole area, all one family.

The Bertram Tuckey family in about 1908. Mrs. Tuckey holds baby Luella; Robert (with puppy), Bert (with bicycle) and father Bertram. At left is Edna Williamson, the children's nursemaid. The Tuckeys lived in the apartment above the drugstore (left) in the Belvedere Land Company building.

Luella Tuckey Mersereau

1908–

Mrs. Mersereau's grandparents began vacationing in a small cottage at the foot of Corinthian Island in the early 1880's, before the arrival of the railroad. Her father was chief engineer on the ferry Ukiah, *and oversaw its rebuilding as the* Eureka *after World War I. Mrs. Mersereau is a very feminine woman whose speech is animated; her hands are constantly in motion. Her memory is remarkable; during our interview in 1976 she could glance at a 60-year-old photo and recall the color and texture of the dress she was wearing in it.*

How long has your family been here in Belvedere?

My parents met in 1886 while their families were weekending in arks at the foot of Corinthian Island. My father's parents had spent summers in their ark at the foot of Corinthian for years. Let me read two letters to you concerning the family ark. The first was written to my mother in 1950.

> My dear Mrs. Tuckey,
> By separate cover, I take much pleasure in sending you a copy of the painting of an old cottage on Corinthian Island, which I believe belonged to an older brother of my husband. The artist who painted the sketch, Mrs. Alice Chittenden, was a friend of mine. In the early days she came often to Belvedere to paint with Mrs. Valentine Rey. Mr. Rey drove the ladies with their paint boxes, easels and stools in a buckboard drawn by two horses. Mr. Rey spent the time reading or walking over the Tiburon hills while the ladies worked on their canvases.I sincerely hope this finds you and your children and grandchildren very well. Do come for tea and a visit when you are in Carmel. Warmest greetings to you dear Mrs. Tuckey from
> Yours sincerely,
> Mary M. Whitmer

Now here is my mother's letter of reply:

> Dear Mary,
> So very kind of you to send me a copy of the painting of the Tuckey's shack on Corinthian Island. Words cannot express my appreciation and thanks. If you should ever decide to part with the original I would dearly love to own it. My husband's father, Mr. Alfred Tuckey, was proprietor of a jeweler's store and factory located in old San Francisco where the Russ Building now stands on Mont-

gomery Street about 1867. My father-in-law built the summer cottage on Corinthian Island about 1880 for his family, a wife, three sons and a daughter. They spent all summer vacations and weekends there until 1889 when he died. The rowboat you see in the painting was used for pleasure and also to carry drinking water from a spring located about where the James Heyneman property is (on Belvedere Island).All the Tuckey family descendants loved Belvedere. The oldest son, Alfred, built one of the first five homes when Belvedere became an incorporated town — it still stands next to Guy Daniels' on the Beach Road. The second son, Harry, moved a shack next to the Belvedere Hotel and it still stands, original. He later bought a home next to Sullivan but it burned down. My husband and I owned our home for thirty-five years. Now my two daughters have located here and own their homes in Belvedere, Adamae Carrol and Luella Mersereau. My sons Bert and Robert wanted to locate here but their wives had other plans.

Now the last page of the letter is missing, but you see it does give us some history of the little shack they used on the weekends and summer time. My parents, Mr. and Mrs. Bertram Tuckey, moved to Tiburon in 1903. Eight years later, they moved into the living quarters above the Belvedere drugstore, in the Belvedere Land Company building. My father was chief engineer on the ferryboat *Ukiah.* He supervised the reconstruction of the ferry, then to be called *Eureka,* at the Hunter's Point yard.

I was on the Sausalito ferryboat when its walking beam came crashing down. There was real panic, people foolishly jumped from the upper deck to the lower deck. Many jumped overboard into the bay, and many were injured. I remember just going to the opposite end of the boat to get away from the pushing crowd. The ferryboat that my father ran came to their rescue and I got on board and went home with my father, much to my mother's relief.

Luella, do you have any photos you could share with me?

Oh, yes. Here is one of my family in front of the Belvedere Land Company apartment, my mother, me as a baby, my brother Robert holding a dog, my brother Bert with the bicycle next to my dad, and the girl on the far left was Edna Williamson — she was hired to take care of us. I think that is Eleanor Masterson next to Bert.

And my brother Robert built this little steam ferryboat and named it *Marin* long before the ferryboat *Marin* was running between Tiburon and Sausalito. You see it here in the lagoon, with smoke coming out of its stack — they burned oily rags to get the smoke. And they rowed madly to make the paddlewheel look like it was working!

Doug Wosser also built his own steam ferryboat so of course Robert and Doug had to have a boat race in the lagoon! Robert and my dad felt that Doug's boat would be faster, so the night before the race Robert and Dad stole out into the night to tie old tin cans and junk to the bottom of Doug's boat. Well, Doug won anyway, even with all the junk in tow! A good time was had by all.

What were some of the things you did every day as a girl?

As a young girl I was given money every day by my mother to buy meat for dinner at Anderson's Meat Market. I walked to Tiburon along Beach Road and over the wooden sidewalk along the foot of Corinthian Island. I was always afraid of losing the money below the sidewalk. Mr. Anderson was a big man with white hair and full eyebrows and he always asked, "What will it be today, a hot dog or a piece of baloney?" He always gave us something when we came in, every day. Mrs. Anderson always sat at a high bookkeeper's desk on a high stool, working on the books; she always wore a green visor as she worked. She was very pleasant.

The other stores in town were Carpenter and Chapman Grocery Store on the water side. And across the street was the J.H. Kelley Grocery, later bought out by Beyries. And there was a Chinese vegetable man. My first memory of him was with the pole and baskets bouncing on his shoulders. Later he had a truck and my brother and I and our friends would steal fruit off the truck when he went to my mother's door with a delivery. My mother and the Chinaman could see what we children were doing, so my mother always asked, "and what else do I owe you for today?"

Did your family always live above the drugstore?

No, we moved to a house on Bella Vista Avenue on the Island. I was going to school by then in the Belvedere schoolhouse. My joy in going to school

This painting, by Alice Chittenden, shows the Alfred Tuckey cottage on the northwest side of Corinthian Island in 1884, before the railroad came to Tiburon. In the background is Mt. Tiburon.

Top: Swimmers in front of the Farr Cottage on Beach Road include John Wosser and Robert Tuckey in front, and Bert Tuckey (second from right); the others are not identified. Below: Luella Tuckey Mersereau, 1983.

was being able to walk to and from school — we even walked home every day for lunch. I walked to school with Su Soon, a young Chinese boy whose family ran the laundry in Belvedere. My brother Robert was always in trouble in school and the teachers would spank him. Mrs. Davenport and Miss Morehead were my teachers. They had to travel everyday from San Rafael to Sausalito by train, then ride the ferry from Sausalito to Belvedere and walk up to the school. I cannot remember either of the teachers being late or needing a substitute.

The old Belvedere school house was better and larger than the new one; it had two classrooms upstairs and a workshop downstairs for the boys and a home ec room for the girls. The boys would always hang around after school to eat all the food the girls had cooked on their cooking days.

After school my brothers and my friends and I would go grass sliding next to McLean Lane. My father made sleds for us and waxed the runners. Ours always seemed to be the fastest. One of my playmates was Romy Piazzoni; they lived across from us on Beach Road. We played on the beach or in the lagoon. Eve Arden and I were friends and we would skinny dip on the west side of the island. We walked over the hill after school and down the fine trails. We would hide behind rocks from passing fishermen. The water on the west side was very clean. The water in Belvedere Cove was polluted because a sewer main had broken.

Were there still arks in the cove?

Yes, and they moved into the lagoon for the winter. Later when the drawbridge was made into a stationary bridge many of the arks became the homes of the Italian gardeners on the east side of the island.

What else did you do after school?

Oh, the old Flemming house, now the Tiburon Vintners, was where I had piano lessons. Miss Mable Wosser was my teacher; I was always in trouble because I did not practice — I had better things to do after school with my friends!

Did the 1906 earthquake and fire have any effect on your family?

Well, a cousin from the city came to live with them. They had a terrible time getting her to leave once she had moved in!

What else did you do as a child?

I remember the children of the island would dress in white gowns and go Christmas caroling every year. That was nice. As we got older we would go to El Campo for picnics and dancing. And later when I met Bunk we used to canoe every Sunday over to Angel Island and picnic on the beach and then paddle around the island. Sometimes we paddled over to California City and once in a while out to Land's End, Fort Baker. After Bunk and I were married we moved to Los Angeles for about seven years, then we came back here to Belvedere, to the house where we live now, and raised Larry and Kathy. So I have been here in Belvedere almost all my life.

Top: Alice Sperling Oldag, 1983. Below: Marie Lepori Cattani, 1985.

Alice Sperling Oldag

1897–

Marie Lepori Cattani

1907–

Alice Oldag and Marie Cattani have been friends and neighbors nearly all their days in Tiburon; their husbands were also close friends. These couples saw the ranches and eventually the trains disappear, and the hills fill up with houses. One of the last old-fashioned stores on Main Street, Oldag's Hardware was a storehouse full of iron, wood, rope, and tools. Set on pilings over the bay, the building had a wood plank floor through which the aroma of saltwater rose to greet the customer. Alice Oldag is a slender woman who loves to talk about the old days in Tiburon; Marie Cattani is small, energetic and friendly. They were interviewed in 1976.

When did you both come to Tiburon?

Mrs. Oldag: I came here in 1932 when I got married. My husband, August Oldag, had the Marine Ways, a boat repair shop on Main Street. At that time it was railroad property and he rented it for $25 or $35 a month, believe it or not, in 1932.

When you got married was he already in business?

Mrs. Oldag: Yes, he came here in 1918.

Did he ever work for the railroad?

Mrs. Oldag: No, although he sometimes made trips by boat to pick up the railroad crews in Sausalito. Once in awhile he would have some passengers, but they would have to be very, very rushed because there was no commuting by bus in those days when he came here.

And when did you arrive, Mrs. Cattani?

Mrs. Cattani: I was a little bride, eighteen years old. I came in 1925 and have been here ever since. My husband, Hugo, worked for the railroad. He was a toolmaker and a machinist and he started to work for the railroad down here in 1922.

Did he talk much about the railroad strike in '24?

Mrs. Cattani: Yes, the men had to go off, they didn't work at all. He mentioned a little of it, that's when I met him, in 1924. We were married a year later; apparently I didn't waste any time.

Mrs. Oldag: Wasn't there a big fence put around the railroad yard at that time?

Mrs. Cattani: Oh, yes, all the way around, a high fence.

Where did you live then, Mrs. Cattani?

Mrs. Cattani: We lived at Mr. Chapman's. He was the postmaster of Tiburon and he had his grocery store there too. It was a great big house with two apartments, and they had one side for his whole family. We lived upstairs. Then we moved to a smaller house. There were two flats, as we called them. We didn't call them apartments in those days. Then we bought this lot next door and built our own house in 1929. That's in the Depression, remember, Al?

Mrs. Oldag: Oh, yes.

Mrs. Cattani: They only let my husband work two or three days a week. We did the work on the house ourselves. The railroad men helped dig out and put in the foundation. After that a very good friend, a carpenter at the railroad, helped my husband.

Could you tell us about Main Street,Tiburon?

Mrs. Oldag: Charlie Thom was a great one for parties. Once they took great big heavy paper and drew shaky-looking storefronts on the paper! They covered the whole fronts of the buildings to look like an old western town. That was more fun.

Was that an annual event?

Mrs. Cattani: No. Just a bunch of screwballs who used to get together.

Mrs. Oldag: Charlie Thom — he was a railroad man — was just having fun; he was a great one for fun. He lived in the old Donahue Building.

Back of the stores on Main Street was all water. Many times when there was a bad storm the waves used to go right across the street into the butcher shop!

Mrs. Cattani: It was really bad in the wintertime downtown, oh, boy!

Mrs. Oldag: And while I think of it, this was before my time, but anytime the ferryboat came in with the weekenders, members of the Corinthian Yacht Club, they had a band there that played the same tune all the time, always the same tune. The band would escort the people to the Corinthian Yacht Club. They would all parade down the street!

Mrs. Cattani: It was the only tune they knew, Alice! And remember the dances we used to have down on the street?

Did you close the street off?

Mrs. Cattani: We didn't have to. There weren't that many people. We didn't have automobiles like now. When I came here in 1925 the population in Tiburon was only 325 people. Believe it or not! Now it is close to seven thousand. All the hills were bare, just cows and old-fashioned houses down on Mar West; they were for the railroad people.

What was down on Main Street then?

Mrs. Oldag: Well, let's see. The barbershop was where Rooney's is now. There was Barr's Garage. And Mr. Barr had an open-air taxi that would take people to Mill Valley to the stores and moving picture shows. My husband's business was a boat house and marine ways next to the McNeil Building. Later he got in the hardware business, but in the early days he repaired local boats.

Mrs. Cattani: At all hours of the night and morning!

Mrs. Oldag: Yes, he had to work with the tides. And then after the McNeil Building was Williamson's Garage—he repaired cars and supplied gasoline for the boats. Then Sam's. Sam was always there, wasn't he, Marie?

Mrs. Cattani: He was just a saloon then.

Mrs. Oldag: Then he graduated to a restaurant.

Were they letting women in saloons at that time?

Mrs. Oldag: Oh, heavens no!

Mrs. Cattani: Oh, yes, Alice! When I came here as a bride I had never been in a saloon in my life. My mother was quite strict. And that is where my husband took me. All the railroad men hung out at Sam Vella's, wives and girlfriends, everybody. Even little children were taken there.

Mrs. Oldag: Oh, yes, that's right. Even now it is old-fashioned — old fixtures and pictures on the walls. And then there was Adams' Hardware Store, and Chapman's post office and grocery store. It didn't amount to much.

And what was at the end of the street?

Mrs. Cattani: Mrs. Walden, remember her?

Mrs. Oldag: Oh, yes, Mrs. Walden's, an ice-cream store. The kids would sit in there by the hour in the afternoon.

Marie Lepori just before her marriage to Hugo Cattani, 1925.

Mrs. Cattani: And across the street was Barr's Garage. And the little barber shop. We didn't have cement walks, it was a wooden boardwalk. Then came Harvey Anderson's butcher shop.

Mrs. Oldag: And Beyries' Grocery Store.

Mrs. Cattani: And then was Mrs. Hunt's. I'll never forget her. It was a colored family that owned that restaurant. Well, when I was married the first thing I did was get pregnant, naturally. I used to have a craving for hot dogs and there weren't any in the house. In the wee hours of the morning my husband went down and knocked at the restaurant window. Mrs. Hunt handed him the bun, the dog, and everything. I never ate anything so fast in my life.

Mrs. Oldag: Oh, she was something. She was a beautiful person!

Mrs. Cattani: Now what came after the Hunts', Alice?

Mrs. Oldag: During the war they entertained the servicemen there. The naval net depot was very active.

Mrs. Cattani: It used to be the old Tiburoner, right?

Mrs. Oldag: Yes, it was a big place, and we had dances. We had lots of fun.

Mrs. Cattani: That was in 1942, after the Hunts went out of business.

Where did you do your shopping? Did they deliver?

Mrs. Oldag: At Chapman's and Billy Beyries'. They delivered, but you went there too.

Mrs. Cattani: We usually carried everything home. In those days we couldn't buy the fresh vegetables we have now. You weren't able to buy French bread in Tiburon. Musso's Bakery wasn't there yet. When did Musso come in, Al? I think it was when the Manteganis bought the McNeil Building. Musso first had a little corner of the McNeil Building.

Mrs. Oldag: Yes, and across the street, where Musso ended up, was a railroad hotel. A lot of men lived there, for there was no good road out of Tiburon then, just an old mud path going north. When my husband moved here in 1918 he just barely got here with the truck, and he even had to take his furniture off the truck to get under the trestle.

Where did your husband live when he first came to Tiburon, Mrs. Oldag?

Mrs. Oldag: In a little houseboat down by the old wharf. The railroad tore it down to put in more piers. Part of the time I lived right on the water too. My life changed. My father passed away and my mother moved in upstairs here. We had lived on the water for ten years or so and it was wonderful. And I was helping my husband downtown with the hardware store.

Were a lot of people living on houseboats?

Mrs. Cattani: Oh, yes. You know, when you go down past Main Street going to Beach Road, those were all arks. And there were even houseboats in the water. You have pictures of them, Alice. Get your pictures, Alice!

Mrs. Oldag: All right.

Mrs. Cattani: You have no idea what this place was like. Down where the banks are and Mantegani's store it was all lagoon, all full of water. The railroad filled it all in. In the olden days there was a place along the lagoon that was known as Little Italy because there were a lot of Italians. That is what they called it. The group where I first lived were practically all Italians.

Did you help with the winemaking?

Mrs. Cattani: No. But I did help my dad in the city. He had a big tank in the basement and my three brothers and I used to get down there and stomp all the grapes. And you knew when the wine was coming because the flies would come too. I used to make my beer downstairs here in my own basement.

Mrs. Oldag: We had Prohibition in those days.

Mrs. Cattani: But I cheated!

Did the town dry up during Prohibition?

Mrs. Oldag: Oh, NO! There was bootlegging like crazy!

Mrs. Cattani: I'll tell you, some of the Italians made their money during that time.

The Italians could make their own wine at that time?

Mrs. Cattani: Oh, yes, but it was the other stuff, that really burns you in here. That is what they made their money on. I tasted some one time. You know those people down in Belvedere, Alice?

Mrs. Oldag: Oh, yes, I know.

Mrs. Cattani: They used to come and get my husband to fix things, and they used to give him a bottle.

Whoo! By accident he spilled it on the rug. You should have seen that spot.

What was the boat business like then?

Mrs. Oldag: Fishing was a real sport over here. My husband rented rowboats and people would go out fishing. A lot of fishermen came over on the ferries on the weekends.

Mrs. Cattani: And the McDonoughs rented boats too. Milt McDonough's father.

Mrs. Oldag: My husband also had three launches, and he would take people out fishing, charter a boat for the day.

So tourists came to spend the day in Tiburon?

Mrs. Cattani: Oh, yes. But we called them weekenders. All along Paradise Drive there were just a few old houses, and all that beach was open. Everybody used to come over. Even I did when I lived in the city with my family. In Keil Cove was a beautiful beach. So we used to bring our food and everything. You could use all the beaches. Then people started to build there.

Did tourists go to El Campo?

Mrs. Oldag: Oh, yes, in the launches. They came by ferry to El Campo from San Francisco and stayed the whole day.

Mrs. Cattani: Now all along Tiburon Boulevard, going north, that was all ranches and cows. We even had cows coming here. Once they had a big fire at the Brazil Ranch, and my husband was with the railroad fire department and Alice's husband was firechief and chief of police in Tiburon. He was all we had.

Mrs. Oldag: He was the first deputy and firechief.

Mrs. Cattani: Well, out at the ranch there was a fire, caused by the manure. That will burn, you know. And they did not have any water there. My husband said they never laughed so much, for they climbed up and poured gallons and gallons of milk into the truck to put out the fire with. Isn't that something? (laughter)

And we used to walk out to the ranches to get our cream. You could buy a whole quart of thick whipping cream for fifteen cents. And come summertime that is what we made all our strawberry shortcakes with, and cream puffs too.

Mrs. Oldag: That milk was wonderful.

Mrs. Oldag: Tiburon had two terrible fires while my husband was here. It burned down twice. Here is a photo of Oldag's boat ways in 1930.

Mrs. Cattani: Is that part of the *Legonia* in that picture, Alice? That *Legonia* was a beautiful boat and it had a history.

Mrs. Oldag: It did that. The *Legonia,* as far as my husband knew, was used as a rum runner. And it was in danger of getting caught so they just let it go in the ocean, I think it was headed for Mexico. And he bought it somehow as salvage and had it made over. Of course it was a documented boat; it was forty feet long. Every year he had to go to the Federal Building to have it documented, to be able to operate it. His other launches were much smaller; they were work boats.

Mrs. Cattani: Here is a picture of what August and Alice owned on the waterfront.

Mrs. Oldag: Oh, yes, we bought it from the railroad and we should have held on to it.

Did you go to the City often?

Mrs. Oldag: Yes. It was easier to get to San Francisco than to Mill Valley.

Mrs. Cattani: When I first came here if you wanted to go north you had to take the *Marin* to Sausalito and then take a train up to San Rafael and north.

Mrs. Oldag: There were no banks when we came here, no private doctor. The only doctor here was the railroad doctor. And there were no telephones.

Mrs. Cattani: No phone. No gas; we had oil. You either used a coal and woodstove, or you had what was called the 'little burner.' You had it set in your stove and you had to pump oil into it. And you had to walk downtown to fill your oil cans. That is how we lived for quite awhile. We had a viaduct then, so we walked right over the top of the train yard to get to downtown.

Did the population swell in the summer months when all the summer people would come?

Mrs. Cattani: Yes, I used to notice it more because the Oldags had the little launches and rowboats, and the summer people used them. And Alice used to say that people would come at two and three o'clock in the morning, knocking at their door, to rent this and that.

Mrs. Oldag: It was kind of silly. Sometimes they were not exactly sober.

Alice and August Oldag in front of their store on Main Street, 1930's.

Oldag's marine ways; Sandy McLean's boat being launched. August Oldag (on the dock, left) wears a white cap.

Mrs. Cattani: After they got through at Vella's, who would be?

Mrs. Oldag: Many of these houseboats that once floated in Belvedere Cove are now little houses on Mar West. They moved them up here. The Polacchi house once floated in the cove.

Mrs. Cattani: Polacchi's sister had a bigger houseboat and they moved that up here too.

Mrs. Oldag: If you look at some of these houses around here they have a funny look. And along San Rafael Avenue there were a lot of houseboats. There were houseboats on both sides of the lagoon.

How did you differentiate between houseboats and arks? We have heard both terms used.

Mrs. Cattani: The houseboat was anchored and floating in the water. And the ark was on pilings, with water underneath, or on land.

Mrs. Oldag: The arks were permanent. I remember when Allen had all of them moved away from San Rafael Avenue.

Mrs. Cattani: These beautiful houseboats, believe me, were the most unsanitary things, because everything went out into the lagoon, just out into the water.

Mrs. Oldag: It's a wonder we didn't all die! We all used to swim in the cove and lagoon.

Mrs. Cattani: And the railroad men, some of the work they had to do was very hot, and on their lunch hour they'd go down where the barge slip was and jump in the water, in that dirty water. Well, let's be polite, we never had refuse service here. I used to take the wheelbarrow and go down to the bay every other night and wheel all my garbage into the bay, so help me. Then later we paid fifty cents a month to have our garbage taken away. Now it is ten dollars for three months. You don't know how grateful I was when they said we were going to have garbage service here. I got pretty tired of wheeling that stuff down to the bay. Everybody did.

Mrs. Oldag: When we lived on the water there was a little hatch where everything went right down into the water.

Mrs. Cattani: I'm telling you, Al, we've had it really tough! And to think I was born and raised in the city, and not used to all this. We had gas, electricity, garbage service, everything. And when I came over here, I'll tell you, I did not know the truth about Tiburon. I was in love and blind. You are when you're young. When I saw how I was going to live, I said, "Oh, my God." I told my mother, we don't have gas or a telephone. Well, she told me I had known what I was doing and that it was too late to change. I cried, and told my husband I was only going to live one year in Tiburon. "You can have it. I'm going back to the city!" I never did. And when I found out we had no way of getting rid of the garbage, oh, gee, that was really it!

What was Tiburon like during the Depression?

Mrs. Cattani: When the train yard was busy the hobos rode the trains into Tiburon and hid out down by the yards. They'd knock at our door, wanting potatoes and coffee.

Mrs. Oldag: They never bothered us. You could leave your doors open all the time!

Mrs. Cattani: Yes, we could go to the city and come home and everything was still there. You do that now and you don't have a house.

Mrs. Oldag: The train and ferryboats were the only transportation to the city; there was no Highway 101. So the hobos ended up here on their way to San Francisco.

Mrs. Cattani: One day while Hugo and I were sitting on the front porch I asked him who put all those x's on our door. I was the lucky one. They had marked our door as a place where they could get something good. And finally I said, no more.

Once around Thanksgiving time, this poor man came and we all thought he was bleeding to death. He was all wrapped up in bandages, with blood everywhere, and he wanted something for Thanksgiving dinner. I gave him a plate of turkey. Well, my husband got wise and followed him, and watched him unwrap the bandages — it was catsup he had all over him! Can you beat that!

Can you tell us about the ferryboats?

Mrs. Oldag: The big ferries were beautifully painted and had lots of beveled glass and hardwood. They were very elegant.

Mrs. Cattani: And they had little restaurants where you could get coffee or something to eat. And beautiful restrooms. When I was nursing my baby, I could go into a private little place in the lounge.

Mrs. Oldag: That was a sad day when they took off the ferryboats and the trains.

Mrs. Cattani: Oh, yes. We cried.

Why was the service discontinued?

Mrs. Oldag: The Greyhound Bus, 1941, right before World War II.

It seems there used to be a real social distinction between Tiburon and Belvedere.

Mrs. Oldag: Yes, there always was. Tiburon was on the wrong side of the tracks!

Mrs. Cattani: And there still is.

Mrs. Oldag: I don't think there is anymore.

Mrs. Cattani: There was a time when Tiburon wanted to combine with the Belvedere school to make it easier. Oh, brother, did Belvedere raise heck! They were not going to combine our children with theirs! Oh, no!

Mrs. Oldag: Well, you see, this was a railroad town.

Mrs. Cattani: And we were of the lower class.

Where did your children go to school?

Mrs. Cattani: Right here in the old Tiburon school, at Mar West and Esperanza. My daughter, Bernie, had Mrs. Grbac for a teacher there. Bernie is now married and living in Tiburon. She went to school with her husband; they grew up together. And they hated each other in school. She married George Mantegani.

Do you remember the codfishery?

Mrs. Oldag: Yes, on the other side of Belvedere, facing Sausalito. I went over to see the big sailing boats. It was smelly.

Mrs. Cattani: Oh, you could smell the fishery in Tiburon when the wind was blowing. Oh, what a smell!

Mrs. Oldag: And then there was a whaling station over there in Richmond and we'd get the fumes from that sometimes too.

Did either of your families belong to the yacht clubs?

Mrs. Oldag: Yes, my husband, August, belonged to the Corinthian Yacht Club.

Did a vegetable man come to your house in a horse and wagon?

Mrs. Oldag: Yes. He was a big husky fellow who looked like a prize fighter, and I was afraid of him. My husband used to tell about the boat that would come down from the river, the delta, and bring watermelons and all kinds of vegetables down.

Mrs. Cattani: Al, do you remember Wedemeyer who used to come around with doughnuts and bread? That is how we got our desserts. That was before Musso came. When Musso walked in with his Rum Cake, you could smell it from Main Street clear up to here!

Mrs. Oldag: He was a very fine baker, a real confectioner. He had a fine position in one of the hotels in San Francisco before he came over here. He was originally from Italy.

Mrs. Cattani: But I tell you, you eat a piece of Musso Rum Cake and you're out for a week! All that filling was rum — you could hardly find the cake. When he first came he was in the Corner Market building and then after he graduated he bought all that property on the corner as you turn into Main Street. He lives upstairs over the building. Here I am like a true Italian, talking with my hands. *(Note: Mr. Musso died in 1985.)*

How did the people of Tiburon socialize?

Mrs. Cattani: The Italians had their own group, and they had their dinners together. But Alice and August Oldag, Hugo and me, Jennie and Donald McLean and Mr. and Mrs. Foster, we all had children.

Mrs. Oldag: We didn't have any children.

Mrs. Cattani: No, but they joined in with us. We used to take turns going to each other's houses. We'd put on shows for each other, or come to my house on Halloween. We had lots of parties with our children; it was more for the kids. What did they have to do here? There was no place to go. So we entertained each other. It was potluck. But our school parties were the best, with Halloween parades and costumes.

Mrs. Oldag: Marie's daughter had the most beautiful costumes.

Mrs. Cattani: My husband made them. He made her first costume for her when she was only five and a half. It was supposed to be an insect made out of colored cellophane. We had the whole thing completed except the wings were not attached. Well, that night there was a big fire up by Foster's, and our husbands had to answer the call. There had been a big gas explosion. Somebody said "don't smoke," and some wise guy lit a cigaret and the bottom of the basement was full of gas! It blew up, and

The first Tiburon Fire Department, 1941. Fire Chief August Oldag is at the wheel; Ed Dunn is on the fender. Standing from left: George Schleicher, Charles Pastori Jr., Donald McLean, Charles Pastori, Sr., Dick Perry, Louis Soldavini, John McNeil, Guy Rhodes, C. Lasham, Hugo Cattani, Anthony Raberio. Kneeling, Arturo Scandroglio. On running board: Dick Williamson and John Musso. Standing right: Mike Barnes, Bert Hooper.

seven of the men were blown out. One of them was Hugo. Also Billy Beyries and McNamara.

And I waited and waited for Hugo to come home that night, and I finally came over here to Alice's, didn't I, Alice? And then Charles Chapman, the oldest son, came here and told me that Hugo was up at Ross Hospital. They took me up to see him. All I saw of him was his nose; he was burnt all over. And the only thing the poor fellow said to me was, "I'm sorry, honey, I didn't finish Bernie's wings." He was in the hospital for quite awhile. But Bernice's costume won a prize.

Mrs. Oldag: Tiburon's fire department was all volunteers from the railroad until about 1940.

Is that when the town started to grow?

Mrs. Oldag: I'd say in the 50's.

Mrs. Cattani: With the buses it was easy to come in and out. You could go to Marin City and transfer to anywhere in Marin County or go over to the city. Yes, about in the 50's, Al.

Mrs. Oldag: I think it was about the time the dairies moved out, all that dairy land opening up.

Mrs. Cattani: It was when Reed School was built where Avilas's dairy was. Now what really gave me the chills was when all that ammunition came in here to be shipped out during the war. And remember how mad we were when all that scrap iron was being shipped to Japan just before the war? Our husbands were on the bomb squad. Whenever the whistle blew my husband had to go down to the train yard; it meant more ammunition was being brought in.

Alice's husband was working for the town in the yard, and Hugo and Mr. Foster were working for the railroad, and oh, how we worried about them. At one time they were thinking of evacuating all of us along here, from the Tiburon school, all the way around to Paradise Drive, because we were closest to the train yard and all that live ammunition. But then the war ended.

Mrs. Oldag: And during those years you had to have identification if you were of Italian or German descent, if you were not a citizen. And there were a lot of Italians here. Some of them couldn't stay here; they had to move over to Mill Valley, because of the ammunition. We were living downtown, and you could not use a telescope or binoculars or a flashlight, because it could be a way of signalling.

Mrs. Cattani: There were submarine nets in the bay; I don't know how many Japanese and German submarines they caught in the bay. They had pictures of them — one was almost to Paradise Drive and the other off the Golden Gate Bridge. They had nets under the water, and I can remember the sirens when they thought they caught one. I still have the hard hat and armband my husband had to wear when he was on the bomb squad. But we are in better times now.

Vickie Pariani, John Polacchi, Rose Pariani Polacchi, 1930's.

Rose Pariani Polacchi

1914–

Rose Polacchi is the daughter of Harry Pariani, one of the gifted Italian gardeners who created many of the beautiful gardens of Belvedere Island. The Pariani gardens and rock walls are still in existence today. Mrs. Polacchi, youthful and strong, with short, white hair and sparkling blue eyes, spoke with great affection of her many friends and her happy childhood in Belvedere. Her great love for her parents was evident as she recalled their life together in vivid detail. This interview was taken in September 1985.

Rose, when did your father, Harry Pariani, come to Belvedere?

My Dad came to the U.S. — it must have been in 1907, I know he came a year after the earthquake — and lived in Palo Alto for about a year. He visited Belvedere and liked the island. He went to work here as a gardener, a handyman. He built rock walls, he made sidewalks, fish ponds, patios — you name it, he did it.

Where did he come from in Italy? Do you know the name of the town?

A village about ninety miles from the Swiss border.

Was your father a gardener there?

No, my father was the last of twelve children and his mother wanted him to go into the priesthood. He didn't like it. He joined the Italian infantry, whatever that was. I had a picture of him; he was a handsome-looking guy with a big handlebar mustache. He served whatever time they had to put in, and then he left. He was 24 or 25 years old when he came to this country. I don't know who paid his passage; it was never discussed.

Did he ever go back to Italy?

Never, no. But my mother, Rosa, had a sister who came here and I remember her living with us, when I was quite young. My aunt did go back and did not like it. She went back to the same village; it was still very primitive there — outhouses, and no running water in the house.

What year did she go back?

It was after I was married, 1934. But then my

mother went back, about ten years after my father had died, and by then things had improved. The houses had electricity and running water and toilets.

Did your father know your mother in Italy?
Back there, yes. He came here and then sent for her, like so many of them did.

Where were they married?
In San Francisco, at St. Peter's and St. Paul's, I guess, that's where all of them went.

What year were you born? Did you have brothers and sisters?
I was born in 1914 and my sister Victoria in 1912. She passed away in 1973.

Do you remember any stories of your parents' passage from Italy?
I often heard my mother say that she came over on a ship and was sick the whole trip.

She came by herself?
No, a group of them came together. At that time there was my father, the two Charlies, and the de Tomasis.

The two Charlies?
Well, they were both tall men, but one was a little taller than the other, so we always referred to them as Big Charlie and Little Charlie. They were well known on the island too. Big Charlie was Charlie Pariani and little Charlie was Carlo de Tomasi.

Was Big Charlie related to your father?
Yes, they were first cousins. My mother and some other women, Annette de Tomasi and others, came over together. They had been sent for by the men they married. Some of the men worked on the island, and some worked for the railroad; other than that there was no work. There were no businesses. There were two restaurants in Tiburon and all the rest were saloons. We were never allowed to go over the bridge when we were kids.

Why not?
They just did not want us away from home. That was the boundary, the Belvedere-Tiburon bridge at the base of Corinthian Island. So for years I did not know the town of Tiburon — until I guess about high school.

Where is your husband John from?
John was from Tiburon, Mar West. His father worked for the railroad; he died when John was young. He had caught the influenza that went around after the war, and that left him weak. Then he had an appendix attack and was operated on and died of what was then called ether pneumonia.

How did his mother support her family?
There was John and his sister Pauline and his mother; she went to work in Tiburon at the H and H cafe and later at the laundry.

Can you tell me about your childhood? Were you a neighbor of Jerry Coleman Halverson?
Well, there were the Fetches, the Zucchis, the de Tomasi's, the Stevens, ah, two blank blanks, the Parianis, the Colemans, the Valentis, the Compagnas, the Reeds, the Oldfields, the Hearsts, the Hiltons, the Canziani, Milani — one or two children in each family except for the Colemans, Stevens, and Beyries. We all lived on what we called Ark Row, below San Rafael Avenue. And all of the arks had long platforms that went out to the water. Because that was our playground, the cove, or lagoon as it was called. And we all had rafts made of old wood that we stole from the railroad discard pile, old redwood ties that were put together with boards, and we had an orange crate box — everything came in wooden boxes — and we had our homemade paddle. And then all of us would get out on that lagoon because it was calm water, nothing rough. All of the kids had a raft and we would go over to the first dairy, the Souza ranch, and sometimes they'd give us fresh milk.

So as children you paddled across the lagoon?
Oh, yes, we'd visit the dairy, then go climb the hills. That was when the hills were beautiful. Lupines and yellow pansies grew wild. And poppies. There was a big creek north of the dairy, and a big deep gully, and you never saw such watercress, and we would say, "People buy it in the stores and it grows wild!" Besides paddling we swam all

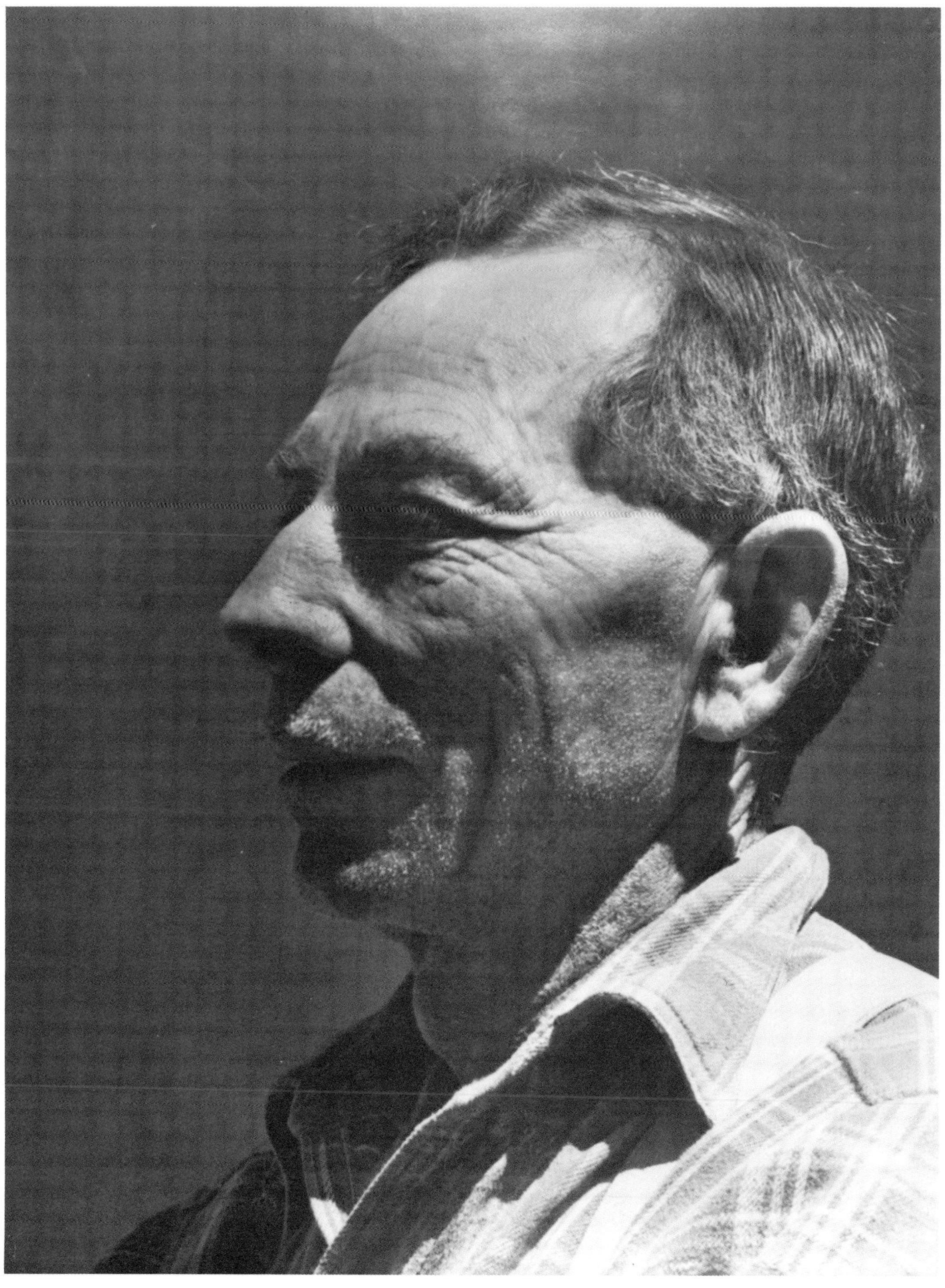

Harry Pariani, 1885–1950.

This view across Beach Road from Corinthian shows the Pacific Motor Boat Club (later the San Francisco Yacht Club), where children of Belvedere and Tiburon went to see movies. Across the lagoon (left center) arks are lined up below San Rafael Avenue. The Parianis' ark was in this area. The picture is undated.

summer; from about the middle of May to the end of September, that is all the kids did.

I also remember movies at the old San Francisco Yacht Club (that is apartments now) every Friday night. We paid five or ten cents. All the kids turned out from Belvedere and Tiburon.

Did your parents have vegetable gardens in the front yard?

Oh, yes, they all did. Out in front on a fifty by twenty foot square area. You would not believe what they grew in there. Squash, peas, string beans, parsley, beets, tomatoes, cucumbers, the works! Every little square had a use. The ground would be turned over and enriched. This went on year after year until 1939 when the land was confiscated and all the arks were either sold or torn down — a lot of them had good lumber in them. You know they had at one time been seaworthy. All the arks had to be moved.

Where did your family go?

Mom and Dad built a house on Acacia, next to the Nordstands, just down below the McLeans. There was the St. Stephen's church, then Carlo de Tomasi, my Mom and Pop's house, and the Nordstands' house, then a public lane. Our house was the second one from the public lane. I have gone up there a couple of times. The yard was all bushy and overgrown, and I have thought, "Oh, God, if Papa saw this he would have a fit." He had a green thumb. If it was growable, he grew it!

Well, we have heard that Harry Pariani was the best!

He had his own little glass house where he started the seeds. He started plants there for his garden and for the ones on the hill. Some of the houses where he worked on the hill had their own greenhouses and he would grow things there. Well, the month of April had this growing, and the month of May had that growing — always something was being rebedded.

How many steady customers did he have?

Oh, he worked for the Heynemanns, the McLeans — that was the D. McLeans that owned the expensive grocery store in San Francisco, the Levinsons, and right at the bottom of the hill Mrs. Payne, and he worked for the Cunninghams, the Mitchells. He worked years for Olive Fetherstonhaugh, who was very fond of my father. She was always making profile pictures of him — he would go pose for her after work, and sit there and have tea with her, and she just loved him. She had a friend in Berkeley, a Mr. Strong, a very famous photographer and painter, and he came over one Sunday and took photos of my father. That is one of them on the wall. You will notice my father had a little mustache, he always wore it, but you can see that he needed a shave, so this photo must have been taken on a weekend, for he did not like to shave on his days off.

I used to go and visit with Olive. I haven't heard from her in a long time — I don't know where time goes.

Now he also worked for, let's see, the Holmeses, the Bridges, the H.B. Allens. The Allens bought the Holmes house. Oh, the Lathrops, Mr. Freer.

That is a lot of people! He must have had younger men working with him.

Yep, he did; I used to keep the books for him. He had Paul de Tomasi work for him and Giulio Mantegani, and a Grbac, not Miriam's husband, but his brother. He had four or five men working for him and he would kind of supervise. He was a hard guy to work for because he did not like slip-shod.

How much did he pay the men?

When I kept the books wages were something like $4.25 a day! Yes! And when he first came to Belvedere he would work a twelve-hour day for less than $2.00! Yes! And then wages slowly improved. In the wintertime there were two or three people that lived in San Francisco and he would go to their San Francisco homes and work there. They would close their summer homes up. Almost all the Belvedere Island residents came about the middle of May and always went back at opera time in September. That would be when the weather was starting to change. For they always had garden parties and big teas and that sort of thing, with guests from the city. And the gardeners did preliminary things like bush trimming and sweeping the paths and so on. The Freers were one of the few families who lived here the whole year round; they were right next to the Boole house. He worked for the Pughs — I went to school with their son Evan. The Richardsons were also year-round people.

Mrs. Holmes had a huge music room and she used to invite all the kids in the village — we were called the village. They always had some kind of play. I remember Punch and Judy. We were just little kids and we were ogle-eyed, you know, to go to this magnificent house. They served us ice cream and cake and that was a real treat!

Did the Holmeses have their children there too?

No, they had no children. This was just for the children of the village! A sort of closing party. The majority of those people, outside of the Mailliards, I don't remember having children.

Did you ever have a job after school?

When I was about eleven I had a paper route, delivering the *Call-Bulletin*. The worst route in the whole area — Corinthian Island! Everybody hated that route and old dummy me took it. I got a BIG $5.00 a month! And I had 45, 46 papers. Two or three of the houses that faced the Belvedere side had two or three hundred stairs. And I had to deliver the paper to their doors or they would chew me out. I accommodated them all.

How did you spend the money? Was it yours to do with as you liked?

It was my money! I don't remember what I did with it — I liked candy in those days, and ice cream.

What did you use for transportation when you travelled out of the area?

We rode the *Marin;* we walked up Belvedere Island and down the lane to the landing because it was shorter than going to Tiburon. We all got a big dime and nickel to spend at the candy store and we went to a show in Sausalito! A dime to get in, a nickel for candy, and twenty cents round-trip fare on the ferryboat! We had a day for thirty-five cents!

And then we took a ferryboat to San Francisco. Belvedere to Sausalito to San Francisco. Or if we were going to San Rafael or Mill Valley we'd take the electric train.

Did you go to St. Hilary's on Sunday?

Yes, we walked. When we walked through Tiburon it was either with Mrs. McKinnon or Mrs. Beyries. We were chaperoned and corralled in a bunch so we did not look this way or that way at what was going on. So we went through Tiburon, over the viaduct, then up the hill. It was a long walk, and there was only one mass, at nine o'clock.

Then did you know Miriam Bradley Grbac?

Oh, yes. Mrs. McKinnon taught us catechism in Belvedere and Mrs. Bradley taught in Tiburon. And every Sunday as a rule, Grandma Bradley, that is what we called her, always had huge pans of yeast buns that she baked in a woodstove, and after church we'd all flock in to Grandma Bradley's and have a bun. We did that for years. And then the priest came by the *Marin* and he would have breakfast at the Bradleys.

Even though you did not go to school with the Tiburon children you were in touch?

Yes, but there was a terrible rivalry between Tiburon and Belvedere. Oh, Belvedere always thought it was better than Tiburon, even those of us who lived in the village. A very strong rivalry, heavens yes. I remember kids like the Bremmers, Tuckeys, the Simontacchis, the Polacchis — another branch, not John's family. They were all big kids, and I mean *big* kids. When they went to grammar school they were as big as the teacher! And if the baseball team played the Tiburon school, oh there was a strong rivalry!

What were your school days like?

We had the first, second, and third grades together in one room, about three or four in each grade. There were about twenty children in a combination classroom. Same thing with the higher grades. So when graduation came in the eighth grade we would have a class of seven or eight students graduating. We walked up the hill about three city blocks to the school.

When you reached the 7th and 8th grades there was a cooking room in the downstairs of the school with little electric plates. All we ever learned to make was fudge and soup. The boys had Mr. Wendridge, who came from Tamalpais High School to teach them woodcraft.

Do you recall the names of your teachers?

Oh, yes. She was a Miss Niven when I first went to school and then she became Mrs. Hodge. She was the Niven whose father owned the orchid place in

Rosa and Harry Pariani in their garden on Acacia Avenue, 1940's.

Larkspur. She was killed in an automobile accident years later; some drunk ran into them.

When you later went to Tam did you ride Bill Barr's bus?

Yep! He was Mr. Sloppy. Although he was a clean man, he could never get all the grease out of his clothes and off his hands or face. He used to come by the upper road at eight o'clock and just beep the horn once or twice and the kids would come running and if you were not there you would be left behind and just be sick that day. He had a schedule to meet. And the same thing at night — the bus left Tam at 3:30; if you missed it you walked home.

The school did not pay for the bus — our parents did. I worked in the bookstore at Tam and that paid for my bus fare for the month.

Did any of the Chinese boys who worked on the island go to school with you?

Oh, yes, they usually lived with the people they worked for, the people that stayed all year round. And they got their board and room and probably something like $15 a month.

Were they orphans from China or San Francisco?

I really don't know. They came from San Francisco. I remember Mrs. Boole had one, and the Crockers. Most of them were in school to learn the language; they had come over from China and their parents were still there. There was a Chinese laundry at the base of the drawbridge; they were the only Chinese that lived there.

Did your mother ever use their service?

No. We did not have a washing machine — my mother had a scrub board and two tubs and she scrubbed with Naptha soap. Then she rinsed and wrung and hung them on the line and prayed that the sun would come out. We had long pulley lines off the house. Monday was always wash day.

Did a Chinese vegetable man come to your house?

Oh, yes! I always felt sorry for him; he came from Sausalito with a pole on his shoulder with hanging baskets. And sometimes he would make two trips back to Sausaltio, back to the warehouse or wherever he kept the stuff, because he brought it over from San Francisco. And he would walk up that island and down those horrible steps and so many of those places like Mrs. Bland's place, hers would be the first Beach Road house; it was a long way down to her door. Later when he got older they had a kind of pulley line and she would write out what she wanted and pulley it up, and he would read it and bring the stuff down. But before that he would walk down and take the order, then walk back and fill it, and walk back down to deliver it. And he did this twice a week. The kids used to steal from him. After awhile he got a horse and buggy and that made it a little easier. Then later he had a truck. I don't know what happened to him.

Belvedere had so many ordinances. You had to have a license to come into Belvedere — you didn't to Tiburon — you had to have a license to peddle and a lot would not pay so they could not come in. Tiburon had a Raleigh Man who sold spices and coffee and that kind of thing from his panel truck, but he was never allowed in Belvedere. Sometimes vegetable peddlers would try to talk their way in, but they were kept out. I don't know if they were protecting the grocery stores or what, but Belvedere did not want tradesmen. But the grocery had no vegetables, just staples — canned goods, sugar, rice. They measured out what you wanted and you carried it home in paper bags. We always had crocks and Mama would put eggs down that would keep for month in some kind of brine. Nobody had iceboxes.

Did your mother have a baking day for bread?

No, it wasn't until 1928 that we could heat water. My father would not put a water vac in the stove. Almost all the places had big woodstoves with stovepipes, but my father would not put one in because he said they were always leaking. So if Mama wanted hot water she had to heat it on the stove in an oblong copper boiler with two handles. It took two people to dump it in the bathtub.

So you had a bathtub in your ark?

Oh, we had a bathroom with a basin and a toilet and a bathtub. As I remember it was a funny toilet — it had a big wooden box way up over your head with a long pull-chain.

We didn't have many comforts but we had a bathtub and heat in the house. I used to be sent to the Livermore Valley for the summer because I was a puny kid. I hated it up there. The first time, I thought I was going into no man's land. They did not have an indoor toilet, or a bathtub, or warm water, or an icebox, and the outside was in the chicken yard! It was a vineyard ranch, they had a cow and my parents thought the air would be good for me.

Did your mother sew or make clothes for you?

No, but she was a meticulous housewife. I'm a disgrace to her! I am! She kept a very clean house; she cooked and she cleaned and she worked on the island and did housework for a good many people up there. She worked for Kadah Rice for years and she worked for... I have not thought of these names in so long it is hard to make them come back. She just cooked and kept us clean. And I wore a school dress and when I came home I had to change into an old dress. We wore middy blouses and short bloomers. If you don't think Vicky and I hated those things!

How long did your father live?

Until 1950.

Did he work up until the day he died?

No. He had quit, sort of. Then he had a bad, bad cold, and then cancer. Dr. Milzner would never operate and he never told him. Because he wasn't going to make Harry suffer. If he had operated it would have been a temporary thing — in six months he would have been right back where he was.

Oh, Dr. Milzner had a greenhouse filled with orchids! His yard had rare wildflowers planted everywhere. Pop used to get a lot of flowers from a nursery down the peninsula, Niles, someplace in Niles. But Dad did not work much that last year of his life. I remember that spring he had planted gorgeous begonias, he had to hold up the flowers with sticks, they were so heavy, they were huge! My mother was never allowed to pick anything from the yard. But somebody would walk by when he was working in the yard and say, "Harry, how do you grow them like that? I've never seen anything so beautiful!" And Pop always cut them one or two with a pocketknife he kept in his pocket. My mother would be furious! Now he had an azalea bush by the back door; when my sister ran for the commute bus she'd pluck one. And he could tell that bush had been molested and he'd raise holy Ned. "If you want it, cut, don't break it!"

How long did your mother live there after your father died?

Until 1952. Then she remarried and she passed away in 1968. That was a shock to me. She was 75. Pop was 65 when he died in 1950, so he was born in 1885.

Did your family make wine?

Yes, Papa did. The grapes came from Ukiah and Willits, never from Napa. They were put on a train to Tiburon. Later wineries would have trucks; the driver would take orders and then come down in a huge truck and there would be so much grape for this house and so much for the next. He had just one big load because he came a long distance; in those days a hundred miles was something. All the families would then work together. One would have the press and all had sheds and big barrels. I can't remember when my father finally quit, but he decided that homemade wine was too risky — sometimes you made a good glass of wine and sometimes, depending on the elements, you ended up with sour wine, and that was always too much vinegar to keep on hand. He learned to buy it in twenty-five gallon barrels and have it sent down from one of the wineries.

As a young girl did you take wine with your meals?

No, I'm a poor Italian, I was the only one that did not.

What was a typical family meal?

Soup, My father started all his meals with soup.

Did he come home for lunch?

Yes, he had a dry lunch with things like cheese and salami; depending on the season he liked string beans cooked crisp and then he put olive oil and vinegar over them with salt and pepper and he would eat that for lunch with a half a loaf of French bread. And at night he would have soup.

Dinner was mostly meat and potatoes, whatever was in season in the garden. There was never any dessert, but sometimes for a treat we would have ice cream from the Belvedere grocery store. They had a soda fountain there and would handpack the

Two of Harry Pariani's gardens: the Bridge house (top) and the Holmes house, later owned by Winnie and Harry Allen.

ice cream, chocolate, vanilla, or strawberry. The strawberry had big chunks of fresh strawberries in it. When Lemuel Allen had the store he loved the kids and always made ice cream cookie cones for us. He had cookies on the counter in big glass jars; he would take out two cookies and put two scoops of ice cream on one cookie and then the second on top. It was all for a nickel.

How was it that your father was such a good gardener? Had his father been a gardener before him?

No. His family had lots of acreage in Italy; they were not rich but not poor either. They had lots of land for farming, cows, rabbits, vegetables, so I guess my father just knew how land was worked. My Dad went to work every morning at five and he did not get home until six or seven. That was a long day. My mother would say, "You'll kill yourself, don't you know the island will always be here?"

I have heard that your father always went around with a cigar in his mouth?

Yes, he did, just a little stub. It was not lit, but always in his mouth; he did not chew it, it was just there. Those cigar butts drove my mother crazy. For at times Dad would just put one of those stubs in his shirt pocket and Mom would find it in the laundry tub. Oh, it would make her mad for she would have to wash the whole tub of clothes again.

What did your dad look like?

He was skinny as a rail and always had to wear suspenders to keep his pants up. He looked like a poor alien; his clothes were always clean, but worn. His pants always had holes in the knees from his always being on the ground. Some of the men wore those awful black pants, but his pants were always corduroy, brown, the color of the soil. His shirts were blue denim in the summer and plaid flannel in the winter. Oh, I miss him! And when you saw him dressed up in a tie you didn't recognize him.

Once a year we would get dressed up and go to Golden Gate Park in San Francisco with a gripful of food, fried chicken, you name it. We'd walk and walk and take in a concert; we took in everything. Then we would go to North Beach to Fior de Italia and have a dinner — they served one big meal. I had to be carried home, I was so tired.

Your dad seemed to love his gardens.

Oh, he did. It was not just a job to him — it was his achievement. People would say, "Who does your garden?" and his customers would always answer with pride, "I have Harry."

Mary Bernard, Queen of the Holy Ghost Festival, 1904.

Mary Bernard Silva

1897–

Mary Silva is proud to be a native daughter of California, as was her mother. She is still active in the gatherings of Marin County's large Portuguese community. As a child, a young girl, and a bride, she lived on all three of the dairy ranches on the Tiburon Peninsula. Her grandfather leased land from the Reeds as early as the 1870's; John Joseph Reed was her uncle's godfather. Mary Silva today, at 87, is a striking woman with snow-white hair and deep-set green eyes. She speaks rapidly, with great excitement, her English charmingly flavored by the Portuguese idiom. This interview took place in her home in Mill Valley in 1975.

Could you begin by telling us when you first came to Tiburon to live, Mrs. Silva?

Well, I was born at the Little Reed Ranch. You call it Del Mar now, isn't that it? We took a ride up there recently to try to find the place where our house was. Just one big eucalyptus is all we could find. But from there looking to the road it was just about the right distance, more or less where the ranch house was. Where my grandparents and parents lived, and where I was born.

When did your grandparents arrive? Where did they come from?

I don't know when. But they arrived pretty young, because they married out here. I imagine my grandfather, Manuel Borges, came at an age when he would be able to make his living, because I don't know of any other ancestors before he came out here. He came from the Azore Islands, the Island they call St. George. My grandmother came from the island called Flores, meaning flowers. I have a map and picture of the islands. My mother told me that they met out here somehow. They came out here young, for they were married young. My grandmother was just thirteen! In those days there was no work, so I guess when you found a meal ticket you got married.

Evidently they had other dairy business before they came here to Tiburon. My mother tells me she was born in Tamalpais Valley in 1879; my grandfather had a dairy there. He also had a dairy at what they call "White Gate," on the ridge above Stinson Beach. And that is where my Uncle Manuel was born, the first boy. John Joseph Reed was his godfather. And from there I don't know where they moved. But then my grandfather ended up at Little

Reeds, and that is where my mother got married. She went to the Reed School.

My mother met my father at the dairy. He probably had come from the old country, from the Azores. But my mother was a native daughter of California. They were the first couple to marry at St. Hilary's in Tiburon. That's what my mother used to tell me.

Did your mother tell you much of her school days at the Reed School?

Oh, yes. She went to school there with Mrs. Wolfe's mother, Mrs. McCombie. My mother had a couple of teachers before Miss Hauss. Miss Hauss was my teacher all the way through. My mother had other teachers but I can't remember their names. All her brothers went to school there.

So I don't know if my father was just a worker or whether he was a partner at the Little Reed Ranch. I think he owned part of it. For they used to form partnerships. They would buy one share, buy and sell. And from there he went down to Hilarita, to another dairy there. I have that picture also. There was the dairy house where the cook cooked for the men, and in back of that, way back by the creek, was a little cottage where my mother lived. That is where my brother John was born.

Hilarita Dairy was closer to Tiburon. And from there I started going to the Tiburon School. I walked right down the railroad tracks. A young fellow at the ranch was going to school, so my mother would let him take me. I remember going down the track and he taking me by the hand. Sometimes my mother and I and my brother would ride up in the milk wagon to see my grandmother at Little Reeds.

That didn't last long. There must have been a change; my father sold what he had at Hilarita and came back to Little Reeds. He used to drive a spring wagon to deliver the milk. The other day I saw on TV a spring wagon with a team just like my father used to deliver the milk, and right away I thought of it. And my mother cooked for the men in the dairy house, where Mary Brazil later took over.

Were there a lot of men living at the dairy house?

Well, there was my father, John Bernard; my grandfather lived in his own house. There must have been two or three more. You know kids don't pay any attention to those things. They lived right in the ranch house, where the cook was. My mother was cooking for the men.

And then the year before the earthquake, in 1905, my Grandmother Borges died. So my mother stopped cooking and went home to take care of her father and my father and us kids. Her brother was just my age and there were two other older ones. And she went there to take care of them, wash, cook, what have you. I went to Reed School.

Now the house you refer to at Little Reeds, was it on the bay side or the dairy side of the road?

On the dairy side, up towards the hills. And the main dairy house was on the opposite side of the road, toward the beach.

Your father delivered milk in a spring wagon?

To Hilarita Station. There was a platform there and the Hilarita Dairy also delivered milk there.

Was there a road between the dairies?

Oh, yes, a dirt road connecting the dairies. If you wanted to go to Tiburon you had to go along the spit, what you call now San Rafael Avenue. We used to call it the spit. Or we'd walk down the railroad track, or take the train from Hilarita down to Tiburon.

And so then a woman came from the Azores to stay at the main dairy house, with this other couple that was her uncle. Well, my grandfather being a widower, they made a match. So my grandfather married this woman and naturally took her home. So we moved out. My father sold his share and we went to Big Reeds, which is the Deffebach property now, at Bel Air. We drove up there the other day. It is so changed I couldn't find where the old house was or anything. My father was the foreman of that dairy. But he worked! He had to get up at two o'clock in the morning and round up the cows. And when a man would quit he had to get out and milk too. And there is where my youngest brother was born, Manuel, who is thirteen years younger than I am. My brother John, in between, was born at Hilarita, ten years earlier. I was born at Little Reeds, John at Hilarita and my youngest brother at Big Reeds. So I got married at Big Reeds in 1913.

Top: Hilarita Ranch house, 1902. The foreman (left) and family of Antone Souza (second left) lived in the house; milkers ate meals prepared by the cook in room at right. Below: Mary Borges Bernard with Mary and John Bernard, Hilarita, 1900.

Why were the dairies called Little Reeds and Big Reeds?

Maybe one had more cows or more acres than the other one.

Where did the name Borges Ranch come from?

From my mother's side of the family. It was my Grandfather Borges' ranch first, then my father took over.

Your father's last name was Bernard?

Yes. It was supposed to be De Souza, but everyone knew him by Bernard. His name legally should be John Bernard De Souza, but he took the name of his godfather and dropped De Souza.

Which was called the Borges Ranch?

Little Reeds. Little Reeds and Big Reeds, that's the way we knew them. And I was married there at Big Reeds, when I was sixteen. My husband, Oliveira, had a delivery business in Mill Valley, a creamery.

How did you meet him?

His sister lived near us.

Where did the workmen live on the ranches?

They had their own house. At Hilarita they had a little cabin or shack where they slept. But they ate at the main house where the cook was. The foreman lived about the same as the men, as far as rank was concerned. We had a separate house to live in but nothing like the homes we have nowadays. The foreman would go do the shopping and order the hay or feed for the cattle.

Were all the dairymen Portuguese?

Yes, at that time they were, for when they came out here they didn't know the language, naturally. And they did not have the opportunities of people who were educated in English. So they'd come to the dairies to get their start. Those fellows would invest a few dollars in a share of the business, because they'd make a little bit more that way. And when they didn't want to work on the dairy any more my father would buy them out. Another guy would come along so he'd sell it to him. That's the way they'd do. That's how my father would do, you know. My grandfather did the same thing.

As I was saying, I was married and my husband had a creamery over in Mill Valley. So I came to live over here. And then he decided to sell the creamery. And we went back beyond Muir Woods, to Frank Valley, to a dairy there. My husband bought into business there and we lived there. I didn't do the cooking though. They had a woman whose husband was his partner and she did the cooking. There was a bunk house there, three or four blocks from the main house; that's where I lived. He would eat at the dairy house and sleep at home. We were there quite a few years. In fact my father also invested in business there.

Then there was a vacancy at Hilarita; they had broken up the dairy there. Mr. Souza and some others. So our cows were brought from Frank Valley down to Hilarita, and I ended up at Hilarita again. So my husband was the foreman there. We were at Hilarita for quite a few years. I ended up cooking for the men, and got twenty dollars a month.

Did you grow your own vegetables?

No. The foreman bought the food for the dairymen from the commission, now it would be called a wholesale house. They bought everything in bulk, in San Francisco, and it was ferried over and came by train. When we were at Big Reeds we got our provisions that way also.

Did you do your other shopping on Main Street?

Yes. My mother said when she was cooking at Little Reeds she would buy twenty-five cents' worth of soup meat; that would be enough for four or five men to eat. It must have been Anderson's meat market.

But when my husband moved his cows to Hilarita from Frank Valley I went to live in a house in Tiburon, by the school up on the hill. We had a hard time pulling the furniture up that hill near old St. Hilary's. The house was between the church and the school. I wasn't there very long because my husband did not like to go up to the dairy and back down again. So there was an ark for sale in Hilarita, an awful run-down old place, right over the water. But we bought it. We painted it. It was a crummy place, I'll have to admit. Of course no inside plumbing. But there was just the two of us. He got an old bathtub from someplace and we put it in the

Left: The John Bernard family, 1903. Right: Mary Bernard Silva, 1950's.

Top: The first Reed School, 1890's. Left: Miss Hauss; Manuel Borges and his sister Mary (mother of Mary Silva) stand behind her. Schoolroom was at left, woodshed at right. Below: Reed School, 1910, from the other side. From left: Mary Brazil, Frank Borges, little cousin Mary Borges, Miss Hauss, Albert Silveira, Mary Bernard, Amilia Silveira, Armond Silveira, Angelina Silveira. Trestle leads to tunnel at left.

bedroom. I used to heat the water and then bring the boiler in and pour it into the tub for our bath. We had a living room and a bedroom and a kitchen. In those years you washed your clothes on a washboard; I still use one to do my little wash. And we had a little vegetable garden right by the water. And a few chickens. The railroad track was right up practically against the back of the ark; we were on the lagoon side of the track. There were a few other arks along there, Italian people. And the weather was not too bad, not too many storms that I remember. You got used to it.

We got so used to the train noise! They had side tracks where they lined up the freight cars. It wasn't even about as far as from here to that wall, about fifteen feet. Sometimes the tracks would be full of cars and next morning they would all be gone and we hadn't even heard it. Or at night there would be no cars there and the next morning the side track was full of cars. They would leave an opening so we could get through.

We had an outhouse, way out over the water, with just two planks connecting it to our back porch. We had to walk over the two planks. Now I wouldn't be able to do it; I would tumble in the water! And the tide went in and out, because there was an opening in the spit.

The Italian family living next to us was the Simontacchi's. I think they worked in the railroad shops down in Tiburon. One of the Italian neighbors had a rowboat. I didn't know how to swim, but the girl did. And she dared me to go on a boat ride with her, so I got in the boat and she rowed and rowed and we went to the underpass where the water went in and out and she tried to get the boat to go through that! But the boat wouldn't go through; we had to duck down in the boat. She wanted to go out into the bay. And I couldn't swim! I was so simple I didn't know what to do. I could have drowned. But I went no more.

How many people did you cook for at the Hilarita Dairy?

Five. Breakfast, lunch, and dinner. We had no gas, no electric. We had a woodstove. The men got up early, at 2:30 in the morning. So they had a cup of coffee and bread and cheese. Then their breakfast was a big meal: beans and eggs, pancakes and eggs. We killed our own hogs, and we had what the Portuguese call *linquesa.* Every day it was beans for breakfast, beans every day. I baked bread three times a week, in big pans, with six loaves in each pan. When the bread was fresh those hardworking men would come in and really go through it. And then for lunch it was always soup and a pudding or pie or cake. And believe it or not at that time I went up over two hundred pounds!

No! But you are so slim!

Now I am, yes. Then I was as wide as I was tall. We were raised to be thrifty. Sometimes I'd make a pudding and everybody had a serving and there was some left. Well, I wasn't going to throw it away. It wasn't enough to serve again. So who ate it? The cook ate it. I'd make a pie or two or a cake and there was a couple of pieces left. You can't serve it, so instead of giving it to the chickens, so who ate it? The cook ate it. It just kept going up and up. See in that picture how big I was?

The dinner was potatoes and fish. The dried fish was either codfish or that other one they call sera. We soaked the fish because it was salted, and we cooked it and made a gravy with a little bit of onion and tomato and thickened it with flour, salt and pepper. Then they would pour that over their boiled potatoes. That was their supper. And bread — that was practically every day. Now they have their roast and legs of lamb and their bread is bought. Of course everything has changed now.

There was no such thing as buying bread then; bread was always made at home. We had our own starter from our homemade yeast. We'd take mashed potatoes and add water and a little flour. Boiled a couple of potatoes and put some of that same water back in the potato, and a little flour and a little starter from before, and the next morning it was up high, and mix that with the flour and knead it, and put a little of the starter back in the bottle for the next batch of bread. We did that every two or three days, so there was no problem with it getting stale, even through we had no refrig. Every other day we baked, two pans of six loaves each. Can you imagine getting a wood stove hot in the morning, hot enough to make a stack of pancakes for the men? Sometimes the wood was wet and it was hard to get it to burn. Oh, we would almost sweat blood! Well, that is the kind of life we had, but we survived.

Along the Tiburon railroad tracks in the early 1920's, many of the arks which had once floated in Belvedere Cove are secured on pilings and occupied by railroad and dairy workers. Belvedere (left) is joined by the spit to Tiburon peninsula. Although wires bring electricity to Tiburon, the highway down to Main Street has not yet been built. Ark dwellers who wanted to go to Main Street either walked down the tracks or rowed to the back doors of the shops.

You were very self-sufficient on the ranches.

You had to be. There was no other way if you wanted to make a living. When my father came out here to start he got $20 or $25 a month.

Did you have your own orchards?

Yes, we had orchards, and we'd go up the line someplace and get tomatoes and then can them ourselves. We didn't go to the store; they didn't have canned food in the store at that timne. It would take a man a whole day to go in the wagon to Novato for big crates of tomatoes.

And up where Hilarita Housing is now, that was all hayfields. They seeded it and plowed it and cut hay for the cows. They had a big fork to pull it into the loft of the barn, and that is what they fed the cows.

So then my husband decided to sell, that's when the Avilas took over the dairy. My husband and I moved back to Big Reeds. See what I was talking about — I just kept going back and forth, back and forth.

Was your father still at Big Reeds when you moved back?

No. He had bought this property here which goes along Alvarado and Elm, this whole block here in Mill Valley. He had moved here. So my husband was the foreman at Big Reeds. I didn't live in the main house or the house I had lived in before. The house I lived in was the last one you can go to in Bel Air. It is still there. The girl who is living in it wanted to show it to me because I described it to her when I had lived there. She said they had made some changes in it. I said I didn't want to go in because I have it pictured in my mind. It was a three-bedroom house with a living room and dining room. It must have been the home of someone wealthy at one time, maybe some of the Reeds. Because from the dining room to the kitchen was an opening so the maid could serve the food through, and on the right of the kitchen was a room for the maid. So it had to be somebody involved in the Reed family, it couldn't be anybody else. The new people had painted it and added a garage.

So we lived there for a while, and then my husband bought a gas station. In the meantime my father gave him a lot, a couple of acres of his land in Mill Valley. So we built a house, which is still here, the last up at the intersection. My husband bought a gas station down where the road turns off to Stinson Beach. I don't remember now why he did it. He worked at the station alone — such a contrast, from cows to a service station! Such a mixed up affair, from one thing to another. Then he wanted me to go down and help him pump gas. He didn't believe I should stay home and take it easy. But my father didn't think that was the place for me. So I decided I wasn't going to go, I was going to stay in my house. So my husband got disgusted and sold the station to his cousin.

My father had owned a big ranch with some other men; it went all the way back to Muir Woods. So they dissolved the partnership and sold the property, and my father bought back nineteen acres. He paid five or six thousand dollars for it. Don't forget that was sixty or sixty-five years ago. Maybe even longer, because my dad has been dead for forty-one years.

There was a little dairy there, so my husband ran that and I lived in the little house and did the cooking. My house here in Mill Valley was vacant. He would sometimes take off with some of his friends and go up to Idaho to buy cattle. And I would stay up there all by myself cooking for the hired man.

I'm kind of a funny person sometimes. I had taken so many bumps and moves and so much work. So I told my husband instead of having a single hired man, get a married man and let her do the cooking for her husband, and I'll go live in my house in Mill Valley. He went right by that house to deliver milk every day. He could stop for breakfast in the morning and at night instead of going back to the ranch stay home. He wasn't about to do that. He wanted me to stay there on the ranch. I wasn't going to stay. So that ended our marriage.

Are these pictures of the ranch?

That was Muir Wood Ranch. That picture shows the little house where I was living, the little bunkhouse in back there. This is my little dog. And that was my little baby, a boy named Edward Anthony Oliveira, born May 18, 1918. He passed away when he was almost two years old, in the flu epidemic, that was in Frank Valley.

Let's go back and fill in some gaps, back to your days as a child going to Reed School.

When I started going to Reed School I was living

Top: Mary Silva's mother with her brothers (from left) Frank, Joe, and Manuel, standing in front of the gate at Big Reed Ranch, about 1913. Below: Hilarita Dairy Ranch, also known as the Souza Ranch, about 1903. The Souza family leased the ranch from the Reed family, 1902–1927. At far right is Antone J. Souza. The rider has brought the cows into the corral for milking. Men hold milking buckets; one has a baby on his arm. Reed School is now on this site.

at Little Reeds, at my grandfather's. I went to school with my uncles. Then when we moved to Big Reeds I went with some of the girls here in the picture, and the teacher, Miss Hauss. She lived right at the ranch, at the foot of the Reed house, in a little cottage by a dirt road that led to the dairy. She walked up to Reed Station and we'd all walk to school along the railroad track and through the tunnel. *(Looking at photos of the old Reed School.)* That is the rear end of it. And yes, this is me *(pointing to a tall, very attractive girl).* I could have been about thirteen or fourteen. I went through the eighth grade; in those days that was where you stopped. I wasn't very old because I married when I was sixteen. I was always a big person for my age, always was. And this one is my uncle, my mother's youngest brother. He is my age — just six months older than me. He is still living, down in Santa Barbara. He's the only one left.

Where was Reed Station?

It was where Bel Air is now, but the tracks, the station, everything has disappeared.

Wasn't it dangerous to get caught in the tunnel with a train coming?

Well we thought so at first, but we found out it wasn't. You know the tunnels had great big timbers that held up the hill, and there was plenty of room between two timbers to get a person in there. Nothing would get you between the two timbers. We'd hear that buzz on the track, and the kids would put their ears down on the rail and say, "Oh-oh, a train is going to come before we get through!" And we would hear that little rumble on the rail. And the teacher would say, "Get in the timbers!" And everyone would get in between timbers. And after the train had gone by the tunnel was all smoky but we'd just follow the train out.

What was the schoolhouse like? Did you have water in the school?

Oh, no! And that was fun for us because two of us would take a bucket and go under the trestle and on the other side there was a water trough for cattle, and a faucet. We would go get water and bring it back in that pail. We did have desks — a couple of single ones, the rest doubles. I know I had a single one.

What did you do for heat?

We had a pot-belly stove. We had a little shed to the side where we kept the wood. When it was raining and stormy and blowing we'd still walk to school. We'd get our feet all wet, and when we got there we'd take off our shoes and stockings and dry them in front of that pot belly stove. That's the way it was.

Were all the children from the dairies?

Yes, they were all dairy children. In that picture, that was the whole school; that was toward the end. Before that there had been more; the McCombies had been there. And others had moved away. Those Silveira boys, there in the picture, they moved away too. They went to Mill Valley school; just like Grace McCombie, they wanted a better education. Miss Hauss was getting pretty old. But us poor little peasants, we were on the ranches; we could not go anywhere else. We had to stay there. I went through the eighth grade there.

Who paid Miss Hauss's salary?

The state. She was a regular school teacher. But she was one of the Reed clan. I don't mean she was related, but it was through them she got the job, I imagine, because she spoke in Spanish like they did. I imagine she was from Mexico also.

What language did you speak in school?

We spoke in English. We might've spoke some Portuguese because the other big girl lived right across the creek from us and we'd get together and play, and I imagine we did speak some Portuguese because my parents couldn't speak anything else.

What kind of clothes did you wear to school?

Just dresses my mother would make, like you saw in the picture. I was so sophisticated, you know! With my big breasts and my waist tightened in and a rat in my hair. At that time people wore rats, long pieces we would roll our hair over. I always had very fine hair and it would never stay up like that. It wasn't until we moved down to Hilarita and we were married that I cut my hair. And for the first few weeks I wore a bonnet so no one would see me with my hair cut.

Did the ranch workers all speak Portuguese?

Oh, yes, that is why I learned the Portuguese, because my father he spoke English but broken, and my mother was a native daughter but mingling with all those Portuguese people on the ranches she was more used to the Portuguese than she was the English. She spoke Portuguese with my father and that is how I learned it.

So you had your own little colony? Did you get together socially?

Yes, once in a while when we were at Big Reeds. We danced. It wasn't an orchestra; they played the fiddle and banjo. We danced the Samaritas, a Portuguese dance. They had a caller, and we had our good times that way. And then at the same dairy were two women and two men working, so there were two more matches. My mother made their wedding dresses; she used to sew very nice. I remember them going to San Rafael to get married. They took the train; they had their veils on and their dresses, and everybody, the whole wedding party, went on the train to the San Rafael church. They got married and came home on the train again and then they had a Samarita in the great big room where they used to cool the milk, where years ago they used to make butter. They had racks where they put those round pans to skim the milk. Now that was all pushed to one side of the room and they'd have the dance and good times.

Now when I got married my husband had a creamery here in Mill Valley. There was a stable right next door. He got a horse and buggy to bring us here to Mill Valley; we got married here, in the old church way up on the hill, and went back to the ranch for the celebration.

Did you and your family use the ferryboats?

Oh, yes, if we went to San Francisco. And I can still vaguely remember riding on the streetcar drawn by horses; I was small but I remember it.

What was the main purpose for going to the City?

Probably to buy clothes. Because you know we didn't have Mill Valley or Corte Madera; these were all dairies around here. I don't know if San Rafael had stores or not. It was much easier to go on the ferryboat to San Francisco and shop there. We would walk down the railroad track into Tiburon and get right on the ferry. They were much bigger than the ones now.

Did you ever come in contact with the men from the codfishery?

Oh, yes. I was at the dairy at Hilarita, cooking for the men, and Mr. and Mrs. Souza lived right opposite the Hilarita Station on the lagoon side. They were retired from the dairy business. So she'd come up and help me with the dishes after the men had had their lunch. And they liked to fish, so lots of times we'd take off and go fishing. We'd walk along the spit and over the hill, because at that time you couldn't go along the waterline. And just about where the spit ends was a little dairy at the base of Belvedere Island. You know they didn't always have milk in containers which they leave at the doors now. They used to have it in a big can and if you wanted a quart of milk they would measure it and pour it out for you. This little dairy had milk but no cows. They bought milk and delivered it in the area. That dairy supplied most of the people in Belvedere and Tiburon. My brother John Bernard worked there.

Anyway we fished right there at the fish yard where they dried the fish. The men did not mind us sitting right on the docks to fish. We would see the men slicing the fish open. I think they were already salted.

Were these workers Portuguese?

Some were Portuguese. It was a mix, mostly English and Italian. And I remember the big ships that brought the fish in, seeing them anchored out in Richardson Bay.

What church did you go to as a child?

When I was a small child in Little Reeds we didn't go at all. We just stayed home on Sundays and that was it. Then we came to Big Reeds and I went to catechism and to mass at the Sisters of Mercy on Strawberry Point. And then when we moved to Mill Valley naturally we had the Mill Valley church.

So you never went to St. Hilary's then?

No, never did. Well, we'd have to walk.

Did your family celebrate the Portuguese holidays?

Oh, yes. We did celebrate and still do. They call

it the Holy Ghost Festival. They still have it, down in Sausalito. A religious procession and all. We just had it. And they used to decorate the cattle. Then they slaughtered those cattle to feed the people. But of course it is entirely different now than it was in those days. Now they don't decorate the cattle. They don't have their own cattle. They go all over asking people to donate cattle, and then they slaughter seven or eight cows. And they have a feed and everything is free. They have a mass at church and they have a queen and a procession and they had a drill team this year and bands.

Well, everything that was Portuguese years ago has gone mixed; now there is nothing that you can say is Portuguese any more. Even the organizations I belong to now, two of them, you had to be of Portuguese descent, you didn't have to speak the language, but you had to be a descendant. But not any more. And you also had to be a Catholic. Now you just have to be a good Christian.

You were a queen once?

I was, in 1904. And I was honored a week ago down in Sausalito; I was the oldest of the bunch and they had the platform all full of queens.

Can we ask how old you are?

Seventy-seven! Yep!

Lester Stone in the 1970's.

Lester Stone

1892–1975

We interviewed Mr. Stone in Alameda in 1975, in a room full of nautical memorabilia, photos, boat models, books, magazines stacked on shelves, tables, floor. A fourth-generation boat builder, he is a man of huge accomplishments; his knowledge of sailing was encyclopedic, and his excitement contagious. The influence he and his father and grandfather had on the design and building of boats in San Francisco Bay is immeasurable. Many of their boats are still sailing today. Twinkling with wit and charm, Lester Stone was the warmest, most gracious man we ever met, a true gentleman.

Can you tell us a little about your family, Mr. Stone? When did you come to Tiburon?

Well, this goes back to ancient history! I was a year old when we moved to Tiburon in 1893. My father, William F. Stone, established a boatshop, his first place of business, just west of the drawbridge, on Beach Road. He built a lot of boats — a lot of boats! He was there, let me see, from 1893 to 1899, and built quite a number of the yachts of that era.

My grandfather, William I. Stone, came from England; Dartmouth was his home. My father, William F. Stone, was born in San Francisco. My grandfather had his boatyard at what is now the Anderson & Cristofani yard in San Francisco. That is where I was born, right in the boatyard.

Was your grandfather a boatbuilder in England?

Yes, and his father was. Four generations of boatbuilders. They were small boatbuilders in England. They built ships' boats, lifeboats, that sort of thing. And then when my grandfather came to San Francisco, the largest boat he ever built was the schooner yacht *Halcyon,* about eighty feet. Then when my dad came along he got into big wooden shipbuilding. I went about as big as they ever went. There was a limit in wood, you know, 250 feet. I know of very few wooden ships much in excess of that. There were some in the first war, but in wood that was about the limit.

When we were in Belvedere my father built boats mainly for people from somewhere else. He didn't build a great many. I would guess maybe an average of two boats a year.

My parents sold their property on Beach Road in 1899. I think there was about 75 to 100 feet of beach frontage. I think he sold it for $600.

Top: The Stone boatworks on Beach Road, 1896. Lester, age four, and Jack Stark stand beside the Nixie, *under construction. The Stones lived in the house behind. Below: Stone boatyard, looking toward Corinthian.*

Do you know who bought the boatyard?

Yes, Pete Swanson. He kept it going as a boatyard for quite a long time, ten or fifteen years. Pete Swanson built a lot of boats over there. He built some very good early power boats; he was almost the pioneer of motorboats in that era.

So in 1899 my father moved to San Francisco, where he started a boatyard at Harbor View, on the site of the present-day St. Francis Yacht Club. He built some very big vessels there. He moved to the Oakland estuary in 1911, when construction began for the 1915 Exposition. I was down in Stanford at that time; I went to Stanford a couple of years, but I left in 1912 and went to work with my dad. I've been here ever since. I sold the place in 1970 to a chap named John Whitset. I spent 58 years of my life on the estuary.

Why did your father move from Belvedere to San Francisco?

He wanted to get into bigger business. In San Francisco he built some very large boats, 250 feet long. You couldn't begin to build boats that size in Belvedere.

Was his business affected much by the 1906 earthquake?

At his yard in San Francisco there was no serious damage. At that time he was building the *Yankee,* and she was knocked down off the blocking along with two or three other boats.

Were you able to continue working afterward?

Yes. The machinery had to be re-aligned; the little office needed minor repairs. If the fire hadn't come along I don't think any of us would have remembered the earthquake. It was the fire that did the damage. I lived out at the end of Union at the time, Union and Lyon, right up against the Presidio Wall. I went with a friend up to the top of the hill there, on Broadway. From there you could get a tremendous view. I went with my friend to his apartment, beyond Van Ness and Lombard, to get a few of his belongings. The fire was about three blocks away, and was eating up about one block in ten to fifteen minutes. It would just race through. We got out of his house when the fire was two blocks away. I saw a continuous line of fire from Telegraph hill to way out in the Mission. It burned for four days, and on the fourth day the wind came up from the west and saved everything west of Van Ness Avenue. It was a terrible, terrible thing! And when you think that in 1915 the City of San Francisco put on this elaborate, never-to-be-equaled show! The Pan Pacific Exposition. Today you could no more equal it than fly. Just think, 1906 to 1915, nine years. Oh, that was just a beautiful exposition, just terrific.

I had a terrific experience at that time. I had the old *Pronto.* This chap, Howard Norton, and I lived aboard the *Pronto* in the yacht harbor in San Francisco and commuted to work in Oakland. We had a little Japanese boy to cook for us, and we were just a couple of kids. You couldn't match the fun we had. Business was very slack at that time, and we lived the life of Reilly, right in the middle of the fair, every night! Other boats were doing the same thing. One was the *Lady Ada,* she belonged to the Zellerbach family; they were there most of the time. And Captain Barnison owned the schooner next to us, just across the float. He was a fine old guy. We were a little noisy once in a while. And the next morning old Captain Barnison would come up on deck and say, "Well, boys, you had quite a good time last night. I came pretty close to coming over." But he never did.

Do you remember Belvedere and Tiburon from when you lived there?

I was only six years old when we left Belvedere, but I have been a member of the Corinthian Yacht Club for the last hundred years! So I practically lived there. My whole life I've been involved over there to some extent. Coming from the old ferryboat I used to walk up to the Corinthian Club, I did that for years and years. We rode over every weekend from Oakland on the old *Jimmy Donahue.*

(Mr. Stone examines an old photo of Beach Road.)

The building here next to the boatshop was later the old Olympic Club, a branch of the San Francisco Club. They had rowing and swimming, kind of a beach club. It was nothing much, just a place to get away; I think it was later abandoned.

The drawbridge was to the left of us. The bridge was lifted with two purchase tackles, one on each corner. Two or three horses pulled it up. The thing was only raised twice a year, to let the boats in and out. They towed the arks in and out at the same time.

Top: Harbor View Boatyard, San Francisco, 1908, on the exact site of today's St. Francis Yacht Club, looking north across the bay. At right: W.F. Stone, Lester's father, third-generation boat-builder.

They had to get out at high tide, because the boats in the lagoon would be on the mud at low tide. The bridge was open for two or three hours, maybe. It was quite an event.

Do you know who built the arks or where they came from?

George Wellington built one ark. My father built the barge for it and they put it in the water, and they had a carpenter, a house builder, build this little cottage. It was a delightful little place, built right on the barge. It had nothing to do with boating; it was just like you had planted a house on this barge. There were potted plants — oh, it was beautiful. The ark colony was lovely.

Do you recall the Night in Venice festivities?

Distinctly! I remember there would be a big barge brought over from San Francisco, anchored in the middle of the cove. The arks would be all around, decorated with Chinese lanterns — see, there was no electricity in those days. Chinese lanterns with candles in them. And on the barge was a band, and there would be singing and band music. Oh, it was beautiful! The whole of Belvedere Island was decorated with lanterns, they were so beautiful. People came over from San Francisco to see it. And of course we knew quite a number of people up on the Island. We used to call it the Island. I guess they don't any more. Well, there were no accommodations for visitors. The Belvedere Hotel was so limited. The cottages next door to the hotel are still there today. The Belvedere Lagoon behind the hotel was a big marsh. I went to the hotel many times as a kid. A little kid of six didn't have many privileges around there.

And there was the old Sonoma House down in Tiburon. Mr. and Mrs. Carpenter were managing it. He later opened a grocery, the Carpenter of Carpenter and Chapman. The Sonoma House was an adjunct to the railroad yards, a boarding house in the early days.

(Mr. Stone looks at another old picture.)

This is Belvedere School, let me see, in 1898. That is when I started to school. Now pick out the good-looking one, that's me. (laughter) That is Miss Boynton, our teacher. I have never forgotten Miss Boynton. She was one of the sweetest... Oh, she was lovely! She was just one of the happy memories. This is Netal Miller; the Miller family lived in Belvedere. This is Tommy Gannan from Tiburon, Jim McLean from Belvedere, and Bess McLean. This is me, with the necktie on. I was six years old then. I value that old picture. This was the whole school, you see, eight classes. I think there are eight children in all.

Here is a picture of the beach at Belvedere. Those two houses above are still there today. The McLeans built those places. Neil McLean was a contractor; he had a lot to do with building the Exposition in 1915. Dan McLean remained in Belvedere until his death. Sandy McLean was quite a character. Poor old Sandy, he was a good guy.

There's Uncle John's place, John Pew, he was a wonderful fellow. He controlled the Union Codfishery; had his office in San Francisco. His house, the Pagoda House, was built about 1890. The old Tropic Bird was there on Beach Road; she just disintegrated, rotted away.

Half the houses on Belvedere must be more than fifty years old, because Belvedere in the early days looked pret'near as it does today.

Did you ever go to El Campo?

Oh, goodness, yes. The excursion boats used to come over, old sternwheelers, with groups from the city, public parties, the bricklayers' union. El Campo was a big picnic ground, with an open dance hall. Groups could rent it for a day or weekend. There was nothing there; you had to bring cooking utensils and food. Sometimes there were pretty wild parties, I remember as a kid. The yacht clubs don't hold any corner on quiet time.

(Looking at more old pictures.)

I remember Burke's old bar room. It was a saloon.

Were women allowed in saloons?

No! Never!

What about women in the yacht club?

Well, in the early days of the CYC women were hardly ever permitted. We used to have Ladies' Day once or twice in the sailing season. There were lady friends on those days, but normally NO!

Here is a picture of the old Corinthian Yacht Club, the little old red clubhouse, on the point of Corinthian Island. It was very much like today's, but on

Top: The Jimmy Donahue *tied up at Tiburon. Below: The drawbridge which gave rise to the name "Opening Day" on San Francisco Bay, 1890's.*

a smaller scale. The upstairs was a big hall with a stage where they had their high jinks. The present clubhouse was built in 1911.

Were you or your father ever Commodore of the CYC?

My father was, I think in 1908–1910.

Could you give us an idea of sailing in your time?

At the CYC we had a regatta on May 30th, Decoration Day, and another on Admission Day, September 9. In the meantime there were races. But in the early days of sailing, racing was not all the time. Now it is ALL THE TIME, night and day! The present yachting people don't know how to enjoy their boats, they don't cruise, they don't go anywhere, they race, race, race! Good gracious, we never missed a weekend of cruising. We'd go up the bay somewhere, Paradise Cove, Napa Slough, Vallejo, the Delta country. Hundreds of trips up in the Delta country.

Your boats were used mainly for pleasure, and racing was secondary?

Oh, strictly. Now it is the other way around. There is too much racing now. I don't know any more about modern racing than a two-year-old baby. I don't know the classifications, I don't know one boat from another.

I was out on opening day last year (1974) in my little boat. There were something like 3500 boats reported in the bay. How many do you think I recognized? Denny Jordan's motorsailor, the *Cordonza*. She was the ONLY boat that I recognized! Now I sat in my little boat and purposely did not get into the parade. We knocked around the upper bay, just jogging around aimlessly. I thought I'd go through Racoon Straits and around west of Angel Island and run for home in Alameda. When we came around the point it was just one mass of sailboats coming down through the straits. I swear it would have been impossible for us to have made our way under sail through this mass of boats. I never thought I would ever see anything like it on San Francisco Bay! And I didn't know one boat or one person aboard any one of them. I used to pass one boat every twenty miles — "There's Bill. There's Tom." Oh, it is so different today. Now there are thousands of boats; we used to think of them in the dozens. And the boats all look exactly alike. I can't tell one from another. One is 23 feet long, the next class is 25 feet long. It has lost its thrill, at least for this old fogey.

You see, this mass of boats has only come upon us in the last ten years; it's all new. I think it's wonderful, but I'd like to see more sailing and less competing. Competition all the time spoils it. We were serious about racing, but we only had seven to ten boats in our class. We cruised everywhere.

Can you tell us about some of the boats you and your father built?

I've got a list here. Some years ago I made a list and I'm glad I did, I couldn't do it today. Here is a partial list of boats built by my grandfather in San Francisco between 1853 and 1893:

Edna	40′ sloop
Queen	42′ sloop yacht
Peerless	45′ schooner yacht
Startled Fawn	45′ schooner yacht
Josie	25′ sloop yacht
Flirt	22′ sloop yacht
Dixie	25′ sloop yacht
White Wings	50′ schooner yacht
Belle	25′ sloop yacht
Mist	22′ sloop yacht
Dawn	35′ sloop yacht
Speedwell	45′ sloop yacht
Emerald	45′ yawl yacht
Cupid	25′ sloop yacht
La Paloma	45′ schooner yacht
Halcyon	82′ schooner yacht
Thetis	130′ sloop yacht
Idler	45′ yawl yacht
Magic	42′ sloop yacht

And here are the boats my father, William F. Stone, built in Belvedere between 1893 and 1899:

Name	Length & Type	Owner
Mary	25′ sloop	H.D. Hawks
Witch	25′ yawl	William Brook
Mignon	33′ sloop	George Biber
Aeolus	35′ sloop	Carl Westerfield
Arituras	35′ aux. yawl	Henry Gorter
Nixie	52′ sloop	George Billings
Emma	39′ sloop	George Taylor
Amigo	34′ sloop	Joseph Matoon
Idler	23′ sloop	Thomas Miller
Gladys	38′ sloop	Thomas Hobron
Tramontana	68′ yawl	H. Simpkins
Presto	33′ sloop	W. F. Stone

Then in San Francisco between 1899 and 1911 he built big vessels, from 100 feet up to 255 feet. And in Oakland after I started we built vessels of 235 and 255 feet. First World War boats too.

Northern Light was the largest yacht we ever built, 114 feet. She had quite a history. We built her for John Borden, a Chicago man. She cost pretty close to $400,000 when I built her in 1927. That was a lot in those days. Today she'd cost two million. I built her just before the stock market crash.

I hope you got paid for the job.

That I did, that I did. And John Borden made a cruise to the Arctic Ocean in her. She was built primarily for that Arctic cruise. They went up as far as navigation would permit, up to Wrangel and Harold Islands. Then he returned and sold or gave the boat to his sister. And she went around the world on a cruise. Eventually *Northern Light* became a pilot schooner up in Boston. Then the second World War came and the government took her over; she was a training ship for Navy boys in Florida. After that she was sold to a fishing outfit up in Newfoundland or Nova Scotia. And I haven't heard of her since.

During World War II we built four minesweepers, two subchasers, and two firetugs for the Navy. It took us about four years to do it, with an average crew of 250 people. After the war it was practically all yachts.

You've designed quite a few boats, haven't you?

Oh yes. *Via* was my design; I built and owned her, 1955-67. The *Waterwitch,* 1926, *Mariles,* named after my wife, *Rascal, Active* — those are all my designs. I also built *Gypsy, Sparrow, Frolic.* In 1937 I built the *Senta* for Bechtel. *Tasko* for Tom Short. *Yankee Doodle* for Leo Tobin; she was his own design. Also *Windward* for Leo Tobin, *Honolulu,* 1949. *Alert* for Ken Bechtel. And the *Galatia* and *Seaweed*. And *Pronto II* was my boat, built her myself and raced her out of the Corinthian Yacht Club, in 1917. Of course, getting to the R class, the *Rascal,* that was the beginning of the end. That was the serious racing. Now with the *Little Rascal* we did nothing but race. She was not fit for or capable of cruising.

You look like a very happy man, Mr. Stone.

Well, my work has been my fun. I spent 58 years here on the estuary having fun. A lot of worries attached to it, but the worries make the fun better. I wouldn't trade my life and experience with anybody!!

The Emerald, *built in 1868 by William I. Stone, Lester's grandfather, sails across Richardson Bay toward Belvedere.*

Photo Credits

Following is a list of those by whose courtesy we have printed photographs. The donors' names are followed by page numbers on which the photographs appear.

Ann and Howard Allen: 28, 34 bottom, 41 top, 186.
David Allen: 4, 26 left, 31, 39, 41 bottom, 79 top & bottom left, 81, 83, 99 bottom, 150 top, 161, 180, 208 bottom.
Marie Louise Bates: 68, 71, 74.
LaVerne and Alfred Bernard: 188, 191 bottom, 193, 198 top.
Marie Cattani: 164 bottom, 167.
Anna-Jean Cole: 43 bottom.
Audrey and Larry Coleman: 58 top & right bottom, 59.
Geraldine Davis: 164 top.
Betty and Aldo deTomasi: 34 top, 46, 49.
Carol and Jack Ericson: 84, 89, 92, 111 top, cover photo.
Olive Fetherstonhaugh: 94.
Miriam Grbac: 106, 109 top, 112.
Jerry Halverson: 54, 63.
Joan and Robert Keefe: 122, 128 top.
Dean and Scotty McLean: 138, 144 bottom.
William McLean: 144 top.
Mary Kathleen Mersereau: 162 bottom.
Luella and Bunk Mersereau: 150 bottom, 158, 162 top.
Philip Molten: 111 bottom.
National Maritime Museum, San Francisco: 66, 211.
Dr. and Mrs. H.W. O'Grady: 126, 202, 206.
Karen Lamoree O'Connor: 134, 137.
Alice Oldag: 170, 171
Rose Polacchi: 176, 179, 183.
Dale Adam Sims: 20, 76, 79 bottom right.
Ray Wolfe, Jr.: 1, 8, 17 bottom.
Edward G. Zelinsky: 117.
Landmarks Society of Belvedere & Tiburon: 13, 17 top, 18, 23, 26 top right & bottom, 37, 43 top, 45, 51, 53, 58 bottom left, 64, 73, 91, 99 top right & left, 103, 105, 109 bottom, 114, 119, 120. 126, 128 bottom, 130, 133, 140, 146, 154, 156, 174, 191, 194, 196, 198 bottom, 204, 208 top.

Sponsors

William R. Adams
Walter and Jane Adler
Lowell and Jean Airola
Kent and Paola Allen
Nancy and James Allen
Andy and Kathy Anderson
Christine McCombie Anderson
Greg and Eloise Armstrong
Edward and Dorothy Ashoff
Annelies Atchley
Kirby and Renee Atterbury
Paula Bacciocco
Howard and Shirley Backen
Mr. and Mrs. Donald Baird
David and Airdrie Barley
Charles and Mary Barnes
Cynthia Bartel
Keith Bartel
Theresa Bartel
Beverly Wright Bastian
Mr. and Mrs. Nicholas L. Bates
Mr. and Mrs. Richard J. Bates
Mr. Lesley A. Bates
Loretta Beckman-Carr
Dr. and Mrs. Russell Bell
Carol and Leslie Benet
Mr. Charles Benet
David B. Bennett
Piper and Miles Berger
Joan and Dick Bergsund
Patricia R. Bertrand
Douglas Black
Richard and Virginia Boesel
Mr. and Mrs. Logan Boles
Fay Boyle
David and Sandra Brewer
Robert and Donna Brill
Tom and Anne Brown
Jeanne Buchanan
George and Edith Bull
Richard J. Burke
John and Usha Burns
Jocelyn and James Cacciatore
Mr. and Mrs. William David Caddell
Clayton and Jane Calender
Dorthy and Enoch Callaway
Marie Canziani Canham
Mr. and Mrs. M. L. Cannon II
Geoffrey and Ruth Ellen Capell
Erik and Anna-Marie Carlsson
Diane Fortini Carothers
Keith Carr
Martin and Jeanette Carr
Marlene Forde Casey
Mary Lee and George Casey
Marie J. Lepon Cattani
Michael and Marie Cavanagh
Jean and Cary Chan
Angela Bartel Chapman
Bryan and Genevieve Chapman
Mrs. J. Robert Christy
Juliet B. Clark
Mr. and Mrs. John B. Clark
Richard and Barbara Clark
Peter and Mimi Clarke
Mr. and Mrs. Robert B. Clelland
Henry and Vera Clouette
George and Mollie Coleman
John H. Coleman
Lawrence and Audrey Coleman
Percy Coleman
Vernon and Mary Coleman
James F. Collbran
Larry Colton
Mr. and Mrs. John C. Colver
George and Dolores Conlan
Dr. and Mrs. Robert H. Conner
Nancy C. Cook
Michael and Michele Cooney
Allen and Jane Cooper
Wendy Bell Corn
Stone and Suzanna Coxhead
Sarah Louise Crabb
Bo and Cathie Dahlstrom
Lenore Jane Davies
Robert A. Davies Jr.
Jagger and Shantala Davis
Mr. and Mrs. Phillip A. De Maria
Aldo and Betty de Tomasi
Elizabeth Anderson de Tomasi
Christina and R. Thomas Decker
Judge and Mrs. Albert F. DeMarco
Jerome T. and Nancy H. Denz
Dominic and Margaret Di Mare
Mr. and Mrs. John L. Diamond
Elaine Dillman
Richard O. Dimmock
Joan and Hillary Don
David and Barbara Donzel

Mr. and Mrs. James M. Doody Jr.
Maxwell and Jan Drever
Larry and Anne Drew
Kathy Duby
George and Monita DuFort
Mrs. H. C. Duncan
Robert and Gayle Dunlap
Eleanor M. and Barbara Egoian
Jean and Alan Ehrenberg
Mr. and Mrs. Theodore L. Eliot
Michael and Nancy Ellick
George and Phyllis Ellman
Norma Emmons
William and Susan Englebright
Drs. Charles and Lois Epstein
Lee and Cathy Epstein
Nat and Celeste Epstein
Carol and Jack Ericson
Mr. and Mrs. Waldo A. Ericson
Mr. and Mrs. Peter Esser
Mr. and Mrs. Reuben Ewing
Fredrick and Doris Falender
Carolyn and Branwell Fanning
Ben and Virginia Farlatti
Artelle and Erwin Farley
Mr. and Mrs. J. Farmont
Mr. and Mrs. Walther H. Feldmann, Jr.
Gregory Felton
Louise Felton
Timothy Felton
Olive Jane Fetherstonhaugh
Mr. and Mrs. Marshall B. Figari
Dorothy R. Figour
John William Fiorito
Judy and Ralph Fleming
Dr. and Mrs. John H. Flint
Carol and David Fluke
Jacqueline and Robert Fonarow
Brandon and Ryan Fong

Carol Forell
Lewis and Anne Foster
Nancy Bickelhaupt Frank
Thomas and Julie Freiburger
Michael Friedman
Mr. and Mrs. Rodney Friedman
Jack and Pat Friesen
Lynn and Evelyn Frisbee
Charles and Laurel Frost
Kenneth and Jane Frost
Gandova Fund
Melissa and Michael Gans
Dr. and Mrs. James M. Gawley
Christie and Ted Gazulis
Lorna Spaulding Gentile
Alexandra Jennifer Gilbert
David and Cynthia Gilbert
Jeanette Linnane Gilbert
Oyvin Gjone
Barbara and George Gnoss
Sheret and George Goddard
Marty and Bob Gordon
Alice and Leslie Graham
Mr. and Mrs. Michael H. Grandin
Mr. and Mrs. Henry B. Grandin, Jr.
Charles Rollin Grant
Mr. and Mrs. Rollin E. Grant
Miriam Bradley Grbac
Mr. and Mrs. Walter J. Griffin
Mr. and Mrs. Richard M. Griffith
Nannette and Robert Griswold
Marshall and Shelby Gross
Max and Patricia Gruenberg
Ralph and Susan Gutierrez
Hadley, Inc.
David H. Haines
Knowles and Sherry Ann Hall
Jennie L. Halvorsen
Stanley Halvorsen

Mr. and Mrs. William R. Hambrecht
Ruthe Hamm
Thomas and Karen Hardesty
Hugh and Muriel Harris
Phyllis and Robert Harris
Carolyn Grant Hart
James and Louise Hart
PK and Toffee Hart
Paul and Ann-Eve Hazen
Gerald and Maureen Hazen
Mr. and Mrs. Jack Heidelberg
Helen Heitkamp
Dr. and Mrs. Simon Henderson
Mr. and Mrs. F. Edward Hevern
Richard and Connie Hildahl
Henry and Peggy Hill
E. Stanley Hobbs, Jr.
Mr. and Mrs. John Hoefer
William J. Holmen
Rick Hopkins
Patricia Hosmer
Mr. and Mrs. David B. Hudnut
Jean and Paul Hull
John B. Huntington, Esquire
Molly Keil Hynes
Dave and Barbara Imrie
Ethel McCombie Irish
Dan Irwin Family
Mrs. Jesse J. Iverson
Berton and Jean Jacobson
Derek B. Jacobson
Henry S. Jacobson
James M. Jacobson
Robert and Gerd Jakob
Helen, Joan and Leland M. Johns
Andrew and Marge Johnson
Mr. and Mrs. Kenneth G. Johnson
Mr. Rudin M. Johnson Jr.
Art Jones

Saburo and Joyce Kami
Gee Kampmeyer
Diane Keaton
Francis V. Keesling, Jr.
Gabrielle D. Keil
Mr. and Mrs. Russell D. Keil
Mr. and Mrs. Russell D. Keil, Jr.
Carol Lee Keller
David King Keller
Joe and Joy Keller
Robert and Dawn Kennedy
Dr. and Mrs. B. W. Kilgore
Frank G. and Ruth P. King
Mr. and Mrs. Hampton L. Kirchmaier
Bill and Janette Knick
Jeff and Marilyn Knight
Dr. and Mrs. Herbert Konkoff
Carl and Mary Kae Krause
Joan Krivda
Al and Joy Kuhn
Jeff Lamoree
Mrs. Mary J. Lang
Mr. and Mrs. Kell Bredsig Larsen
Kelly Lavik
Ned Lawrence Family
David and Sally Mathews Legge
Jane B. Lehman
Mr. and Mrs. Ted Lehmann
Susan R. Lehman
Jim and Emily Levorsen
Miss Hania Lewicka
Katherine Lewis
Mr. and Mrs. Carl T. Lewis
Ronald Earl Lindemann
Tiberio P. Lizza
Mr. and Mrs. Randall Longfield
Myron and Hector Lost
Richard and Molley Lowry
Ken and Joan Lucas
Ed and Roberta Lupton
Edward Lynch
Leslie and Diane Lynch
Natalie and Walter Machette
Mrs. Claude MacKenzie
Mr. and Mrs. Lachlan MacLean
Shirley S. Maddocks
Jim and Sonja Mahoney
Donald and Jayne Mann
David and Kathleen Marba
Paul S. Marcucci
Marin County Free Library
Bob and Penny Marshall
Brian Richard Matas
Dr. Peter and Leslie Mathews
Larry and Jan Mathews
Edwige Louise Maxwell
George S. May
Mr. and Mrs. R. G. Mayberry
Bill and Genny Mc Lean
Sue Mc Lean
Dr. and Mrs. Richard C. McAuliffe
Bruce and Gwen McCauley
Adam C. McClure
Jack C. McClure
Mr. and Mrs. Horace R. McCombie
Milton S. McDonogh
Pete McFarland
Terry Pritchett McGuinness
Dr. and Mrs. Malcolm B. McIlroy
Betty McKegney
Scotty and Deane McLean
Lee and Deborah Meisel
Laurence B. and Mary K. Mersereau
Mr. and Mrs. Lawrence Mersereau
Mr. and Mrs. Kenneth Metzger
Ralph Y. Meyers
Mr. and Mrs. George Michals
Mr. and Mrs. William C. Milks, III
Brad and Helen Miller
Marissa Jane Miller
Richard and Regina Miller
Sheldon Miller
Suzi Mitchell Miller
Louise Montgomery Mirata
James and Janet Mitchell
Shirley and Allen Mitchell
Vera Moitoza
Philip Molten
Patrick Morris Family
Chris Morrison
Keith Morrison
Jay Morton
Roy and Barbara Murphy
Nancy and DB Murray
Bill and Mary Myers
Arlene Merino Nielsen
Donna J. Noble
Virginia and Robert Norlen
Paul and Gloria Norman
Jerry and Judy Nowlin
John Jeffrey O'Connor
Karen Lamoree O'Connor
Kevin Robert O'Connor
Tracy Anne O'Connor
James Hunt O'Connor,II
Dr. H.W. and Ethel O'Grady
August and Alice Oldag
Jean Johnston Oller
Mary T. and Floyd H. Osborn
Mr. and Mrs. Eldon Ottenheimer
Mr. & Mrs. Lee A. Otterson
Justine C. Oyster
Andrew L. Pansini
Gertie and Harold Parker

George Wesley Parrish
Alfred J. and Kay Pellicciarini
J. Michael Phelps
Frank J. Pipgras
Margot Plant
John and Rose Polacchi
Jeanne and Tom Price
Edith McLean Purvine
Mr. and Mrs. Thomas D. Quilici
Eugene H. Quinn
Eugene Rauscher Family
Lander Reeves
Joe Regelski
Mr. and Mrs. Carl Reichardt
Trudy and Neil Reid
Barbara Grant Retelle
Harilyn and Fred Reusche
Jane Ann Rey
Robert and Alice Rey
Sybil and James Reynolds
Mr. and Mrs. E. R. Rice, III
Charles M. Richardson, Jr.
Jerry and Suzanne Riessen
Mr. and Mrs. Donald Ring
Ellen and Jack Rising
Dr. Theodore Rist, Jr.
Dexter and Brenda Roberts
Mac and Jan Rogers
Maureen and Rick Roland
Fred and Judy Rose
Arthur and Joan Ross
Bruce and Sylvia Ross
Stephen and Holly Roulac

Mr. and Mrs. Nathan D. Rowley
Mr. and Mrs. Jack Barton Roxton
Margaret Sanford Rumsey
Mr. Peter A. Salz
John E. Sanford
Edie and John Schaller
Capt. and Jane Schellenberg
Richard and Zoila Schoenbrun
Mr. and Mrs. M. Shamsavari
Mr. and Mrs. Donald Hawkins Shannon
Stuart Silloway
Franklyn and Jamie Silva
M. and V. Silveria
Starr and Don Simon
Whit K. Simpson
Dale Adams Sims
Richard M. Sims, Jr.
Ed and Irene Slisky
Alaister and Consuelo Smith
Janie and Syd Smith
Mr. Carter B. Smith
William and Jodie Smith
Robert and Helen Solinger
The Sperling Sisters
Joan Murman Stark
Marilyn C. Steinau
Jean Fourt Sternberg
Anna Conley Stock
Ruth and Lawrence Stotter
Martha Summers
Kate Supple
Mrs. Frederic Supple
Fredric and Joan Sweger

Lewis and Trudy Taich
Wataru and Yanie Takahashi
Jerry and Elizabeth Talbot
Elizabeth and Alexander Tarics
Mr. and Mrs. James L. Taylor
David and Louise Teather
Rufus G. Thayer
Mr. and Mrs. Paul Thimmig
Tiburon Land Company
Tides Foundation
Dick and Dorothy Trezevant
Karl and Jean Tulp
Margo Turkington
Henry van Bergen
Dr. and Mrs. Theodore van Ravenswaay
G. S. Vincent
Helen G. Warren
Mr. and Mrs. Kenneth Washburn
Mr. and Mrs. T. C. Wellman
Effie E. Westervelt
Lawrence and Ann Wheat
Dan and Jan Williams
James G. and Joan H. Wilson
Joyce E. Wilson
Vickie and Harry Winblad
The Wolfe Gallery
Jack and Marilyn Yelverton
Gregory and Claudia Yuhas
Jack and Delia Yuhas
Michael and Alice Yuhas
Michael and Beryl Yuhas
Mr. and Mrs. Edward G. Zelinsky
Mrs. Fred Zelinsky